CCSN LIBRARY
3 1193 00
Heffern
1955-
The n
D0482687

The Naked Truth

The Naked Truth

A Working Woman's Manifesto on Business and What Really Matters

Margaret Heffernan

Published by Jossey-Bass
A Wiley Imprint
989 Market Street, San Francisco, CA 94103-1741 www.josseybass.com

Permission credits appear on page 263.

Library of Congress Cataloging-in-Publication Data

Heffernan, Margaret, 1955–
The naked truth : a working woman's manifesto on business and what really matters / Margaret Heffernan.—1st ed.
p. cm.
Includes bibliographical references and index.
ISBN 0-7879-7143-X (alk. paper)
1. Women executives—Interviews. 2. Businesswomen—Interviews. 3. Women employees—Promotions. 4. Achievement motivation in women. 5. Success—Psychological aspects. 6. Ability. 7. Success in business. I. Title: Working woman's manifesto on business and what really matters. II. Title.
HD6054.3.H435 2004
658.4'09'082—dc22

2004007900

Printed in the United States of America
FIRST EDITION
HB Printing 10 9 8 7 6 5 4 3 2 1

Contents

To Lindsay

Preface

In 2002, I wrote an article for *Fast Company* magazine. I had a sense that some weird things were happening in women's careers and I wanted to test the waters, to see if what I thought was going on was as ubiquitous as I imagined. I discussed some of these issues with the magazine's founder, Alan Webber, who invited me to write something. He said if it was any good he'd publish it.

When the article appeared in *Fast Company,* I was entirely unprepared for the response. I was inundated with email, from all over America and, eventually, all over the world. Thousands of emails from women stuck, frustrated, angry, disillusioned, disappointed, and, in some cases, disappearing. Many of the letters were passionate accounts of the obstacles these women had encountered—obstacles that no one had warned them about. Some of the letters were cries for help; others were practical solutions.

I spent four months doing almost nothing more than answering my email. The letters were too personal and too passionate to warrant an automated reply—and there was too much to learn from them. When the tide subsided, I sat down and listed every correspondent and her location, industry, age, and position. When I came to write this book, I started with a sample from this group, chosen to ensure that I looked at issues that transcended any particular age or place or job. My correspondents—many of whom I've now met, many of whom introduced me to yet more extraordinary women—form the basis of this book.

My *Fast Company* experiment confirmed—beyond my wildest imaginings—what I had seen in my own career and the careers of many women I'd worked with and for: that women are still abused, undervalued, and alienated in a business world that still can't recognize and respect them; that the pressure to align personal and work values is urgent and unrelenting; and that many women are inventing solutions that, if they were shared, could make us a lot less lonely. I'd always known women preferred solving problems to reporting them, but I'd never imagined so many smart, creative solutions.

My meetings and correspondence with so many women also delineated the fundamental pattern of women's careers: we start off promisingly, do well—and then, as we gain some seniority and power, weird things start to happen to us. What worked before suddenly isn't effective any more. If we can understand the pattern here, and know that it is systemic, not personal, we can work through it and emerge with personal power, freedom, and a true sense of having crafted our lives. We can see what's happening to us, make some choices, know when to leave (and how), and go on to craft careers that map meaningfully to the values we refuse to surrender. The shape of this book mirrors that pattern: from how we decide what we want to be when we grow up, through the bad things we encounter, to the gaining of power, creation of a life, and the making of big decisions about staying and going.

There is a lot about money in this book. Not because I believe that money is the only reason to work or the only reward that work brings. I don't. (In fact, I'm staggered that after decades of research showing that money is *not* a primary motivator for work, most corporations still manage their employees as though it were.) Women in this book come from the for-profit and non-profit worlds and pursue rewarding careers in both. But the economic independence of women is a vital issue for us if we are going to change our present circumstances, in which the poor, for the most part, are women; in which we are paid less, have a lower standard of living, and retire on less. No one who respects and admires women can be satisfied with a state of affairs in which women remain dependent on, and loyal to, institutions and companies that continually let them down. We can't wait for those institutions and companies to fix this; we have to take responsibility for our financial independence. We have to make informed choices and understand the financial repercussions of our decisions.

Facing some of the truths in this book will take nerve. It's disappointing to find that stereotypes, harassment, and discrimination are still with us. But it's exhilarating to find women fighting through those obstacles to evolve their own concept of power, to craft a blend of work and life that really does satisfy, to design career paths that do not require the splitting of personal values from work values, and to run companies that give the entire business community a different view of how work can be done. These women, all with successful careers, know that telling the naked truth about what business is, and could be, is the only way to make it better for everyone.

Boston and Farrington Gurney
July 2004

MARGARET HEFFERNAN

Participants

The names of some participants have been changed to protect their careers.

Linda Alepin, senior executive at IBM and Amdahl Corporations. CEO, Pebblesoft Learning Inc. Partner, Center for New Futures. California. Mother.

Paige Arnof-Fenn, CEO, Mavens & Moguls. Worked in Wall Street, for Procter & Gamble and Coca-Cola. Boston.

Cathy Aston, mid-level manager in one of the big three finance companies. Midwest. Mother.

Jacqueline de Baer, managing director, Jacqueline de Baer PLC. London. Mother.

Kimberly Bunting, CEO/President, Business Access LLC. Texas. Mother.

Chris Carosella, SVP for Fortune 100 company. Now CEO, Bold Strategies. Colorado.

Betsy Cohen, VP, consumer products. Midwest. Mother.

Ruth Cohen, medical practitioner. Boston. Mother.

Donna Collins, consultant in health care industry. California. Mother.

Margaret Consentino, left Fortune 100 company where she was VP/general manager. California.

Dee Copelan, senior manager, Fortune 500 company. California.

Elaine Davis, VP, GlaxoSmithKline. California. Mother.

Ann Day, VP, international marketing for consumer electronics giant. Boston.

Karla Diehl, COO, industrial automation company. Tennessee. Mother.

Liz Dolan, senior marketer for Nike, author and radio host of NPR's *Satellite Sisters.*

Risa Edelstein, serial entrepreneur. Currently CEO, vintageFresh LLC. Massachusetts. Mother.

Susan Ellis, director, customer care for cosmetics company. New York.

Nancy Frank, partner, Goldrush Communications LLC. California. Mother.

Holly Godwin, project manager for Fortune 100 company. Texas. Mother.

Adrian Guglielmo, CEO, Diversity Partners. New York. Mother.

C. J. Hathaway, CEO, CJ Hathaway Associates, an event planning business. California.

Jennifer Herron, robotics engineer, defense industry. Colorado.

Kathleen Holmgren, SVP, Sun Microsystems.

Bronwen Hughes, VP, Clinical Development and Regulatory Affairs. Colorado. Mother.

Suzy Hurt, MBA. Senior manager in manufacturing industry. Oklahoma. Mother.

Diane Jacobsen, trained and practiced as architect, then became senior client manager for consulting firm, now managing director. California. Single parent.

Heather Johnston, architect, runs her own firm. Washington.

Lynne Kingsbury, business development, Fortune 100 software company. Massachusetts.

Alison Knight, senior consultant, natural gas industries. Texas. Mother.

Jana La Sorte, CEO, Janlyn PR. New York.

Mary Linfield, VP, software industry. Colorado. Stepmother.

Jennifer Mack, business studies student. United Kingdom.

Lise Markham, CEO. California. Mother.

Pamela Matthews, Wall Street banker. New York. Mother.

John McGarr, healthcare strategist, In-Sync Consumers Insights Inc. Canada. Father.

Jason Miles, MBA, senior analyst, enterprise risk management, Fortune 100 company. Virginia.

Amy Millman, president, Springboard Ventures. Washington, D.C. Mother.

Meena Naidu, transport economist. Project leader, aid and economic development. London.

Linda Phillips, managing director and lawyer. Has run business affairs and talent businesses in the United States and the United Kingdom. London. Mother.

Karen Price, project manager in the engineering and construction industries. Ohio. Mother.

Melodie Reagan, SVP, Level 3. Colorado.

Gail Rebuck, CEO, Random House, United Kingdom. Mother.

Bonnie Reitz, CEO, Inside Out. Previously SVP, sales, marketing, and distribution for Continental Airlines. Florida.

Glenda Roberts, director, mergers, acquisitions, and joint ventures for Microsoft Sales and Marketing Group. Washington. Mother.

Jane Saddler, software project manager. Texas. Also a single parent.

Clare Scriven, partner in Midwest investment firm. Colorado. Mother.

Jeff Seager, software architect. Washington.

Dominique Senequier, CEO, AXA Private Equity. Paris.

Kate Shaw, CEO, financial management. Boston. Mother

Joan Silver, Ph.D., national learning director, financial services. Boston.

Heidi Smith, MBA, has worked in advertising and information technology. Michigan.

Mary Giery Smith, technical writer, aerospace industry. Virginia. Mother.

Cindy Solomon, VP, sales and marketing, Playtex. Colorado.

Teresa Spangler, president, Creative Leadership Adventures, LLC. Prior to that, senior positions at Red Hat Inc. and PictureTel Corporation. North Carolina. Mother.

Glenda Stone, CEO, Aurora Gender Capital. Founder, BusyGirl Network. Winner of the 2002 European Women of Achievement award for outstanding entrepreneurialism. London.

Yvonne Strachan, head of Equality Unit, Scotland.

Sharon Tunstall, head of HR at Nike and Universal Music Group. Now head of HR at New York ad agency. New York.

Michelle Turchin, MBA and speaks several languages. Recently left for-profit world to become director of learning for leading educational non-profit. New York.

Carol Vallone, CEO, WebCT. Massachusetts. Mother.

Sally West, CEO, Tykra. California.

Cindy Wilson, runs her own international event planning and management company. California. Mother.

Fiona Wilson, VP, CMGI. Now adjunct professor at Simmons College and studying for Ph.D. Boston.

The Naked Truth

requires an entirely abnormal degree of adjustment, adaptation, compromise, and conformity. A business world designed by women would look very different but, because these are our training grounds, we struggle to learn from them what we can—while holding on for dear life to who we are and what we care about. Doing this is tough because women have very few role models — which is both a curse and a blessing. It's a curse because it means that there are very few examples to emulate; it's a blessing because it means that women have the opportunity to invent unique, original ways of working that allow them to remain true to themselves.

But the problem is—or has been—that women face their challenges alone. And when they do that, they usually start by blaming themselves. When the system doesn't work, they are more likely to think they have failed than that the system has failed them. At the moment when we need help and support most, we retreat, nursing our injuries in private. And yet when you look at women's careers, these setbacks are pretty predictable, occurring in a pattern that it is hard for any career entirely to avoid. Knowing that, it is possible to stand back and see that what is happening isn't personal, that it's happened to lots of other women—and that they've crafted solutions they can share.

Because what we have going for us is our honesty. Honesty about mistakes and honesty about successes. Honesty about the bastards who've obstructed us and the angels who've befriended us. As I've talked to hundreds of women around the world, I'm struck by the truthfulness, modesty, and humor with which they relate their trials and tribulations—and the array of nervy, original solutions they've invented. The obstacles we face fall into discernible patterns; the responses vary enormously in their style and chutzpah, and they represent a formidable force in the war against discouragement, discrimination, and distractions. This wealth of experience and creativity—the naked truth about our experience in business—is the foundation of this book. Everyone who has contributed to it loves doing business her way—not like men but as unique, powerful women holding fast to the values and beliefs that make our lives worth living.

The women in this book believe passionately in sharing—and they've been enormously generous in sharing their experiences of frustration, anger, failure, mistakes, and triumphs. They share these so that others don't have to learn from scratch what they have discovered the hard way. One of them wrote to me, "I think of this as like Linux or open-source programming—we're just so much smarter together." So this book is a sharing of code: the codes we've all devised to unlock our potential, avert discrimination, and keep our spirits high.

It does not feature interviews with high-profile, famous CEOs, and this is deliberate. Tremendous as these women are, few of them believe that they can afford to be as truthful as they'd like about their experiences. Their profile is their stock price, and they tread a fine line in order to be accepted. Female CEOs understand that their gender remains an issue and that it subliminally informs the way in which they are questioned, challenged, and profiled. Much that they share in private informs this book, but little can be attributed. Likewise, some of the names of individuals and companies have had to be obscured. Even in this day and age, women fear reprisals. They want the naked truth to be known but they recognize that it is still not welcomed in many quarters.

We proceed with optimism. Although this book contains some horror stories, it is not a book of complaint. Women are problem solvers, so there are many, many solutions here. Every one of them may not feel comfortable or appropriate to every reader—but they are all available for women to try, to imitate, to learn from. Every woman here has significant achievements behind her and in front of her; every woman here wants other women to succeed. We all believe that business offers tremendous careers for women—and that women offer tremendous opportunities for business. Who and what we are has never been more important, relevant, and necessary.

A flurry of research, by the business community and by scientists, has identified real differences that women bring to relationships, society, and the workplace. Business commentators in particular point to the superb alignment between our innate abilities and the demands made by fluid, chaotic economies in which change is a constant. In doing so, they give women heart and make us feel more sure-footed, more confident that our differences are assets, not liabilities. But the same commentators continue to underestimate how much is ranged against us, how subtle and systemic the narcissistic machismo of business continues to be. Many men, and some women too, wonder why we haven't achieved more. I hope that, after reading this book, they'll see the truth: we are achieving far more than the system tells us we can.

I watch my children growing up with a more positive view of business than I had. I hope they see that business can be exhilarating, creative, and fulfilling and that it is a powerful, productive way to change the world. Most of all, I hope they start as I continue: with generosity, hope, and faith that women can, and will, change the game.

Chapter One

Start Smart

Our deepest fear is not that we are inadequate. Our deepest fear is that we are powerful beyond measure. It is our light, not our darkness, that most frightens us.
—NELSON MANDELA

What do you want to be when you grow up? It is a question we ask children of all ages, not because we are prepared to take the answer seriously but because we believe the response is a gateway to the child's inner fantasies and obsessions. As we get older, all that changes is that we expect the answer to get serious. Saying you want to be a saint at age five is cute but at age twenty-five it starts to sound neurotic and—worst sin of all—impractical.

The question persists across generations because it works: it *does* show us what we value, dream about, care for. And we aspire to work at professions that express these. Finding the right work means knowing who you are—but work, quite often, is also the way that we find out. "What do I want to be when I grow up? How should I know? I'm twenty-two, I haven't done very much yet—and I'm supposed to decide the rest of my life *now*?"

I would like to be able to offer a formula for figuring out how to identify your life's work. However, although my business career has taught me a lot about women in business and a lot about myself, nothing I've learned produced a quick and easy formula. What women are and what they want is too complex, personal, and rich to be stereotyped. I've done great and hideous jobs, I've worked for peanuts and I've made millions. I've worked in Europe and the United States for gurus and psychopaths and with legions of brilliant men and women. I've learned a lot about what I like and don't like and how to tell the difference. I've learned that opportunism is good, but not good enough, and that there are smart ways of thinking about our careers that help us more quickly reach the places where we really want to be.

What I have learned too is that the journey is different for women. Although it looks like men's and women's careers have become increasingly similar, huge and important distinctions remain. Women are still paid less than men, they advance less easily, they are more likely to leave large corporations to run their own business. Corporate career structures, built by men for men, are anachronistic and wholly out of sync with what women do, need, and value. Women will all tell you that a big part of our careers involves navigating the shoals of preconceptions, stereotypes, and projections that we are born into.

I remember sitting in a room full of brilliant women at a leading investment bank. Together, they probably had more degrees than the government and more intelligence than their board of directors. What was their problem? They didn't know how good they were. Anxious, demoralized, and demotivated by a toxic environment that measured them only by how successfully they imitated men, they found it hard to take themselves seriously as women with unique talents, skills, and opportunities. That experience has been repeated the world over, in every industry I can think of. It's way past time for women to take ourselves seriously, know how good we are, be comfortable with our own energy, skills, and talents—and make sure we put ourselves in positions where these are used, admired, respected, and compensated appropriately.

Karen Price

I am 35, graduated summa cum laude with a BS in civil engineering, I have an MBA, and this past January I left my six-figure management job and a promising career because I couldn't stand it anymore. I felt like a failure for quitting, but I had reached the end of my rope. I wasn't entirely sure what was wrong, I just knew that I felt like part of me was dying. What I thought was success instead had became a death trap.

Karen didn't make mistakes. She got qualified, she was smart, she worked hard. In the eyes of others, she was very successful. Why isn't this a happy ending—yet?

Karen's experience is not unusual. All over the world, girls are going into business. We start off smart, enthusiastic, and optimistic—we work hard and are immensely dedicated. And we succeed. For the first few years, we get accolades, encouragement, and promotions. But as we get more and more power, weird things start to happen. The style and tactics that seemed so successful suddenly stop getting results. We encounter resistance and hostility. Our lives get harder to manage. We enter an Alice-in-Wonderland place where friends become enemies, values become liabilities, success makes us vulnerable and choices feel like strait jackets. We feel that we must have done something wrong somehow and, in our confusion and humiliation, we withdraw, lose confidence—and so find success even more elusive. *The problem,* we think, *must be me. What have I done wrong?*

Nothing. We've done nothing wrong. Being smart and working hard are entry-level requirements. But they won't protect you from the weird experience of being a business woman in a world that remains dominated by men and their values. The companies we see today were built by men for men. Reluctantly, grudgingly, they granted women access—at first just to lowly positions but eventually, when it served men's self-interest, to more powerful positions. We called this progress. But everything comes at a price. The price was that we had to behave in ways that men could be comfortable with: we mustn't frighten them, threaten them, usurp them, or in any way disturb their universe. In other words, we were allowed in as long as we didn't *change* anything. We became gatecrashers.

Because we didn't build the business environment we now move in, it doesn't derive from or express our style or thinking habits. So, sooner or later, every woman is faced with a choice. We can either assimilate—keep working hard to blend in, avoid attention or offense, in order to be accepted—or we can leave the party altogether and go to, or build, a different and more congenial place. That choice is unavoidable, decisive, and utterly personal. Every woman makes it, consciously or unconsciously. Our decision derives from who we are and will define who we become.

Once we understand this, we start to see that most of the difficulties we face aren't our fault. They go with the territory. We can't avoid them; we just have to decide how to deal with them. Whatever we decide, our decision is made easier when we see that we aren't alone, that we can reach out to others for context and advice—context that demonstrates that our challenges aren't exceptional or personal, and advice drawn from the repeated experience of women who've handled the same setbacks. We can overcome any of the challenges hurled at us—it's just a lot easier when we see that we aren't alone and we haven't failed. No woman has ever enjoyed a successful career without help.

What will protect you is knowing that perfect paths aren't an option. Almost no woman has had a wholly unimpeded career; in fact, careers are beginning to look more and more irregular, interrupted, and individual. In choosing a career, what's essential is to remember who you are and what you value, to stay very focused on finding work that is consistent with that, and to be prepared to leave when your identity and values feel like they are dying. Sounds simple, feels hard. The big challenge is not to be successful in business, but to be successful while remaining the woman you want to be.

Ten careers in a lifetime. A hundred thousand hours. That is what a working life is estimated to be. How are you going to spend them? I've had eight careers: radio production, television production, television business affairs, CEO, consultant, business owner, interactive consumer product developer, writer. And I'm not nearly done yet—or at least I don't think I am. Oh, and there's also wife, mother, sister, daughter, friend. Do those count? I think so—even if I didn't choose all of them.

A career is not a job. A career is a path along which you grow. So, when I had my radio production career, I had a different job every year. Same with television. As CEO, I ran several different companies, in different markets. Careers are about growth, development, learning more, making more. But where do you start? And does it matter?

Just because you will have ten careers doesn't mean that choosing them doesn't matter—although it may not be the kind of life-or-death decision that your parents imagined. Because the days of joining one firm—or even one industry—are mostly over, your choice isn't going to make or break you for the rest of your life. You can—you should—experiment. You must make mistakes. What's important is that you put yourself in a place where you can learn, you do learn, you recover quickly from mistakes, you engage with work you value—and you get out if you feel you're dying.

I knew none of this when I started.

Which Way Should I Go? Asked Alice

Before you can begin to think about your career, you have to think about yourself. How important is your career? How important are you to yourself? Are you prepared and able to take seriously what happens to you—or are you prepared to leave this to others?

These sound like absurd questions. I wish they were. But of the many hurdles women face in their careers, the very first is the challenge of taking ourselves seriously. Our expectations for ourselves derive from a myriad of sources—none more potent than our families.

Donna Collins

I was nudged into becoming a registered nurse by my dad. I guess I didn't have exposure to the kind of professionals that may have made me think on a grander scale of ambitions. I had straight A's in honor classes and got accepted to all the colleges I applied to. I wish I'd known there are other careers for women or that I could have applied to Ivy League schools. I was still living my family's expectations of me. I wish I had more exposure to female role models that could have helped me stretch my reach.

Women often start out with ambitions well below their capabilities and we do so because we don't take ourselves, our careers, seriously. We don't plan, we don't think. I've talked to hundreds of women who will say their careers "just happened" or their careers just chose them. They describe themselves as passive characters swept along in someone else's narrative—but they're describing a central activity of their lives. We do ourselves a disservice when we fail to take ourselves seriously—and we set ourselves up to be trivialized by others.

I left a great university with a good degree—and started work as a secretary. This was dumb. I wasn't taking myself seriously. None of my male peers would have contemplated taking such a miserable job. And I was miserable, for years. Miserable enough that I started doing that job badly, which is dangerous because you don't ever get promoted for poor performance, no matter how great your degree is. Underestimating our capabilities and not putting together a bold, ambitious career plan is the recurrent feature of women's careers. We drift—and find ourselves in places we didn't plan and don't like.

Chris Carosella

> I started as a receptionist in a financial institution . . . no particular reason, it was just a job. One promotion led to another and another. I moved around in the industry, always performed well. It wasn't until I escaped that I realized I had been in a corporate cult. I found out who I was after I left the toxic culture that I had been in for eleven years.

Chris became a senior vice president when she was thirty. Don't our stories prove the Cinderella myth—that you can start at the bottom and end up at the ball? No, they don't. Although legends abound of women starting in lowly positions and clambering to the top, they are grossly misleading, omitting all the pain and humiliation and anger that such career paths provoke. And the legends always leave out the women who didn't make it but were abandoned to badly paid jobs. One of the many reasons women fail to make it to the top is because they start so close to the bottom. Starting down there just makes the journey harder and longer. And makes it more likely you will end up in a place you would never have chosen for yourself if you had taken the time to think about it.

Cindy Solomon

> I started as assistant product manager and went up through the system to VP of Sales and Marketing. I did this in 3 years and I'm not that good! What was I thinking? I kept thinking I would be happier in the next job and then the next job. I had no one to talk to because I was the only woman at my level. It is horribly depressing to realize that the assumptions you based your life and work on are based on other people.

Lacking a plan, failing to take ourselves seriously, means we find ourselves fulfilling the needs and expectations of others—satisfying family or corporate goals rather than our own. This passivity bedevils women because so many norms of femininity revolve around putting others first, not being pushy, not being ambitious. Ambitious women are regularly portrayed as sexless harridans, greedy, obsessed with power—who wants to be like them?

Well, no one, of course. But taking ourselves seriously is not selfish or greedy or wrong. In fact, quite the opposite: failing to do so wastes our gifts and diminishes our contribution. We can do more, for ourselves and for those we love, when we put ourselves in places where we can succeed.

Who Am I?

The successful career requires knowing what you want and knowing how to get it. Of these, the second part is easier. Knowing what you want requires tremendous self-knowledge and self-examination. But at the beginning of a career, without a lot of experience, what can you know?

Quite a lot, as it turns out. You've done something—exams, jobs, projects. When you reflect on those, what have you done best? Don't just guess—ask people. They'll have insights you will never see yourself. Think about the work you've done that you are most proud of: what made that so satisfying? Think about work you've failed at or just not enjoyed: what are its characteristics? Depending on how much experience you've had, you may not be able to come up with very complete answers, but once you start asking these questions, you will begin to note how you perform, where you thrive, and where you don't. Start to track how you work and to identify where you get stuck. A career that builds on your strengths is a great place to start—it may be all you need to know. The women with the smoothest careers are those who've followed their passions, regardless of discouragement or obstruction. Love isn't everything but it's a powerful motive.

Linda Alepin

My passion for technology started with my love of crossword puzzles. I found my first primitive programming courses to be the same sort of challenge—make all the words fit! I did sort of choose it "blindly" but having chosen well, I guess I do not see what I might have known that would have helped that choice.

Jennifer Herron

I love to watch machines move. I chose engineering because I liked to know how things worked and I was good at maths and sciences.

Think about how you like to work. Do you enjoy speed? My dumb job as a secretary taught me one thing: I worked in an office that produced two radio programs—an hour and a half of original programming—every day. I loved that pace. Later on, when I was given a year to produce a one-hour film, I should have either said no or changed the schedule; it was too much time and I did poor work when asked to slow down. In broadcasting, time is considered a luxury, but for me it was a burden.

Do you like working alone or in teams? If you love teams, all kinds of work will be wrong for you—and if you like working alone, project work will drive you demented. Are you practical or conceptual—do you like ideas or getting things done? Women have such a tremendous reputation for pragmatism and multitasking that we are more likely to be assigned project work than conceptual planning—you can only fight these preconceptions if you know yourself well. Sometimes, of course, the only way to find out is to try something different and see how you thrive.

Interviewing hundreds of people throughout my career, I've regularly asked them how competitive they were. Most of them didn't know what to say. I didn't really care what the answer was; what is important about being competitive is *knowing* whether you are or not. Not everyone is competitive but I am constantly amazed by how many people are—especially, how many women are. Deeply, intrinsically, ineradicably competitive. They won't tell you so because it doesn't feel quite nice—but if you are very competitive, downplaying it is like driving with the brakes on. Unleashing it is exhilarating.

Heather Johnston

I started racing bikes; I showed up for a training ride and discovered a bunch of people who weren't threatened by a smart, tough, talented woman—they thought it was cool. They actually expected it of me! Suddenly I realized I was motivated by competition; I had power, athletic talent, and a thirst for speed and fast machines. This was fun and not very ladylike—and for once, altogether acceptable. This was revolutionary. I was getting respect for being no-holds-barred Real, as opposed to Proper. The experience drove me to dig deep and find the energetic, powerful, talented, creative girl I'd hidden away at age 11 when that got dangerous, and find new expression for her. It was great. Ultimately, the experience of rediscovering my talent and power, and finding a way to embrace them, gave me my whole spirit back, and that led to the courage to start my company.

I've met more women who were competitive than weren't—and I've met more women who didn't know it than did. And after underestimating themselves, the most recurrent error I've seen women make is getting their own competitive quotient wrong. Knowing this about yourself makes choosing the right career a great deal easier.

Stereotypes suggest that men are more competitive than women; I have found this to be entirely untrue. Stereotypes equally suggest that certain "masculine" hard-core business profit-and-loss disciplines—finance, engineering, sales—are competitive, while the "softer," "feminine" disciplines of marketing, design, and operations are not. Also untrue. Competitiveness isn't intrinsically good or bad, masculine or feminine—but it is fundamental to your work style and to the kind of environment in which you can thrive.

Much of the same discomfort that attaches to competitiveness attaches to ambition. How ambitious are you? Do you feel the need to achieve? Like competitiveness, there isn't a right answer—but you must know this about yourself or you'll start in the wrong place. Line positions involving profit and loss—such as sales, marketing, and manufacturing—offer a lot of power. Staff jobs (HR, legal, strategy, research and development) do not; for ambitious women, they will be the wrong place to start. Women running companies mostly come through line positions, not staff positions.[1] But staff positions are the "caring" ones—looking after people, looking after the company—so women easily gravitate there. The fact that *66 percent* of women work in these areas must be related to how few women end up at the top of organizations.[2]

What kinds of environments do you enjoy? Do you thrive on chaos or do you need total clarity about tasks and responsibilities? Do you enjoy spontaneity or does the absence of direction make you feel anxious and worried? You don't need any work experience to answer questions like these—you will know from family life, parties, and vacations. Think about where you've been happiest; did that pleasure come from careful planning or pure opportunism? If you like spontaneity and are one of those women who can always see what needs doing, you will love start-ups; if you prefer clear instructions, more traditional organizations will suit you better.

C. J. Hathaway

> For me small companies were much better because they afforded me opportunity. I've always been a person who looks around to see what isn't working or what isn't getting done—and then I'd jump in and take them on. In small or start up companies, that has allowed me to expand my responsibilities, and in some cases even create positions for myself that hadn't existed previously.

It is, of course, possible to enjoy both order and chaos. Daphne Kuo worked for me as a finance VP and had the closest thing I've ever seen to a perfect c.v. She alternated big companies—Toshiba, Johnson & Johnson, Fidelity—with start-ups. She loved both and learned from both. Start-ups gave her the opportunity to take on massive new responsibilities; established businesses confirmed those skills. She brought innovation to more staid workplaces and a real sense of process to brand-new companies that sorely needed them.

My father always maintained that the best way to choose a place to work was to think about the people you would be working with. You will spend so much time with them; are they your kinds of people? Would you want to be stuck on a transatlantic flight with them? Your peers don't have to become your best friends (although if you choose well, some of them may). But you will spend too much of your life with them to devote that time to uncongenial colleagues. And if you don't like them, they probably won't like you. Work is hard enough without having to pretend a compatibility that isn't there.

These are all questions that you will ask yourself over and over again. Experience will refine your answers, maybe even change them completely. Different jobs will reveal to you aspects of your talent and personality you didn't see before. But some of the most important questions to ask yourself as you set out on a career are these: What are my values? What do I care about? Where can I find work and colleagues that I respect? All individuals and all businesses have values. Values congruence—aligning what you value with what your company values—produces a great deal more satisfaction in work; working for people you don't respect, on projects that you don't feel are important, is a recipe for frustration and failure.

We all want to do great work, on something we believe in, that we can be proud of, with people we respect. Although I started in a bad job, I discovered that the company offered much of what I was looking for: the products were tremendous, the values (of public service broadcasting) made me feel my work was worthwhile, and the people were a blast. Once I changed jobs (which I could do easily because the corporation was still expanding), I was in the right place. And there were a lot of women around in positions of power.

One of the key issues for women is finding companies that respect them. When you visit a business, look around. Do you see women in positions of power? Are they treated with respect? When you talk to them, do you get the impression that they are expressing who they are—or hiding it? Are they all wearing the same predictable protective coloration—dark suits, helmet hair—or are they allowed to be feminine? What can your network and research tell you about them? Go online and look at the board of directors—do you see any women there?[3] If there are no women at the top of the organization, it will be hard (and sometimes, though not always, impossible) to be taken seriously. Yes, you can be the first; is this your goal? Do you want to start your career with a fight?

Chris Carosella

> I never had a plan to go into financial services. I wish I had known how few women ever made it to senior positions. I wish I would have made a conscious decision to determine what my values were and how I could find work in an area that was something I was passionate about.

Values aren't the same as money—but how important money is to you will be an important determinant in the career choices you make. Why? After sex, money is the most personal, complex, mystifying part of our lives. People find it hard to talk about, to understand, and to manage. I always thought money didn't matter to me because I didn't like the men who were driven by it. Their passion for money struck me as cold, greedy, inhuman—so my career was never driven by financial goals. I just did work that I loved. I wasn't rich, I just always lived within my means. But as I grew older, I became afraid—afraid of what my retirement would look like. I would take my children to the McDonald's near Quincy Market in Boston, and watch a woman working there—red-haired, in her late sixties—and panic that that would be me one day. I had few savings. I had never really thought about how I would live if I didn't work.

That redhead changed my life. I decided that I did want to make money. Not to be driven by it and not to let it dominate my life. But I wanted to make enough money not to be afraid. And enough money to be able to make choices—about where I worked, what I would (and would not) put up with, about where I lived. Making money gave me freedom I could not have had otherwise, and having choices made my life feel like it was mine—not the company's, not my family's, but mine. It was a wonderful feeling.

By contrast, I recall with horror watching a friend ask her husband if she could buy a drink. A grown woman asking permission like a child? But she had no money of her own. I've never entirely understood where today's women got the idea that they weren't responsible for their own financial health. We take responsibility for ourselves, for our children, for our employees. Money is about responsibility too; will you take responsibility for your own financial security? If you won't, you become dependent.

Jana La Sorte

> My father is military so we all followed his life, my mom in particular. His money, his job location changes, his timetable all ruled our lives. My parents fought constantly about money so the only teaching I received was that money caused problems. And that whoever had the most money, had the most power. I understood early on that I wanted my own money so I did not have to be subject to anyone else's rules or fight with anyone about what I could/could not buy. And, of course, to have my own power ultimately.

Having her own money was just one aspect of Jana's independence that led to her also having her own company. She is quite clear that she is responsible for her own financial well-being. This doesn't make her cold or unfeminine—it makes her secure.

There is no evidence that money makes people happy. You should never take a job, or a career, just for the money. But in a world where we regularly see divorce, layoffs, and early illness and death, we can see that financial dependence is a highly dangerous road to take. Women are poorer than men. In part this is because we are less well paid and because we have babies. But it is also an inevitable consequence when we don't take money seriously. We take responsibility for our finances if we care about independence, security, and being able to work the way we want to. Having money, and being very good at making money, gives Carol Vallone the power she needs to run her business according to her values. It allows her values and her money to be in sync.

Carol Vallone

> I have the massively large house and all of the trappings that would indicate money, position, that sort of stuff. And maybe once you have that, you don't care about it any more. So money is definitely important to me but important as it relates to my other purposes. The ultimate importance to me is you can do business this way: you can be passionate, you can work in an alternative way *and* you can make money. Money as it relates to having a comfortable lifestyle is important to me but having those other pieces is the *most* important to me. The amount of money itself doesn't quite do it for me.

Thinking about values helps you to ask the fundamental question: where do I belong? This is a particularly critical question for women who still will encounter many companies where they will be made to feel they do not belong. Companies that do not value us as different but will judge our success only by how far we succeed in assimilating male behaviors, standards, and values. It's no fun working where you aren't wanted or appreciated—gatecrashers are too worried about being discovered to enjoy the party. You will find that you belong in a place that has values similar to your own, that values you as a woman and does not try to turn you into a man.

Values can be hard to think about—they're so abstract and nebulous, hard to see in real, concrete terms. Sometimes the best way to think about them is to visualize what a particular job would look and feel like. On leaving university, I was offered a job with a prestigious investment bank. Like most graduates, I would start as an analyst—in my case, I was to be analyzing the brewing industry, which was big business and reasonably attractive to someone who enjoyed drinking. The pay was great, there was a clear career path, and I knew my father would be pleased as punch. But then I tried to visualize what my life would be like in year one and then in year five. I saw a suburban house, a car, roses at the door, a leather briefcase, smart suits. I knew I couldn't do it. I didn't feel that I belonged in that picture.

Some industries are better than others. Many senior women have succeeded in retail, consumer products, and the media. Other industries, notably financial services, continue to be characterized by macho cultures that celebrate and reward bullying, intimidation, and late nights. But even industries that look inimical to women have good companies—I know women who've enjoyed great careers in aerospace and the car industry—so you will get greater insight by looking at individual businesses. What do stand out are individual companies—and your plan needs to find those. Monica Leuchtefeld, who runs global e-commerce for Office Depot, maintains that the company matters more than anything—and many successful women agree with her.

Betsy Cohen

I looked for the largest company that had good training programs and good products that I believed in. I thought that a brand management career was the stepping stone to general management, and that has been true. I wish I had known how long it really takes to work oneself upward in a big company, as that has been frustrating because a large company has so many talented people and no one leapfrogs upward. Maybe smaller or more flexible companies can accommodate faster upward movement.

Big or small, old or new, what matters is uncovering those companies where your values and your ambition don't have to be suppressed, where you can be appreciated by the contribution you make to work you believe in.

What's Your Plan?

Actress and writer Anna Deveare Smith says that whenever she hears women complaining, she asks, "What's your plan?" It's an invaluable mantra. When you have a sense of what you want to do, or where, what's your plan to get there? Knowing what you want is the hard part—getting it can be, maybe not easy, but easier, if you have a plan.

Since so many successful women claim their careers "just happened" to them, why do you need a plan? Because without one you can fall into career drift—satisfying other people, achieving other people's goals, building success in areas you don't really relate to. Without a plan, you absorb your company's plan, or your parents' plan—and find yourself, years later, wondering why you are doing a job that feels like a death trap.

Plans help us to work smart. Without them, we just outwork everyone around us; we throw quantity instead of quality at the problem.

Cindy Solomon

I began my career fresh out of college with only two firm expectations . . . first, that I would get a job and second that I could pay off my student loans and support myself. No one ever mentioned that I was supposed to like the work, find a company where I could excel over time, etc. Additionally, I never addressed my career and my career moves proactively, I simply worked until I dropped and hoped that it would get me promoted.

I neglected my entire life for too many years because I was seeking to achieve the only way I knew how, which was to outwork everyone else. If I were to do it again and approach it the way I mention above, I would out-think the organizations and the opportunities rather than out-work them. That would have allowed me to, if not have it all, at least have some life while I was achieving my work goals.

Plans save us time and energy. They stop us from making commitments to people we don't like and projects we don't enjoy. But most of all, plans work. At the age of fourteen, I fell in love with Shakespeare and became utterly determined to become a theatre director. At the age of fifteen, as an American living in London, I sought out Anne Barton, an academic married to the preeminent director of Shakespeare. I thought that as a fellow American and Shakespeare enthusiast she would be able to help me—and she did. On her advice, I graduated from high school a year early and applied to and was accepted by the top London school that sent more girls to Oxford and Cambridge than any other school in England. I overcame their prejudice against American education to apply for and win early admission to Cambridge University, where all of my idols had trained. And, when I got there, I started directing plays. I had a plan. The plan worked.

The problem I encountered next was something I had not planned for: I discovered that I hated directing plays. What I should have done next was make another plan. Instead, I drifted and became a secretary. When eventually I made another plan, that worked too.

Whenever I've had a plan, I've made progress; when I didn't, I drifted. Plans work because they focus your mind and attention and also because they help you to identify and articulate what you want. Once you can do that, you can ask people to help you—and they will if they can. If you can't say what you want, people may want to help but not know how.

Plans focus what you want and make you think about the skills you need to get there. Do you have those skills or do you need to develop them? Does that mean school or experience? Who do you know who can help you? Who do they know? Who can give you insight into whether or not your goals are achievable and appropriate and, if they are, how you reach them? Marjorie Scardino, the CEO of Pearson, says you should have a plan and "execute it violently." She points out that we plan most major aspects of our lives—we plan weddings and vacations and maternity leaves. Why on earth would we *not* plan a career?

Plans don't stop when you get the first job or when you get the big job. Plans keep your career moving on your terms—not anyone else's.

Cindy Solomon

The mentoring I give to younger women now includes the following things that I would have done very differently not only from the start, once I was with a company.

1. Ensure that the due diligence you do on every job move includes whether you like the actual work and whether the company has proved in words and deeds that they are willing to work with you to meet your goals (no better way to get at this information than to ask to interview some of their mid level managing women).

2. Once you are in a job, determine what you want to learn from it, what achievements you hope to have within it, what your skill sets will be when you've achieved your goals and where you will be challenged next. I also suggest that women look at the financial contributions they are making to their company every six to twelve months and ensure that they are being adequately compensated.
3. As soon as you hit the door of each job within each company, find a male mentor to get you up to speed on the relationships and real decision making processes. This will also ensure that someone is out there in the "boys network" giving you unintended positive PR.

If we start smart, and stay smart, our working lives become easier and we feel in charge of them, not dependent on the whims of men and markets. I'm struck that the most dynamic women I know are fearless in identifying goals for themselves and figuring out how to achieve them. They don't wait for good fortune to strike; they go out and make it for themselves. And knowing what they want helps them to get out of bad situations fast.

Many women, asked to explain their careers, will come out with the demure response: it was luck. This is immensely frustrating to hear because it suggests that you can't really *do* anything; you either have luck or you don't. They attribute their success to luck because they don't want to appear to boast or to appear to be too calculating—or perhaps because they don't want to share what they know. But it turns out that luck isn't quite as arbitrary as it appears. Recent studies show that people who consider themselves to be lucky are simply more observant than those who consider themselves to be unlucky. Experiments show that when a person who considers herself lucky and a person who considers herself unlucky walk down the same street, it is the "lucky" person who spots the coin.

Having a plan makes you more observant because you know what you are looking for and are better attuned to find it. You have a better-defined sense of what is useful to you. And plans get you to where luck happens; I may have discovered that I hated directing plays, but Cambridge was not a bad place to be while I reconsidered. If your plan lands you among smart people in a place where you belong, your "luck" often does the rest.

You have to know what you want. You need a plan to get it. You need "luck." And you need to take risks. When asked how she had managed to combine a dazzling scientific career with successful business and broadcasting ventures, Susan Greenfield said, "I took risks. I decided to say 'yes' to everything that wasn't life-threatening. I used to say, 'Boats are safest in harbor but that's not what they're built for.' Those who risk nothing, risk more." She is fifty-three years old, a baroness, a lecturer at Oxford University and director of the Royal Institution, one of Britain's most ancient and admired establishments. She also runs several businesses and has twenty-one honorary degrees. In careers, just as in investing, you find a risk/reward trade-off.

In my own life, my big successes have come from deviating from the norm—doing something unexpected that involved significant degrees of uncertainty. Leaving broadcasting, having babies, leaving England, starting new companies, leaving America. I'm not sure I experienced these decisions as risks—at the time, I felt I could not decide differently. But their outcomes were uncertain and, compared to my peers' career choices, they were risky.

When we take risks and they work to our advantage, we call that luck. When they don't work to our advantage, we call them mistakes. I learned I didn't like directing plays; it was a good thing to know, and analyzing why eventually sent me off in a more fruitful direction. Mistakes in a career are really just learning.

Paige Arnof-Fenn

I would say I have learned something really important in every job. But every day in those jobs would not be described as a day or an experience I loved. But it was incredibly important that I learn in those roles. I was an analyst on Wall Street. It was difficult mentally and emotionally. I decided to leave Wall Street and I think I have done better with the opportunities. I don't think you have to like every job but you have to learn from every job.

Paige took herself from Wall Street to Procter & Gamble to Coca-Cola; she has had a rich and varied career, characterized by companies she's passionate about and colleagues she admires. She is now CEO of Mavens & Moguls, a new business that she believes can grow to be as big as she wants it to be.

Paige Arnof-Fenn

> I think people are always in transition. That is the reality of the economy today. There is no lifetime employment or staying in that job forever. If you are doing something you love, learning new things, and adding value to the world at large, it is as if you are walking around with a toolkit adding to that skill set. How you spend your time is what really matters—and doing something with it.
>
> You have to be true to yourself and know what your true north is. It never works if you go against that. If it means you have to leave a job or a company to go where you are more in sync with your value systems and beliefs, do it.

A career is not a plan for life—at best, it may be only your plan for the next chapter of your career. But if it is in tune with your values, the story will be rich in experience and make sense. Be ambitious with your plan; successful women always set themselves goals that are a bit of a stretch: not impossible but not too easy either. If you aren't ambitious for yourself, no one else will be. Most men still regularly assume that other men are ambitious and expect them to want more—responsibility, pay, promotion. They do not regularly make the same assumptions about women but tend to underestimate what we do and what we want. They will continue to make that mistake unless we signal our ambitions, needs, and goals clearly. It's not a bad habit to start thinking well of yourself.

Think about how much of a fighter you are or want to be. You may not know this until you find yourself in the midst of a battle, but the question is almost bound to arise at some point in your career. Do you want to stay and slug it out, or do you want to work someplace where you are accepted and appreciated for the woman you are? It takes a lot of confidence to fight your way through toxic environments and hostile industries—if you can do it, the sense of accomplishment is immense. But it isn't for everyone. Many women enter financial services thinking they won't mind the fight. They leave in droves when they discover otherwise.

When you find yourself somewhere you don't want to be, don't feel ashamed. Call it learning, not a mistake, and analyze what you've learned before you make the next plan. That way, however bad the experience, you will have extracted value from it. The most successful women are the best learners.

Talking to successful women about their careers, I've heard hundreds of hair-raising stories about awful men they've worked for, ludicrous tests they've been put through, enormous challenges they've overcome. But I've always heard laughter too. Because once they've come through these ordeals, what remains is amusement and joy. Amusement at the absurd obstacle race we still run; joy when we find the work, the colleagues that bring out the best in us. Joy too at the discovery that, after all that, we've discovered what we should have known all along: we *are* worthy. There is nothing we cannot do. We just have to set our minds to it.

■ ■ ■

I used to find that the only time I got for thinking was while traveling on a plane or train, and I came to value this time for providing the space I needed to ask myself questions about where I was and where I was going. At the end of all but the last chapter, therefore, are some questions to reflect on when you next find yourself on a plane or train or stuck in traffic. They are timeless questions and, over the years, your answers may well change.

Travel Thoughts

- What do you believe in? How would you describe your values? Do they relate to your work? What work would match those values more closely?
- How important is money to you?
- How competitive are you?
- How ambitious are you? For what?
- Where do you imagine you want to work?
- What's your plan? What skills do you need to achieve it? Who do you know that can help? Have you told them what you want?

Chapter Two

Geishas, Bitches, Guys—and the Invisible Woman

First they ignore you, then they ridicule you, then they fight you, and then you win.
—GANDHI

When women first got into business, we knew we'd have to work hard not to disrupt the status quo. As gatecrashers, we were so eager to get in that we agreed. To be good girls, behave, not rock the boat. We did that by conforming to roles that men were used to, roles that made *them* feel comfortable. At first, this took the shape of severe women in stout shoes and ruthlessly tied-back hair: by being totally sexless and quasi-military, we looked like a safe pair of hands. Gradually this gave way to pink blouses with bows that were our stand-in for ties. But the clothes were merely the external signs of what was happening at a deeper level: we were absorbing lessons about how to behave in ways that would not aggravate or threaten men. Like new immigrants, we assimilated in order not to be thrown out.

While these pressures have changed and, in some cases, lessened, they are still with us. It is rare to find a company in which full-fledged femininity is encouraged or even tolerated. In a world in which 85 percent of all purchases are influenced by women, requiring female employees to modify their femininity might look like commercial suicide. Our market power means that it is clearly in the interest of business to see us, and hear us, as we are—not as men want us to be. The business argument that says women should be encouraged, supported, listened to, and taken seriously *as women* is unequivocal. But this isn't what happens.

Instead, it is inevitable that, in the course of a woman's career, she will be treated as a stereotype. Sometimes this is obvious; sometimes it is so subtle we don't notice it happening. Sometimes, even without meaning to, we play along with the stereotype because it seems to make our lives easier. What's really important about stereotypes is to be able to identify them, see what is happening to you, and deal with it in a way that feels authentic. It's not easy but it has to be done.

It has to be done because falling into a stereotype has concrete consequences. The number one reason given by women for being held back from advancement is male stereotyping and preconceptions of women. In research studies, when asked to explain why they couldn't progress within their organization, 66 percent of women reported feeling trapped by the way that their male colleagues perceived them and expected them to behave.[1] Stereotypes force women into behaviors that are self-limiting; stereotypes either curtail or trivialize our power so that we aren't as effective as we want to be, and we can't achieve the results we are capable of. In being what other people want us to be, we lose confidence and the chance to be ourselves.

In my experience, there are four main stereotypes women tend to fall into: geisha, invisible woman, bitch, and guy. I have been sucked into three of these; if you are really unlucky, you may experience them all. I've never known anyone to escape all four. But when you can see what's happening, you are in a far better position to negotiate your way out of it and to develop your own authentic style. All over the world are women who've fought their way through this nonsense and emerged whole. It can be done.

Geishas

No matter how senior, seasoned, and experienced we are, it's astonishing how quickly and easily women are expected to serve men.

Cindy Solomon

I worked for a great start up; we grew exponentially and, after about 5 years, we were bought out. So I go to Detroit to chat about a VP spot with the new owners. But all guys. So I'm sitting waiting

> for my interview with Bob, and a kid about five or six years younger than me came out of a meeting, didn't see a secretary but saw me and asked me to get coffee. Sure I said—how many? Eleven. No problem. So I get the coffee, take it into the conference room—full of all white guys, all 40 with all little round glasses. I set the tray down and ask Bob, "Is there anything else I can do for you?" And of course he does a huge double take (*What are you doing?!*). And I tell him, "That gentleman asked me to get you guys coffee."
>
> Bob was horrified—he was such a good man—and said "You see why I need you here." And maybe if it had been 10 years ago I would have taken it. But I just couldn't be the only woman again.

Cindy couldn't take it because she knew that men who *automatically* treat women as geishas find it hard to learn to take them seriously. This means starting with a huge handicap. But when you are young and pretty and just starting in your career, it can be hard not to enjoy the fact that men like how you look. There's nothing wrong with that; just be careful about the assumptions that go with it. For some men, being pretty turns you into an ornament, not a peer. It means you may be expected to be charming but never to ask directly for anything for yourself, never to negotiate as an equal. That, in turn, can force you into behaviors that cost you pay and promotion. So what starts as innocuous or flattering turns into a box of preconceptions you can't get out of.

> *Pamela Matthews*
>
> When you start out in banking, you are a slut or a geisha. The pretty young things fresh off of the college campus. And you get all kinds of attention because you are fit and cute. At that point, your career goes along fine because you are junior and you are NON-THREATENING!

Many men think of women as geishas in order to keep them at a distance, to trivialize their skills. Fiona Wilson once worked for a man who wasn't particularly well organized, creative, or well regarded. That she was all of these things made her potentially quite threatening to him. He found a way of complimenting her that, at the same time, put her firmly in her place.

Fiona Wilson

I have an MBA and a ton of international experience. I had a ton more real life work experience than my boss. But you know what he valued? My charm. That's what he said. MY CHARM!! Not my brain. Not my MBA. Not years of experience with blue chip international clients. But my charm.

Some men get very confused by women at work. Used to thinking of us as potential girlfriends, lovers, wives, they're not quite sure how to work with us as serious peers. Confused, unimaginative, or defensive, they resort to the geisha stereotype.

Jennifer Herron

I try to be gregarious in an effort to make business contacts. But depending on the man, it is sometimes interpreted as "now I am here to serve you personally." And it turns into a Geisha situation. There is no business discussion—they want to talk about where I went to school and where I am from. Like my life is their business? Also, many men find it fascinating that a woman is an engineer. "Oh my God, you know how to run a CNC mill and use power tools?" It gets rather annoying when you are trying to talk business and they want to discuss their fascination.

The problem with this kind of stereotyping is that it can become self-fulfilling and self-perpetuating: when you are treated as a geisha, it becomes pretty easy to start acting like one—because that puts men at their ease.

Ann Day

Just smile more . . . that was a piece of advice I got from a board member at the company I work for—finishing with "it's always better when you smile."

What's Ann supposed to do—scowl? Of course not. But the more she smiles, the more she gets thought of as "that nice girl with the lovely smile." Before you know where you are, even though you didn't *start* as a geisha, you can find that you've turned into one.

Geisha stereotyping is pernicious not just because it's insulting but because it puts you into a role in which it's hard to find a way to be taken more seriously. Too brusque and you'll get labeled a bitch or a guy (of which more later.) Too pleasant and you're stuck in your geisha role. It's also pernicious because you need an ego of steel for it not to get to you; it's hard to take yourself seriously if your colleagues do not.

Diane Jacobsen trained and practiced as an architect—a tough career with notably few female leaders. Harder still, being an architect means working with contractors and builders.

Diane Jacobsen

> Contractors—whoa!! I quit architecture because I got so sick of them. I was so sick of being called honey and sweetie and being disrespected and talked down to by people who had less knowledge, less education and less experience than I did—and they would do so just because they were men. And I did come up with some good come backs, I had some great quips and used them regularly but that would just incense them and I would become a target and they would try to see if they could get to me.

When she retrained for a career in high-tech design, Diane brought with her years of experience in knowing what she can change—and what she can't.

Diane Jacobsen

> Just yesterday I asked to be removed from a project because we got a new project sponsor who just came on board and who is probably one of the worst misogynists I've ever known. And there's no win with this man. I am damned if I stay and damned if I leave. So I just asked to be removed.

It's hard for me to imagine anyone less geisha-like than Diane. A single mother, she's smart, tough, energetic, with a passion for solving hard problems. She brings tremendous technical and managerial experience to multimillion-dollar projects. But she still got asked to look after visiting wives at corporate dinners. She finally left this company—which shows how hard it can be to fix or avoid this kind of treatment.

Geisha behavior contributes directly to our being undervalued and underpaid. Geishas aren't taken seriously as breadwinners, which also means their need for promotion is not considered. For as long as we have been in the workplace, women have been underpaid; currently a woman's average earnings are $36,716 compared to a man's earnings of $52,908. In the United Kingdom, women are paid an average of £20,314 compared to a man's £28,065.[2] In both places, it is against the law to pay men and women differently. The fact that these anomalies persist is due to many factors—not least the stereotype that sees the man as breadwinner and the woman as providing a secondary, therefore less critical, income.

Sometimes, consciously or unconsciously, we collude in this devaluing process.

Jeff Seager

I was in a position to write a review for a woman who was working for me but reporting to someone else (her manager). Her performance was exemplary, I wrote a glowing review and recommended that she be promoted. I later found out that when she had her review with her manager, she let him convince her that there were other people (males) in her group that deserved the reward more than her. I was livid about this because she'd out-performed everyone in her group, but she let her boss push her into accepting an outcome he wanted.

My wife Claire has seen the same thing; take two equally performing people, one male and one female and the male will always say that his performance was 150 percent and the female that it was maybe 50 percent at best. Another woman I work with, also doing exceptionally high quality work, also apologizes all the time. You can hear the "I'm sorry I performed so well, I didn't mean it" between the lines. One might argue that this is just a matter of selfconfidence, but I've seen it much more in women than men so I've got to think there's a cultural component to the behavior.

The cultural component Jeff refers to is deep: an ancient definition of femininity that is about not asking, not standing up for ourselves. Much in our history and upbringing discourages girls from making demands; femininity is all about being sensitive to the needs of others. I once made a film about Cheltenham Ladies' College, one of the first progressive girls' schools in England. Girls there were instructed not to ask for things—the salt or sugar, for example—because good girls were supposed to *intuit needs*. Thus, girls learned two life lessons: do not ask, and always serve. Perfect geisha training. I'll never forget interviewing Beryl Baynham, who attended CLC as a student and now works there as a teacher. She recalled how, as a student, she'd waited outside a teacher's office, struggling to find the confidence to knock on the door and ask for something. She prayed the teacher would emerge, relieving her of having to make a direct request. As I interviewed her, Beryl brought the room to a frozen silence: "I'm really a very boring person. I always have been. I have never done the things I wanted to do, I was too afraid to ask. I always felt that if what I wanted didn't come my way, that that was my fault so, well, nothing really happened in my life."[3] After all these years, I've remembered Beryl Baynham because she crystallizes the way that many smart women feel at work: frozen in that moment at the door, wanting, but not daring, to ask.

Learning not to ask for things is the psychological equivalent of foot binding; it devastates women's abilities to reach their goals. Over and over again, around the world, I encounter the same issue: women don't ask. The consequences are appalling. I'll never forget a conference where a woman working in the telecommunications industry confessed, "I gave raises to the men and not to the women. I had a budget for these raises—but it was the guys who always asked for them. I didn't give them to women because the women never asked. I see now that this was wrong—but why didn't they ask?"

Women don't ask because we cling to the belief that hard work and a pleasant demeanor will garner raises and promotions. But they don't—which is why women still earn 76 cents to a man's dollar or 82 pence to a man's pound.[4] They garner smiles, even affection—everyone likes a geisha—but they don't elicit money or power.

A recent study showed that 7 percent of female graduates negotiate for a higher salary than that initially offered, whereas 57 percent of male graduates do. And the negotiation works, yielding a 7 percent pay increase.[5] This accumulates, of course: the higher pay represents higher value, so those with the high salaries get better assignments and more promotions. Being a geisha isn't just demeaning, it's expensive. By not negotiating a first salary, it's estimated that a woman loses more than $500,000 by age sixty—and by repeatedly not negotiating, a woman earns $1 million less over the course of her career.

But it's not just the money. In not asking, we concede that our role is just a social one. We don't ask in part because asking feels pushy, overbearing, aggressive. Asking seems to threaten the relationship—but that relationship isn't a professional one. It's the geisha relationship.[6]

Chris Carosella

Women are taught at an early age to be nice, share credit, wait for people to give us recognition and hold back part of ourselves so boys will like us. While there's certainly nothing wrong with being nice and sharing credit, there is a wide spectrum of how to do that. I like to hear women talking proudly about their accomplishments, not denying themselves for anyone. It isn't about arrogance; it's about confidence, self-acceptance, power and strengths.

When we feel that we cannot ask, we can be tempted into other behaviors to try to get what we want—more "traditional" ways that feel less disruptive and don't require new paradigms. Agnes Peters, a television director, was notorious for her so-called negotiation style. At the least provocation, her eyes would well with tears. Budget discussions, rough cut viewings, anything approaching a negotiation. When her cameraman wanted to quit for the day and she needed another shot, when union rules said it was time to send the orchestra home—out came the tears. With women, it never worked. But with many men, it worked a treat. They were terrified of full-blown tears—and more frightened still of being caught with a weeping woman. So they caved in.

But the problem such geishas have is that, by trading on an outmoded model of femininity, they make it impossible for men to take them seriously as thinking, sentient adults. They have crippled power: enough for small victories but not for big ones. As such, their potential is limited by the stereotype they've adopted. Agnes got to make films, but she never rose in her position; no one would ever have dreamt of giving her real power because, ultimately, no one would take her seriously. Behaving like a little girl meant that was what men thought she was.

Crying may get you what you want but it doesn't mean you're taken seriously. In fact, it usually makes matter worse because now men are afraid of your emotion. I recall a frank conversation with a bunch of men at London Business School: this was the single subject they most wanted to learn about from me—how to cope with *their* fear of women's tears. It was a curious conversation because they were so convinced that the slightest criticism would provoke floods. That fantasy in itself demonstrated how much more powerful than women they feel—and how afraid they are of their power. Because they were afraid of emotion, these male managers never gave their female employees the quality of honest assessment that they gave to men. But we know that feedback is an essential element of every executive's success—some claim it is the most important form of business education in a career. So, out of their fear of emotion, men's "gentility" set women up to fail. When asked how they ought to handle things, I told them that, if they overcame their fantasies of intimidating power, they'd find that most women don't cry. Most women would rather do almost anything than weep in front of their boss. And if they do, how terrible is that? Why should women pay the price of men's cowardice?

By the same token, flaunting sexuality to get what we want doesn't really work either. Is it possible to get ahead by sleeping around? Some women still think so; 10 percent of women say they have had a fling with their manager—but, of those, only 12 percent were promoted.[7] Is this real power? I don't think so—because it isn't yours. The problem with geisha power is that it can be taken away at a whim. It's really just dependency.

Joan Silver

At the insurance company where I worked, the head of HR was a reasonably smart person but, for the role she played—HR for 50,000 people—you have to be more than 37 years old! You need more experience, seasoning. And knowing the culture of the place, I thought "Oh God, she must be sleeping with the CEO"—and then blamed myself for being cynical! But it wasn't three hours later that someone told me that this was actually going on. This kind of behavior is the fodder of organizational life. It is bad for the men. It is bad for the women. It is bad for the organization. No one wins—especially ambitious women.

Chris Carosella

My boss was married but he had affairs all over the place. He tried to persuade me once to hire a woman he was having an affair with so that they could be closer geographically. I refused and told him

> that this woman would affect productivity and make it harder for me to reach my targets and that would impact my bonus. He said, "You refuse?" I said, "Yup." He said, "What if I make you?" I said I'd complain to HR. He did eventually get his woman a job—in a division where bonuses did not depend on the bottom line.

Every aspect of the geisha role has a small positive and a big negative for women. It's nice to be admired when you're pretty—but it doesn't mean you're respected for your competence. Not asking for things feels easier—but it costs pay and promotion. Crying may enable you to get your way—but at the price of honest feedback and respect. Sleeping with the boss may get you the promotion—but earns resentment and dependency.

The first step to escaping geishadom is to recognize that this is the box you are being urged into. Watch the behaviors that are rewarded and ask yourself: how seriously is she being taken? How seriously am I being taken? How might my behavior contribute to my own trivialization? If you find that you're expected to assume the role of a geisha, there are certain key things you can do to gently force yourself out of this box. Asked to get the coffee? Ask a guy to come along and help you. That way you both do it. Do the same with smiling: I will if you will. Any time you feel you're asked to do something less than serious just because you are female, make sure you get the guy to do it too.

Practice asking—for promotions, for pay. Role-play with friends. It may feel awkward at first, but will put you in a far stronger position when the time comes for the real thing. One of the smartest recommendations I've ever come across was Elaine Davis's suggestion to keep a journal of your contributions. Regularly—weekly, if it's easier to remember—write down what you've achieved, obstacles overcome, crises averted. This will have multiple benefits: it will remind you what you've done (useful for building your confidence as well as for résumés and job interviews) and it will be essential when you need to articulate *why* you should be rewarded. "Please" is not an argument; contributions are. Don't stand frozen outside the door: walk in with the understanding that all you are doing is conducting a business negotiation. Start with small things that you need for work—the small negotiations build confidence for the big ones. Don't simper; know your facts; do the deal for the client that is you.

Geisha behavior persists in corporations because men like it and we don't blow past it. But we can. All of these strategies work without turning you into someone or something that you're not. And they'll earn you respect.

The Invisible Woman

One of the most effective ways to escape being treated as a geisha is to make yourself disappear. This sounds a little weird—but it is something women have learned to do well. Perhaps the best, most extreme example I've come across is the story of Yevgenia Borisova, a Russian journalist who was trying to tell the true story of the war in Chechnya. Refused official accreditation, she was not officially allowed to be in one of the most dangerous places on earth. Nevertheless, she went—traveled with Russian and Chechnyan soldiers, sailing through checkpoints. No one ever asked her for her papers or challenged her presence. What makes this even more remarkable is that she was traveling with a big, cumbersome satellite phone. But because she was a woman, no one saw her.

It isn't just in Chechnya that such weird things take place. I can't really explain how this happens, but it does: men just don't see women. We think that we are perfectly visible—only to marvel as we see our projects, ideas, innovations, promotions, power dematerialize before our eyes. My husband Lindsay is one of the least territorial, most liberated men I know. He adores and respects women and gets along with them, at work and socially, very well. Yet the other day, when he came home and ran into some workmen laying new carpet in our home, he gave them instructions, gave them some keys, and saw them out. He came upstairs and told me what he'd done—which was the opposite of what I'd told them and the reverse of what I wanted. Lindsay had done what men always do—walk in, see other guys, and assume that the real deal is just between them.

Lindsay doesn't do this any more—but the story repeats itself the world over. Women who travel with a male assistant get used to big questions being addressed to him. Women at meetings get used to seeing their ideas ignored—and then stolen. Individually, each instance seems so petty that complaint seems overblown—but the accretion of these insults undermines confidence and skills.

In environments where visibility and achievement are the crucial ingredients of evaluation and promotion, each time we are invisible we lose a piece of our worth.

Our talent for invisibility makes us fantastic interstitial managers: people who—no matter how crazy the organizational structure—fill in the gaps and get things done. Interstitial people are invaluable—as a CEO, I knew who my interstitial players were and they absolutely made things happen. The problem is that, in most organizations, this skill commands no respect at all. Appraisal and reward systems aren't set up to recognize invisible achievement. Sharon Barnes contrasted a man and a woman implementing a new computer system. The woman trained everyone gradually and converted her entire team to the new system without a hitch. No drama, no crisis. Her male counterpart delayed and provided no training whatsoever. So when the new system came online, his staff came out in open revolt. He swiftly laid on a company lunch and emergency consultant training to deal with the crisis—winning a bonus and letter of commendation for himself. The woman's work was better—but it was invisible. Dramatic rescues—the stuff of action heroes—reap rewards, whereas just making things work does not.[8]

Heidi Smith

> I used to work at an IT company among mostly men and it seemed like the Christmas party, birthdays and holidays always fell to women. While I admired the effort that was made to make the environment more hospitable, the tradeoff was that it seemed to marginalize the women in this hard driving atmosphere. I also think that women in many instances solve problems before they occur—and then do not get the recognition for this in light of their male counterparts that let problems fester. By women being attuned to the nuances they can often see difficult situations before they arise—and yet they have a hard time taking credit for that or promoting it.

Knowing that they enter male bastions on sufferance, women often encourage their own invisibility. Being off the radar screen means we don't get attacked, so it's a lot easier to get things done. Women often describe themselves as "subversive" or "spies," "working underground"—meaning that, in often intensely political environments, being invisible is their way of getting things done. But the problem with invisibility is that it means we get neither benefit nor credit for our achievements. For our confidence, this is debilitating. Invisible to others, our successes become invisible to *us;* we fail to internalize them and value them as ours. And, naturally, that means that our colleagues and bosses forget about them too.

> *Jason Miles*
>
> There is one ally that I made over the past year. She is a very strong, professional woman who impressed me from the moment I met her. She treats others with respect, accepts any challenge thrown her way and always gets the job done, and done well. Sadly, I observed over time that she was given neither the credit nor the respect that she deserved from her chain of command. In one situation a project that she had contributed heavily to was nominated for an excellence award that my company gives out to only a handful of efforts each year. However, her name was left off of the nomination that was communicated to the entire company. The management team's reaction was first to acknowledge privately that she had been left off, and second to assign someone to give her a short pep talk to minimize the morale impact. Later when the project team (all except her) won the award there was no additional follow-up to include her.

Part of being invisible is not being heard. Whole studies have been written on this, proving that women can articulate good, smart ideas—and never be heard.[9] We all have experienced seeing our best strategies and ideas stolen. I worked once for a boss who was drowning in a complex and endless negotiation. When I offered him a negotiating strategy that looked like it could cut through the knots and make us a lot of money, he embraced it eagerly—too eagerly, making it clear that he accepted it as his own. Claiming and defending it as his territory, he lost my loyalty, my commitment, my enthusiasm. Would it matter in my career? Not necessarily. But it mattered to me. I had been invisible before; I did not want to be invisible again. I love contributing to something greater than myself—but in an environment in which achievement is measured and rewarded, I've never understood why saintly self-sacrifice should be expected of women but disdained in men.

Of course, we are trained from an early age not to boast, so we rarely complain of this kind of treatment. When we do, it feels like ego or vanity, a desperate plea for praise. But it isn't—it is a plea for confirmation that we exist and a demand that our value be recognized. Pay and bonuses depend on a full appreciation of our contribution; these have to be seen before they can be rewarded. Women continue to be underpaid in part because who we are and what we contribute is unseen and unheard.

> *Joan Silver*
>
> I was asked to work with Kathy, a senior woman in our organization. For a period of time she had been the first and only woman in the group. Kathy was a quiet, thoughtful individual. Very smart. In meetings, when she tried to offer an opinion, she would be talked over or ignored. When she did get an opportunity to provide input, she was often patronized and then her idea ignored. Inevitably the same idea or input would later be raised by one of her male colleagues. The group would immediately hop aboard the idea as something great. The male colleague would get credit for her idea. As a result, she chose to sit back and made the assumption that eventually her male colleagues would stumble upon things for themselves. The boss wanted her to be more aggressive and speak up. What he was saying was that he wanted her to be more like the men so that they would be more comfortable. We provided her with some strategies for being heard—she learned to keep going when interrupted, to tell them they were interrupting and that it was rude. She learned to do it and was heard more.

The best tip I've ever come across for combating this kind of corporate deafness came from Geraldine Laybourne, when she worked at MTV.[10] She and a colleague made a point of confirming each other at meetings. They would echo *and* attribute good ideas—"I think Mary's idea is a good one"—to ensure that it was heard and its author remembered. What's so smart about this tactic is that it makes everyone look good: both the person with the smart idea and the person generous enough to identify its author correctly. It's so smart it can be catching; you start to look churlish if you *don't* do it. Generosity is enormously, surprisingly powerful.

Lots of other tactics work—reiterating ideas and advice afterward in memos, following up discussions to reinforce your position. Some women find idiosyncratic, but memorable, ways of drawing attention to themselves—like having a sign that says "I just did something wonderful. Ask me about it." What started as an office gag has become a way of generating conversations that reinforce achievements.[11]

The habit of keeping a journal of accomplishments comes in handy here too; the first person you must be visible to is yourself. Internalizing your contributions is an essential first step to ensuring that other people see them and see you. Of course, sometimes men don't see you because they just don't want to. They'd prefer that you not be there and prefer that you not be heard. This can be pretty intimidating, so it's essential that, when challenged, you can use your accomplishments to defend your ground.

Chris Carosella

A former vice chairman of the company spoke at a management meeting where I was one of only six women out of approximately 250 senior managers from the 26 capital businesses. After he spoke, he came over to me and asked why I was there. Since so few women were there, he wanted to know what made us eligible for the meeting. I told him I was the SVP of customer service. He chuckled, said I must have "a department full of women" and stated our experience has been that women bring too much baggage to the office. I explained that one of the reasons our company had achieved its financial targets for that year was because the new customer service department, which consisted of men *and* women, fixed the bleeding of lost premiums and rebuilt relationships with customers and the sales force. He was surprised to learn from me that our department had received national recognition for our innovative solutions to complex problems.

After the vice chair walked away, the head of HR from our business ran over and wanted to know what the discussion was about in case he had to "do damage control" for me. When I relayed my conversation, he indicated he was worried I might be "too honest" with someone at the highest levels and that it might hurt my career.

Daring to be honest, to be visible, put Chris's career at risk. But silence would have put it at risk too. We have to be very committed to our own visibility.

It takes nerve: to be seen, you have to want to be seen. This sounds obvious, but I think women sometimes will their own invisibility—I know I have. We just want to do the work, get on with it, and not have to mess with anyone who's a little threatened by our presence. Many women actively seek out a conformist style so concertedly that, in trying to avoid comment, they avoid being seen at all. The helmet haircut, the nice gray suit, sensible pumps. Armies of uniform women marching up and down Wall Street, hiding. Planning to meet an email correspondent once, I said, "You will recognize me because I have long hair and carry a large red bag." "Oh," she said, "I just look ordinary." She could not see herself distinctively enough to describe an individual.

And as women, we have a fantastic array of choices as to *how* we want to be seen. If clothes are a language, what do you want to say? It's a waste to say nothing. Consciously or unconsciously, I always dressed more expensively than my job allowed or required. Only later did I realize that it was my way of showing that I could go higher. Others recommend that you dress "as you want to be paid."[12] I'd suggest you dress as you want to be paid next year.

Blending into a bland corporate environment helps to make you invisible—but developing a personal style is a powerful way to maintain a personality. The red handbag helped me do that. It was practical, stylish, and identifiable. People who saw it saw me. I wasn't invisible. And when they saw me, I had a chance of being heard.

Of course work clothes are different from leisure clothes and every culture has a comfort zone that you must be aware of. But how many people do you look forward to *seeing* at work? Why not *be* one of those people? Madeleine Albright's brooches offered just the tiniest hint, in a very male, very staid environment, that under the suit was a real person with wit and naughtiness. It isn't just the creative directors who can make visual statements. Be memorable. Your clothes and accessories should articulate you, be about your style and not about fashion. How can anyone remember you if they can't see who you are? If you cannot bring your personality to work and have it seen, do you really want to be there? As Sharon Whitely said, "A peacock that sits on his tail feathers is just a turkey."[13]

There's so much to admire in women like Andrea Jung, CEO of Avon; Myrtle Potter, COO of Genentech; and Stacey Snider, chairman of Universal Pictures. But one of the many things I love about these women is that, on their way to the top, they haven't cut their hair. Most women do and I've known women who have been counseled to do so—specifically to advance their careers! Hair is the classic symbol of sexuality; it declares our femininity.

Apparently this so rattles men that they'd prefer it went away. But no more. After years of helmet hair, we are finally seeing that we do not have to disguise our gender. We can, and will, be visible women and proud of it.

Bitch

If you're not a pretty little geisha and you're not invisible, the chances are that, one day, you will be called a bitch. The first time that this happened to me was when I was working for a company that built software for Intuit. Much bigger and richer than we were, the company was tough to work with. As they kept asking for us to absorb more of the risk and expense, I kept saying no and explaining why. After the conference call was over, they didn't hang up because we heard their private conversation: "God that woman's a bitch."

Tough men are idolized; strong women are demonized. The extremes are sometimes so great as to be ludicrous—as when Dawn Steel, production head at Columbia Pictures, was named one of the worst bosses in Hollywood by *California* magazine. She was selected in preference to a man who killed two of his migrant workers, then tried to flush them down the toilet! What was it that Dawn Steel did that was so terrible? Sometimes she yelled at people.

Men receive accolades for being decisive, powerful, effective, strong. But when women demonstrate the same qualities we can be labeled strident, intimidating, aggressive. These criticisms regularly surface when we make the mistake of catching an error or recommending a better strategy. When our competence threatens men, some of them retaliate by attacking our femininity.

Susan Ellis

When I worked in Columbus, Ohio, I had such an asshole for a boss. About my age or younger. Knew nothing and had no experience. He was very controlling and insecure. And I would argue with him: "There's a better way to do it so our numbers are better." And he got so frustrated with me and would have fired me if he could have, just to get me out of his face. Instead, he said, "You are entirely too aggressive for a woman!" Well. I thought "thank god—goodbye." Because who says those types of words? It is ridiculous! At what point do you become "too aggressive for a woman"? At the time I thought there was something wrong with me. I am not woman enough for this job. There is a level of femininity for this job? I am supposed to manage it so you smile and give me a cup of tea???? I did not want to stick around and find out. So inappropriate and so unacceptable. He could have taken issue and said I am your boss and I am sick of arguing. I have said that to people; he could have said that. But to make it personal and about me being a woman . . . that's weird.

Susan refused to be a geisha, and when this made her boss uncomfortable, she was made to feel that that was her fault. He believed that it was her responsibility to pander to his concept of femininity. When she didn't, she was the one with the problem.

As Joan Silver coached a female executive who was trying to become visible, she learned that she'd escaped one stereotype—only to face another. Now that the executive could be heard, she made her male colleagues very uncomfortable.

Joan Silver

She learned to stand her ground and was heard more. As she got more confident, her boss started getting uncomfortable. She was becoming "contentious" and "undermining his authority." She became more open and more comfortable with taking a stand—and he didn't like it. She eventually left the organization—she got scooped away by a competitor.

In very masculine cultures, like the one Chris Carosella worked in for eleven years, doing anything that may look like you are *more* competent than a man is a recipe for insults.

Chris Carosella

My reputation was built on turning around poor performing branches and regions. As a result, I was promoted and transferred frequently. Each move was an opportunity to fix problems that resulted from inept management and each time it was a male predecessor. Since I was always the first female in each role, it was no surprise to me that I was referred to as a "bitch."

When I took over the Southern region, expenses were out of control—and I found out that this was because so much was being spent on strip clubs. Sales guys were blatantly putting "Lap Dancing" and "Gold Club" on their expenses. At first I thought they were just busting my chops. Then I find it's all for real! Expenses were way out of control because of strip clubs—so I stopped it. One of the guys described me as "There's that bitch that won't pay for . . ." Some of the men went over my head to complain, saying it would lose us business. But it didn't. At $500 a throw, it was *costing* us the business!

Being called a bitch carries with it two problems—beyond the insult of the term. When we are called bitches, our defenses persuade us we are being labeled for our expertise and competence. We start to think being a bitch is perhaps not so bad after all. If standing my ground and refusing to be walked over makes me a bitch—then, yes, we say, I'm a bitch. This kind of defensiveness is perfectly understandable—but if we get stuck in this role, we can became so tough, so impervious that we lose our talent for normal, human relationships. When we concede to the stereotype, we run the very real risk that it will take us over.

The other problem is that "bitch" suggests that you have done something wrong—and therefore should be punished. Bitches, after all, aren't really suitable for inclusion in polite society. So the label is used to exclude us.

Meena Naidu

Apparently it's OK when things are going well and I'm "nice" but men in particular are usually very unhappy when they screw up, resulting in me pointing out the error in their ways. I have been abused orally, been bitched about by men in team meetings where I was not present and have had my manager not talk to me for almost 3 months simply because I didn't turn out to be the weak and demure creature that he was looking for.

To be a bitch is to be alone—isolated as a deliberate punishment or by the tough veneer the stereotype requires. Isolation, of course, ultimately makes it impossible for us to succeed and to be happy.

Pamela Matthews

Things get dicey as you start to reach the more senior levels (vice president and up) and you become a threat to the men—your peers and the senior guys. If you are tough—tough with junior

> people, tough in meetings—you are a bitch but you have respect. You have NO friends at work and everyone talks behind your back but you are respected. You can advance but it must be very lonely. That's not me, I could not take on this persona. It's not worth it to me. But there is no acceptance of other ways to be successful.

Isolation is a very bad career move. You need your networks, you need allies, we all need friends. The exclusion and isolation that comes with being a bitch is a profound career penalty, meaning you can get tough assignments, you can do them well—but bitches never make it to the top table.

So pervasive is the bitch stereotype that companies can now send such "difficult" women on courses to modify their behavior. Courses to retrain so-called "bully broads" are designed to cure us of the habit of being tough, forceful, and direct—all words that, in a male lexicon, would be complimentary and essential qualities for advancement. But these courses advise women to smile, speak more softly, and use self-deprecation or stammering when speaking! (This despite all the evidence that it is just those habits that cause women to be routinely undervalued and underpaid, and their achievements to go unnoticed.) They even recommend that women talk slowly and even walk slowly so they don't rush past people, and to be comfortable crying at work.[14] It's just trading one stereotype (bully broad) for another (geisha) and calling it progress. As Robin Gerber argues, "Women who are confidently competent, who gain power through the strength of their convictions, who put determination behind their ideas and communicate clearly and directly aren't bully broads—they're leaders."[15]

I don't think that the solution to being called a bitch is to become a geisha. I think the most important thing you can do is not let the epithet get to you: don't let it turn you into a bitch. Think hard about all those aspects in your life in which you clearly are not a bitch. Don't worry too much about persuading the guys how nice you are, but make sure you're confident in yourself, in your relationships. Although being called a bitch carries with it a grudging respect, it's a lonely role to fall into—not least because no woman relishes the label. It leaves us in a place where we can be competent but not a colleague, successful but not satisfied.

Guy

We don't want to be invisible, we don't want to be geishas or bitches, but we do want to fit in. So we assimilate as profoundly as we can: we behave like men.

> *Meena Naidu*
>
> My general view is it's incredibly frustrating to be categorized because it suggests that you are a one dimensional person and men find it difficult when we move between categories. The problem with these categories is that they turn a valid trait into something negative. If I want to be feminine and wear makeup and a skirt, then I am a geisha. If I pull someone up on a mistake or assert a view, then I am a bitch. And if I simply try to "fit in" then I must be a hard person who thinks it is acceptable for men to make derogatory comments towards women (which I am assured don't relate to me) or must feign interest in boys' joys—must we get the penis implant?!?!

The pressure to behave like a man is insidious, profound and hard to resist. Male colleagues would put their arms around my shoulders and beam, "Good ole Margaret, she's one of the boys!" and I'd take it as the compliment it was meant to be. When conversations about Microsoft inevitably led to discussions of whether to "open the kimono," no one was embarrassed by my being in the room. Because I was a CEO, they didn't see me as a woman—they saw a man.

Everywhere I go, I hear women tell me that, in order to progress, they must assimilate. They have to learn to act like a guy. The grim stares of female CEOs in business magazines say loud and clear: I can be as mean and tough as you guys can; just try me. It doesn't look like much fun—and it isn't. Running my first company in England, a core part of my job was to negotiate agreements with the labor unions. One of the union bosses took me out to lunch at a Chinese restaurant and ordered the most gruesome items on the menu: webbed chickens' feet, ducks' tongues, lambs' testicles. The challenge was obvious and I rose to it. I wasn't going to let him intimidate me—so I ate everything. But whereas I used to tell that story with pride, I now realize that I just fell into his trap. He tested me as a guy and I passed, as a guy. A far better response would have been simply to order my own dishes, food I preferred. I should have refused to do the guy thing.

Such macho tests are a regular feature of corporate life. Can you work through the night? Stomach the red-eye? Investment bankers closing M&A deals, engineers writing code, journalists in war zones, and doctors sawing bones: it's an endless experience of hazing to see if we can really cut the mustard. When you're competitive, as I am, these tests and rituals are hard to resist until you are confident enough to know that yes, I can do it and no, I don't want to. I'll order off of my own menu, thank you.

The other three stereotypes—being a geisha, a bitch, or just plain invisible—limit how far up in an organization we can get. Being a guy does not—which is the reason ambitious women fall into this stereotype after successfully avoiding the others. As guys, we train ourselves never to draw attention to our gender; we wear the corporate uniform, arrive super-early, leave really late, and, if we are mothers, learn never to mention our children. But while it may bring substantial rewards, being a guy does nothing for our spirit. Men may accept us as one of them—but we aren't one of them, and we know it. So we're left feeling neither female nor male. Faking it diminishes us as human beings.

Joan Silver has worked with executive women who had all the professional skills they needed, had experienced considerable success within their corporations—but who still felt that something, somewhere, wasn't quite right. One of them felt she could never comfortably bring her whole personality to work.

Joan Silver

Meetings always left her feeling "less than." She went to a male colleague and asked him about this.

"I just don't fit in here."

He just said, "Why don't you behave like us?"

But they were all allowed to be *individuals*! Why did she have to change and they didn't?

"I couldn't do my best work because I was too busy trying to be someone else. I didn't want to pretend. I couldn't do great work pretending to be something I'm not."

When we act like guys, we may be playing a leading role, but it's still playacting and leaves us feeling that our work, and our achievements, belong to some other "guy" we don't much respect. They belong to some other person, the person at work, the person that isn't really me.

Karen Price

> Once, I was having problems with two male peers in my organization. They kept interfering with decisions that I had made on the project I was running. They were usurping my authority and treating me like someone who could be walked all over. So I walked into the one man's office while they were both in there, closed the door, looked them square in the eye, and cussed them both up one side and down the other!! I used almost every swear word I know. They both sat and stared at me with their mouths practically hanging open. When I was done, the one man, who is a good ole southern boy, said "Damn Karen, I didn't know you had that in you," and his compadre replied "Well Richard, you'd do the same thing if it was your project wouldn't you?" "Yup," was the reply. I never had another problem with those two. I was accepted into their male management club. I was proud of myself at this moment for my brashness and the effect but, in hindsight, I gave up a piece of my womanhood it seemed. I had been playing "one of the guys" for so long, I didn't realize what I was giving up.

Being a guy at work means that you are very cautious about all aspects of your femininity; that you are, in effect, locking away a big part of who you are.

Karen Price

> I wanted to be accepted by men because it seemed that they controlled success. So many female characteristics are perceived as weak. If I was socializing with women, I was careful to never get too close, never to act too girly. I would never allow myself to work the company bake sale or even make something that showed I was good in the kitchen. I was so afraid of being perceived as "one of the girls" instead of "one of the boys." I was harsher and tougher than I ever liked being. I was a hybrid between woman and man. But I saw myself as behaving very masculinely. I had to be more tough and less caring than is my true nature.

You can't be a guy and be one of the girls. The worst consequence of aping male behavior at work is the way women often treat other women. Women who are desperate to fit in often prove what real guys they are by treating other women badly. It happens a lot. I remember a female boss of mine proving her "manhood" by demanding that I deliver her dry cleaning. After I refused, she regularly blocked all efforts I made to train myself. Such memories stick in the minds of women forever because they feel like such betrayals. Women look to each other for support, encouragement, and mentoring and are dismayed to find instead Queen Bees who want nothing feminine near them to remind them uncomfortably of who and what they really are, or were.

I worked as a guy for a lot of my career and, while I don't think I was especially horrid to women, I know that I didn't give them the support and encouragement many of them deserved. I was good at developing the psychological camouflage that won me kudos and rewards. Only later did I start to see this behavior as intrinsically false, a well-integrated but nonetheless stressful and lonely lie. Having seen that, retrieving my true self became a matter of urgency.

How, and when, did I stop being a guy? I think I changed when I found myself working for a guy with such exceptional machismo that I knew I couldn't work his way. No one would ever win with him on his terms so I had to work with him on my own terms. And there was one evening when I found myself telling the story about the Chinese food—and instead of feeling proud of how tough I was, I suddenly just felt very, very stupid.

Did I walk into the office the next morning a changed woman? Of course not. But I did two things. I started giving myself permission to be myself—I turned the self-editing machine off. Not only did the sky not fall—my work got better. My relationships improved. Work felt different. The other thing that I did was, when I found myself getting into head-to-head arguments with someone, I'd ease off and say something positive to them. Instead of pursuing the debate to the point where I'd crush them, I enlisted their support in resolving the issue. Helping them made them want to help me; collaborating replaced stalemate and sadism. It was the negotiating equivalent of ordering my own food: when I didn't like the terms of the discussion, I changed them. It was so much more effective—and I felt fantastic.

The Chinese restaurant lunch took place ten years ago. It took a long time to turn a mistake into learning. And I'm aware, even now, that I sometimes revert to old, bad behavior. But I'm getting there. Perhaps one reason I persevere is because I see now how profoundly liberating it can be once we transcend stereotypes to become our own person. Nowhere, I think, did I see this more clearly than at a recent business school conference. It was full of smart, inquiring MBA students, eager to understand more about business and how to manage their careers. But they'd already absorbed so much: the cropped hair, the suits, the personality firmly under control: not too loud, not too fast, not too kind, self-editing their generosity. It made the conference quite depressing. But then Susan Greenfield spoke. She's a founding director of a company developing treatments for Alzheimer's disease and her work was recognized with the Golden Plate award from the Academy of Achievement in Washington, D.C. She wears miniskirts, she has long blond hair and a great big smile, and she sparkles. She even dares to talk about her figure. She's a girl—lively, funny, straightforward, pulling no punches. But most of all, she's her own woman. So she gave the MBAs permission to be female too. In that one moment, the power and energy they'd bottled up came pouring out and transformed the room. This, I thought, is what women can be.

Whether her male scientist peers will forgive her for it remains to be seen. Escaping stereotypes is an exceptionally hard part of our careers—maybe even the hardest—because, as Meena Naidu says, stereotypes take something valid about us and turn it into something shallow and trivial. We want to go about our business without having to blow our own trumpets—but that doesn't mean we are willing to sacrifice rewards and promotion. We want to please people—but that doesn't mean we will be pleasers at any cost. We want to stand up for what we know is right—that doesn't mean we are unfeeling. And we want to be accepted as competent and confident—while remaining female and feminine. Every stereotype costs us in real terms: in salaries, in promotion, in recognition, in opportunity. And every stereotype costs us in psychic terms too: it is exceptionally hard work to hang onto an identity that receives no reinforcement, or negative reinforcement, every day that we go to work.

I'm not sure that it is possible to escape stereotypes altogether, but I am convinced that we can combat their consequences. Pay, promotion, recognition all depend on tactics like journaling, reinforcing each other at meetings, teaching ourselves to negotiate, and underlining our achievements through memos, reports, and even idiosyncratic gestures. These all help to deepen the regard in which we are held by our colleagues and ourselves. But many women find that it's hard to escape a stereotype once you're defined by it, and they come to feel that the only way to change the way they're regarded is to change jobs. If, after all your efforts, you feel that way too, make sure that every step you take next defines who you really are—not who the guys want you to be.

Travel Thoughts

- Are you proud of the way that you work? Are you proud of the way you are treated at work?
- How seriously do your peers take you?
- Can you be heard at work? If not, why not? Can people see you? Who at work will amplify and support what you say?
- What have you achieved in the last three months? What benefit was it to the business? Who knows about it?

Chapter Three

Balls to the Wall: Toxic Bosses and Hostile Environments

Above all things, never think that you're not good enough yourself. My belief is that in life people will take you very much at your own reckoning.
—ANTHONY TROLLOPE

We may evade stereotypes. That changes us, but it doesn't necessarily change the men around us who continue to view women as inferior beings. Not all men are like this, of course—the business world holds lots of men who respect us and want us to succeed. But it also still features plenty of men who don't want to work with women, don't see why they should, and will do everything they can to get women out of their ambit. Some of this is conscious; much of it is not.

> *Chris Carosella*
>
> I was the only woman on the senior management team of this company. Eleven men plus me. At my first senior staff meeting, I disagreed with a comment one of my colleagues made about a strategic issue. After the meeting was over, he said, "Chris, don't you know you're just the cunt at the table? No one cares what you think."

Toxic bosses and hostile environments derive from the same thing: the attitude that defines "normal" as "male."

Jennifer Mack

> I was in a seminar on, of all things, cultural awareness, and we had a presentation from a guy from Rolls Royce. Someone asked him what it took to succeed in the company. His answer was: "Testosterone. Testosterone. Testosterone." That was in 2004.

Men with attitudes like these see women as anomalies, to be gotten rid of or humiliated into place. Such a mind-set can never regard women as peers or superiors. Misogyny in the workplace is a very uncomfortable subject for everyone to discuss: for men, because no one likes scrutiny or blame; for women, because we don't like to complain and we keep hoping that, by acting like equals, eventually we will be treated as equals.

Because I know readers will complain that not all men are like this, I will reiterate: not all men are misogynists, not all corporations are toxic, not all bosses are macho. But it's a blessed career indeed that never encounters these issues.

How do they manifest themselves? The most overt form of managerial machismo is sexual harassment. The old boys' network still runs much of our business lives and is not nearly as accessible, open, and inclusive as it should be. Toxic bosses judge their female employees by how masculine they are, questioning and finding fault with anything that makes them different from men. Pay discrimination remains, relentlessly, a crucial issue—and discrimination against mothers (in pay and promotion) has proved systemically hard to eradicate. The obvious external result is low pay and slow advancement for women; the less visible signs are loss of confidence, undermining of competence, and, sometimes, rage.

Denying the existence or importance of these things convinces no one. Worse, if we don't identify the instances of misogyny in the workplace, we fall into the trap of taking them personally. You start to think that you are the problem. And then, of course, your confidence, enthusiasm, and commitment falter further. Being able to see these for what they are, identifying them so that you don't take them personally, is key to dealing with them.

Because we *can* deal with them. While newspapers are full of stories of women opting out, the less-told story is of women persisting and finding ways to do good work *and* hold their heads high. Sometimes you do have to leave—but sometimes you can stay, work smart, and find a way of working that diminishes no one.

Sexual Harassment

A lot of sexism has gone underground, so it's rare to find yourself in a confrontation as direct as the one that Chris described. But with 50 to 80 percent of women saying they have been sexually harassed in the workplace, that problem not only hasn't gone away, it remains a persistent feature of women's careers.[1]

Lise Markham

It used to be a chauvinist was clearly marked by the wife-beater T-shirt, invisible to the naked eye but clearly defined by most women in the workforce. In time, those men smart enough to know what "politically correct" was changed their outside behavior but still had the misogynist lurking deep within. Promotions would come and go to male co-workers in the ensuing years but the women would not suspect sexism because the boss outwardly was so pro-female.

I worked for several companies, both large and small, private and publicly traded, where I was the first woman in the division or entire company to be hired. Unwanted sexual harassment was rampant in both. The men who protested this kind of behavior the most, were often the guiltiest themselves. Almost 70% of the problems I dealt with as the boss myself were sexually based and of those, 90% were unwanted, illegal actions by a male superior over a female. Many women believe reporting such behavior now is viewed as not being a team player; not playing along which one must do to get ahead.

Reporting this behavior is so frowned upon—by men *and* women—that it is estimated that only 5 percent of women experiencing harassment step forward to make a complaint. Nevertheless, for those women who do have the nerve to report this behavior, awards are on the increase. In the United Kingdom, the cost of awards rose by 33 percent in 2000.[2] Women like Angelica Graham, a twenty-one-year-old sales trainee who got a job working for Ralph Marriott. He asked to see her pubic hair, tugged at her skirt zipper, tried to feel around her crotch, pinched her bottom until she screamed, and finally remarked, "She's a fit one, I wouldn't mind giving her one." This was in Angelica's first week at work. The court accepted medical evidence that estimated it would take two-and-a-half years before she could work again. Mr. Marriott was ordered to pay $10,000 personally and his company was ordered to pay $220,000.[3]

Harassment typically befalls women at the outset of their careers; they are young, pretty, and vulnerable. In one-third of cases, it comes from the director or owner of their organization and/or their ultimate manager. The company Angelica worked for had no written policy on sex discrimination or harassment or equal opportunities in general. Nor did it provide training or advice to employees about sexual harassment or warn them against it. The only aspect of Angelica's case that isn't typical is the speed with which she acted; most cases are brought by women who have put up with sexual harassment for over twelve months.[4]

Angelica's company sold cars; some have dismissed the seriousness of the story by seeing it as specific to the industry—they ask, "What can you expect of car salesmen?" But at the other end of the spectrum, the pattern of harassment and discrimination repeats itself. Kate Bleasdale founded and was CEO of Match Holdings, a healthcare recruitment company. She built the company from a $35,000 loan to a business worth $275 million—but was dismissed before the company went public. Her award of $3.5 million—the United Kingdom's highest-ever award for sexual discrimination—seems small compensation for losing the company she built from scratch. In the court case, it transpired that one of the concerns of her new chairman, Sir Tim Chessells, was that "he had never worked with a female chief executive and didn't really know how to interact with one . . . and whether that meant he had to alter the way that he behaved in the boardroom." Bleasdale alleged that Sir Tim told her he was uncomfortable about having to "alter his approach, as there would be a woman present. At all meetings he curtailed what I was saying, gave knowing looks to other non-executive directors, and always spoke to me while wagging his finger at me in an extraordinarily aggressive manner . . . He simply did not believe a woman should be in the boardroom, let alone be running the company." In another incident, Bleasdale alleged that the chairman leered at her breasts and looked her up and down so obviously that she went to the lavatory to check if her trouser zipper was undone. She was twice asked if she was pregnant. The accumulation of these incidents was tremendously destructive: "I'm still not the person I used to be. I was confident, dynamic, full of energy, able to keep ten balls in the air. I ran around, doing home, doing work. I was very goal-oriented, making sure things were running efficiently."[5] Bleasdale spent over a year at home on antidepressants.

Whole industries have had their reputations tarnished as their cultures have tolerated, encouraged, and rewarded the macho behaviors of which harassment is a crucial part. Just under one-third (32 percent) of women on Wall Street say they have experienced sexual harassment. Thirteen percent say they receive unwelcome sexual attention at work and that sexist comments are tolerated in their firm. Smith Barney became infamous for its Boom Boom Room, a so-called party room where managers carried guns, and men hung toilets on the ceiling, drank Bloody Marys from a barrel, and routinely subjected women to lewd pranks.

I am always amazed by how often men bring up the subject of sexual harassment, only to make a joke of it. I've heard CEOs, lords, and chairmen laugh about how foolish regulations are and how maddening it is for them not to be able to compliment a woman on her dress or hair style. But of course, compliments don't constitute harassment because compliments don't have the intent or the effect that harassment has. Sexual harassment in particular, and sexism at work in general, is "about keeping women in their place by creating a hostile environment."[6] Kate Bleasdale has lost confidence because that is what harassment does—chips away at our sense of self-worth and achievement. That is what it's for.

Meena Naidu

I was taken out to lunch about 3 weeks ago by the team leader of a project which I am supposed to be working on. He has the direct power to get me on and off projects. The way he propositioned me was so clever I didn't even see it coming till it was there. I told him I thought it would be complicated and perhaps not a good idea. He didn't seem to be deterred by the situation. He is very keen to get me out on a project with him, which means we will both be out of the country together—you can imagine what he will try on. At the end of the day, if I have to leave the project I will. I know that if my company finds out, they won't be happy about the situation but they will probably pull me off rather than him because he is more senior.

> I am constantly hit on by men (colleagues, clients and stakeholders) which forces me to question the value placed on me. Am I on a team because I am good at my job or because I happen to be one of the few females around who is young and not totally ugly and with large breasts? Does that mean it will be easier for me to get interviews? No matter how much I want it to be how good I am, I always question it. A male colleague of mine mentioned only last week (when I asked him his views on my new female director) that men first assess the attractiveness of women and competency is the last thing they review.

Meena eventually dealt with her team leader. First, she went to the head of HR, who didn't see what the problem was. Then she went to the head of the company, who did. Meena was put in charge of the project and the company introduced a sexual harassment policy. The incident forced the company to look at these issues and it emerged stronger, and fairer, as a consequence. I'm impressed by Meena not just because she had the nerve and skill to solve her problem, but because she made the whole company better when she did.

Looking back on my career, I can see that I experienced some sexual harassment but that I didn't recognize it as such. I just thought the middle-aged, married middle managers were flirting and that that was pretty stupid of them. Because I was in a job I didn't much care for, I wasn't afraid; that I might lose my job for rebuffing them never occurred to me. But being pestered by your boss can make your job an obstacle course.

Linda Phillips

> I was always, always being pursued by the head of the studio. And it wasn't subtle. "I can be a very, very good friend," he would growl, "but a very bad enemy." He invited me to his house one night and of course it didn't occur to me 'til I got there that there would be no one else there. I managed to keep him at bay, but it wasn't easy and he never, ever stopped.
>
> Until finally, I had this great idea. The next time he came on to me, I said, "You know I really, really like you. I think you are one of the sexiest, handsomest men I have ever known." (He was famously ugly.) "But you know what I need right now? I need commitment. I need someone who will be there for me on Christmas morning." And I never heard from him again. *(laughs)*

Linda's strategy worked because she gave her boss the decision to stop pursuing her—and because she wasn't afraid. Bullies prey on fear. The *British Medical Journal* recently ran an editorial about workplace bullying. "A deadly combination of economic rationalism, increasing competition, 'downsizing,' and the current fashion for tough, dynamic, 'macho' management styles have created a culture in which bullying can thrive, producing toxic workplaces and nurturing a silent epidemic."[7] The costs of this epidemic have been estimated at billions of dollars per year. Those costs are estimated on the basis of days lost through illness. They don't take into account the awards made to the few women who work up the courage to take their bullies to court.

Bullies generally intimidate as a cover for their own inadequacy. So women caught in bullying cultures find that the more competent they are, the more they disturb and enrage the bully, who only feels powerful when others look weak. When Kate Bleasdale regretted that she was no longer the confident, dynamic, efficient person she had been as a CEO, interviewer Jasper Gerard commented, "If she is no longer that, *she is probably easier to live with.*"[8] In other words, it's nicer for men when women lose their confidence, competence, and power. Where do such attitudes come from? From the male assumption that women are intrinsically lightweight—toys to be played with, not peers to be taken seriously—and the world is easier for men when women know their place.

The Old Boys' Club

As women become more senior, or just older, the threat of harassment may recede. It goes away in part because we're no longer seen as nymphets and in part because we don't look, or act, so vulnerable. Instead, something else starts to happen. We are subjected to environments and behaviors that tell us we don't really count.

Chris Carosella

It gets worse when you go out of town. You get what they call "out of town stuff"—meaning screwing around. "It's okay," they told me, "We never tell these women our real names. Our wives'll never find out." There was even one guy who said he played around—but then told me that he'd always slip away at the last minute.

"They think I've joined in," he told me.

"Why is it so important?" I asked.

"It's a guy thing, peer pressure I guess."

But while one poor guy is caving in to peer pressure, the women all around are hearing the same depressing message from men: we lie to women; women are playthings, to be used and discarded if they don't please us. In hearing stories like these, whose side are we supposed to be on? Conversations like this serve one purpose: to exclude women from the mainstream.

It is human nature—alas—that people tend to like people who are like themselves. This is as true of women as of men. But since men already hold the center of power in most corporations, the consequence for women is that we tend to get shut out. Men like men like themselves—and that isn't us. So we are excluded in all kinds of ways. Companies that tolerate, endorse, or even encourage exclusive behavior by men are hostile environments for women. This doesn't mean that they are impossible to work in—but it does mean that we aren't welcome and we will find it hard to build support of the kind that every career requires.

Asked to name the most significant factors holding them back from advancement, women in a recent survey cited "male stereotyping and preconceptions of women (33 percent)" and "exclusion from informal networks of communications (41 percent)" as the top two.[9] The "informal networks of communications" is what we call the old boys' club. Like all clubs, this one selects members on the basis of how similar they are to each other; the whole point of being together is to reinforce and advance one another. The old boys' clubs are intrinsically narcissistic, judging themselves by each other—not by any external reference. They aren't about diversity or challenge or innovation—and they are still alive and well, as the head of HR at CMGI told me (before she herself was replaced by a man). "It's all about access. The guys golf together, they drink together, they piss together. Sometimes they let you in, sometimes they don't. *They* choose. It's how everything gets done."

Kate Bleasdale understood why she had to be expelled—she didn't fit into the club. "I think that if I had been a man with a few gray hairs, fitted into the club, then it would have been much less threatening."

Not all hostile environments are blatantly sexist. We are excluded just by being ignored, our voice left unheard.

Bronwen Hughes trained as a nurse and then moved into pharmaceutical research and development. She's a bubbly, vivacious blond with a fantastic sense of humor and a string of achievements that testify to her focused, pragmatic intelligence.

Bronwen Hughes

After about four years, I became the first non-MD to be in a senior position running a major international clinical development program. I'm very proud of that, since it was viewed as groundbreaking in the organization and a lot of people called me to thank me for changing the culture and opening up the opportunities for men and women. I was the first woman ever to give a presentation to the board! They couldn't believe it and kept saying, "we've never had a woman here before" and I just said, "Well, you'd better get used to it."

Then there was a change from Germany whereby German physicians were sent over to run the medical division. They brought with them very traditional views about women in the workplace. I was asked to join a team of seventeen, working with Boston Consulting Group on reengineering. And I said, "You can't do this to me! I need some camaraderie!" But there weren't any other women. I was just completely alone. I'd be flying back and forth to Germany for meetings and the guy leading it just didn't pay *any* attention to me. I tried everything: jokes, being nice, being funny, being serious. I used to come home from the meetings in tears and John would always be patching me up and helping me get back in the ring. Finally, at the end of one session, I went to the guy and said "Look, I've had enough of this. You have to take me seriously. You have to listen to what I have to say." And then I phoned my boss and said "Now you have to phone him and tell him the same thing!"—which he did.

Then we were doing the implementation and it was murder! And I got an offer to join another firm and I took it. When I told them, they said "you can't do this to us!" But I was NEVER going back! *(laughs)*

The hostility Bronwen experienced was implicitly sexist and she knew it. She didn't take it personally but she saw that staying was futile. She can laugh now because she got out in time to stay whole, confident, herself.

There are other ways that the old boys' club sometimes excludes us. Sometimes it is just by making the price of inclusion way too high. Some of their rituals are so alienating that we opt out of them ourselves. I remember company conferences where the guys thought it would be fun, after a lot of heavy drinking, to race rental cars around the hotel car park. By going to bed early with a book, I cut myself out of the gang, excluded myself from the network. I knew it had professional consequences: I could either join in, doing something I hated and thought was stupid—or I could be honest but count myself out. I was the only female CEO in the group.

Even when we overcome our repugnance and do join in, we don't fool ourselves that we really belong. We do things we hate but it doesn't really make us feel any better.

Pamela Matthews

> I am off to the Masters this year on a client entertainment event. I've spoken out to a lot of people about my view on the whole issue. It has cost me in that I am now isolated on this issue and it is a mark against me and a mark that separates me from everyone else. As you can imagine, I am the only woman in my group and the only one with client coverage responsibilities. I would find this an uncomfortable event even without the current controversy related to the Masters. I will feel a traitor of sorts walking in while women are protesting at the gates. Also, it involves staying in a house with six other men—awkward. And the whispered form of entertainment at night is the myriad of strip bars in Augusta. I am torn because I think it would hurt my client relationships to not go and will also hurt my positioning internally, as my peers will be "bonding" with my boss and then I would be left out of all the fun stories they will refer to.

Pamela did find somewhere else to stay. And she excluded herself from the strip clubs. She fulfilled her client responsibilities and did come back with her own "funny story." It was all about the anti–Martha Burk beer bottles being consumed in the clubhouse.

But not all exclusions are our choice. I vividly remember discovering that I was the only one of my peers not invited to a dinner with Wall Street investors. Had I been forgotten or deliberately excluded? Should I make a fuss—or would that make me look petty and hysterical? In the event, I decided to leave it until or unless it happened again. I let back channels know I was annoyed. Nowadays, I would make it a point to comment on every exclusion, to let men know that I won't be sidelined. But it's still hard to resist the feeling that at meetings, at conferences, on golf courses, women are gatecrashers.

Sally West

> I've also had experiences where I was passed over for an invitation to a management meeting because I somehow wasn't really necessary for the meeting—yet every other male individual who was connected was invited. Given my high-level position, I did not accept not participating in the meeting, so I booked a ticket (charged to the company) and still attended the meeting. Difficult because although you've still fought and attended, you end up being constantly on the defensive; not conducive to optimum productivity.

I think Sally did the right thing—refuse to be excluded. Only by acting worthy do we stand a chance of being seen as worthy. But much of this kind of exclusion is so subtle that standing up for ourselves feels like an overreaction. It's so easy to explain it away as careless or unimportant. Which is what it would be if it happened rarely, to very few women. But it happens all the time and we do get the message.

Exclusion is serious because a big part of being able to work effectively, and of being able to *enjoy* work, involves having friends, allies, supporters. So many women have asked me: why should guys have their old boys' network and not us? But in hostile environments, women aren't allowed to build that kind of power base. When, occasionally, we do find female peers, even that is derided. Marty Johnson, CEO of the American Red Cross, spent much of her career in the U.S. Navy where, she says, she avoided fraternizing (her term) with other females lest they be accused of plotting.[10] In the United Kingdom, Paul Routledge, a newspaper columnist, recently reported that male journalists covering Parliament regularly refer to their female colleagues as "the lezzie lobby."[11] His sneering derision of the rare camaraderie women can find at work is, alas, not untypical.

> *Pamela Matthews*
>
> There is one other woman here who has kids—she works in PR. And I can talk to her sometimes. But then the guys always refer to her as "your friend" with that little lesbian overtone! This is a very juvenile industry.

The old boys' network sounds so benign; if it were inclusive instead of exclusive, it would be. But in many industries and many companies, it isn't. It's a wall around power and influence that we cannot breach. If we try, we are mocked, derided, belittled—or made to accept behaviors we find repugnant.

Toxic Bosses

Toxic bosses represent a leadership style that works by humiliating those who don't conform. Women are not their only victims—many men are subjected to a style that demonstrates power by crushing those around them. But women are more often victimized by toxic bosses because they stick out, have less support, and therefore are easier to pick on. Bosses who are toxic to women assume that they can't possibly be up to the job and so keep looking for areas of weakness. They expect to find these in anything that looks overtly "female" because the female, to them, represents something aberrant. Toxic bosses assume that the norm is male and that anything that is different must be inferior.

> I am concerned that you are building a company with too much of a female orientation. We are very strong in female subject promotions on the homepage and very weak on the male subjects. For instance, we seem to be strong on promoting gossip, cooking, stars, TV dramas, etc., but much lighter on the major sporting events, business, financial markets, science, autos, etc. Your employee population and Board of Directors composition seem to reflect this, as well.

This was emailed to me by David Wetherell, CEO of CMGI and the lead investor in my Internet company. It is an amazing insight into one man's preconceptions of "female" subjects (the trivial stuff) and "male" subjects (the serious stuff). Although I was a CEO of one of his companies, he apparently didn't think I could have any interest in business, finance, science, sport, or cars. How I could do my job if all I knew about was gossip, cooking, stars, and TV drama? The board of directors he worried about was, miraculously, half female, though the employee population was not. What probably caught his attention was that women occupied many of the senior positions. Why should this be a matter of "concern" unless one assumes that women are intrinsically foolish, dangerous, or incompetent?

David might be alone in his willingness to commit such thoughts to posterity, but he's not alone in having them. Although I never experienced sexual harassment of any kind working for his companies, I did recognize the toxic environment that was built up by men who claim to like women but like them as ornaments, not as power wielders. Toxic bosses aren't overtly, outrageously sexist and they aren't impossible to work for. But their leadership poisons the atmosphere, creating alienating, macho environments in which it's tough for women to thrive.

The companies run by toxic environments are usually characterized by a value system that we find pretty strange. The number of hours worked becomes a contest: did you work though the night? Do you answer a 4 A.M. email? Can you stomach the red-eye twice in one week? It's all about endurance, strength, toughness. Toxic bosses assume women can't take this stuff and draw the conclusion that therefore our work will be inferior. It's a hideous trap because a lot of this work style is just plain stupid. So we're trapped: if we challenge it, we look weak; if we conform, we aren't working smart. It's very hard to think straight when you feel you're constantly on the run.

Glenda Roberts manages mergers and acquisitions for Microsoft. She is a gorgeous black woman, with a tiny waist and a big beautiful brain. Coming from Texas at a time when young black women weren't exactly dominating the math department, she's had to contend with harassment and toxic bosses—and still keep her competence and humor visible to all. Before she came to Microsoft, she knew all about toxic bosses.

Glenda Roberts

You can tell you have a toxic boss if, when you get up in the morning, you have a knot in your stomach. If you find that his way of winning is to humiliate you and micromanage you—to treat you like you're some little kid. At that point, it's really important to tell somebody (I call this the Anita Hill phenomenon). Tell somebody so you can hear yourself describe what is happening to you—and so you can get some visibility onto the bad behavior. And keep a journal: write down everything that happens so you know you aren't losing your mind and you have the facts when you need them.

Glenda knows what she's talking about: you can't know at the outset how you will want to deal with a toxic boss. There may be reasons to stay. But you must ensure you aren't alone and you must ensure you do what it takes (confiding in others, keeping a journal) to protect yourself. This doesn't mean you have to go to court; it just means you have put in place what you need to stay sane and protected. Otherwise, you will start to think that you are in the wrong and, as your confidence fades, so too will your competence—and then they've won.

Macho management styles persist because they look so tough and conform to an old male paradigm in which power is dominance. As such, they humiliate both men and women—that is their purpose and their pleasure—but women pay a higher price because our refusal to emulate this style is interpreted as a genetic weakness.

Sharon Tunstall

I was head of HR at Nike and I often refer to this as the best and worst job I've ever had. I totally respected the brand and marketing approaches; I worked with smart and fun people. Unfortunately my boss wasn't one of those people. He definitely fit into the toxic boss category. This man "liked me" but just couldn't identify with a woman in a senior management role; he was comfortable with women on a personal level but just didn't know how to interact with them professionally. He would make comments about my earrings being too large; my car (a Mercedes) being the wrong image for Nike; my style being too "soft." Yet I was told I exceeded his expectations in terms of what I was able to accomplish in the first year and he would praise my accomplishments with "I can't believe you have done so much in such a short period of time." Though I was successful to a point (my peers really didn't want me to leave, many of them men) I couldn't break through the barrier the president created between the two of us. After almost three years and his numerous criticisms of my "style" I left.

People argue that these instances are too subtle, too personal to be taken seriously as management issues. But the mind-sets behind these attitudes betray a systemic discrimination against and dislike of women that has tangible outcomes. Men who don't like women don't promote us, don't encourage us, don't give us the honest feedback we need to succeed.

Joan Silver

In professional life, men are evaluated by one another for their "potential." Women are evaluated by their male colleagues by the results they deliver. A recent organizational example—a senior group evaluated the professional support staff (analysts). The men evaluated the men, especially those who had not produced results, by saying things like "He worked really hard. He is in a tough industry. He's a really good guy. I think we have to give him a break." The men evaluated the women in similar circumstances saying things like "She doesn't seem to be able to keep up. She didn't produce the results we need. She isn't aggressive enough to get the job done."

Mary Linfield

My current boss is a good ole Oklahoma boy. I talk to him for two minutes—and he's yawning! My input is just not considered. He clearly doesn't want me in his office. What's so frustrating is that he has put me in the right job; I am competent to make some good decisions. But I take the yawning personally. He's being insulting. We have a meeting this afternoon. If I feel I am not heard, I'll go. I'm already looking. What else can I do?

If you are working for a toxic boss, it's crucial to identify whether he is symptomatic of the culture.

Elaine Davis

Good cultures eventually expel toxic bosses and colleagues. So then your job is really just to outlast them. When I found myself in this kind of situation, I thought long and hard about this and decided that I liked the company a lot—so I stayed. And eventually the guy was weeded out.

Elaine did a smart thing: she differentiated a toxic boss from an otherwise wholesome environment. Outlasting these guys isn't easy but, if you are working in a great place, it can be worth it. I once worked for a real screamer—his trademark was throwing phones at the wall—but six months later, the same job with a different boss turned into a joy.

Pay Discrimination

Some of the trivial aspects of exclusion have to be ignored—I soon gave up even trying to change the banal golfing conversations that initiated every Monday morning CEO meeting. You can't fight everything—and although many management practices may be toxic, they aren't illegal. But other aspects of discrimination are too serious, too fundamental to be overlooked. If you stay, you have to win these. Once again, the issue of equal pay raises its ugly head. At CMGI, I knew that I was paid substantially less than my peers. But I couldn't do anything about it without jeopardizing the position of the person who had told me. When the company's proxy statement came through the mail, I saw the evidence in black and white. I fired off a furious email. A week later my pay was doubled.

It's easy now to see this as a neat, tidy victory that proves we can win in these confrontations. It certainly was a victory. But at the time, I was angry, hurt, insulted, betrayed, very tempted to quit. Like Pamela, like Kate, I had worked my ass off. I was disciplined, determined, focused, and—incredibly—loyal. But the people I was loyal to knew that they were treating me unfairly and they knew that this was illegal. It saved them money they didn't need or notice. Why did they do it? Because they could. Because I wasn't one of them.

I've spoken to too many women to think my case was unique—some of their stories make me look almost polite by comparison. What these stories show is that discrimination is not personal but can be endemic. Wal-Mart, the biggest employer in America, appears to do the same thing on a far grander scale. The guys who run the company (twelve out of the fourteen directors are male, as are twenty of the twenty-two top managers) are too smart to remove women from management entirely, but their true attitudes are shown by where they put, and how they pay, the bulk of their female employees, as shown in Table 3.1.

Table 3.1. Wal-Mart Employment Statistics.

Job	*No. of Employees*	*Percent Who Are Women*	*Male Salaries*	*Female Salaries*
Regional VP	39	10	$419,400	$279,800
District Manager	508	10	$239,500	$177,100
Store Manager	3,241	14	$105,700	$89,300
Asst Manager	18,731	36	$39,800	$37,300
Management Trainee	1,203	41	$23,200	$22,400
Department Head	63,747	78	$23,500	$21,700
Sales Associate	100,003	68	$16,500	$15,100
Cashier	50,987	93	$14,500	$13,800

Source: Plaintiff's evidence in discrimination suit. Data: Richard Drogin, *Business Week,* March 3, 2003.

What so amazes me about this is that the discrimination operates on several levels: more women in worse jobs *and* with worse pay. Women huddled at the bottom of the pyramid.

Because many successful men assume that a woman's income is the second salary in the household, they often think that it is therefore not so important. Men are breadwinners but a woman's wages are just for extras. Although it shouldn't matter whether we are breadwinners are not, salary is not trivial for any woman I've ever met. Of course it funds our essentials—but it is also, in our culture, a measure of our worth. And too often our paychecks say that we are worth less.

I've spoken to many women who know that they are underpaid, compared to their peers, yet do not complain. They feel uncomfortable pointing out that their employer is behaving illegally. They fear recrimination. Sometimes they hope it is an oversight and will, magically, be fixed one day. Many are in jobs that they otherwise love, and they don't want to leave just to make a point. I don't think anyone can tell them that they are doing the wrong thing. But accepting being underpaid tells your company that you agree that women are worth less than men—or you accept that you personally are worth less than your male peers. It's hard to win anything after a concession like that.

Mothers

If women overall don't feel welcome in the higher echelons of power, this is as nothing compared with how they are made to feel when they become mothers. The mommy track represents the assumption that, once women have had children, they won't be as eager or as capable of doing serious, high-powered work. If you have trouble being taken seriously as a woman, being taken seriously as a mother is a new, higher hurdle.

Kate Shaw

The first day I came back to work after my son was born, my [male] assistant was sitting in my desk! I went to my boss and asked him what was going on. He said that he just assumed that, now I was a mom, I wouldn't want to work so hard so I'd give some of my accounts to Sean.

"Hang on a second," I said, "let me get this straight. You think that because I have two mouths to feed now instead of one—I don't need to work as hard?"

My brain was just buzzing I was so furious. He kind of stammered and didn't know what to say and I was just ready to explode.

"I'll tell you what," I said, "I am going to go home now and you are going to think about this conversation. And then I'm going to come back tomorrow and we'll start all over again."

I went home just fuming—I couldn't sleep all night I was so mad and so scared and so insulted. And I came in the next morning and Sean had moved back to his desk and I got back to work and worked my ass off.

How I wish that, earlier in my career, I'd had Kate's line: "*You* are going to think about this conversation." She got out before exploding—but she firmly placed the problem where it belonged: on her boss's shoulders, not her own.

If our salaries are often considered secondary, once we are mothers it is often assumed that our jobs are now secondary too. This has inevitable consequences for our promotions and our pay.

Pamela Matthews

I came in from maternity leave for my review and asked where I was ranked. In the 2nd quartile, they said. But then, when I came back

> to work full time, I found that what I was being paid was "well below average." Why—when my performance was *above* average? I was told I lacked marketing skills—but *none* of my work involved marketing, so how would they know? All HR wanted to know was whether I'd sue.
>
> I talked to my manager, who was very supportive, so I decided I'd try to make it work; but then I was moved to a crap job with tons of travel and no guaranteed pay! You cannot believe what is happening to you—and everyone knew it was going on.
>
> Everyone is perfectly cordial on an everyday basis—however the women are consistently getting paid less and promoted at a slower rate. It takes women a few years to catch on to this trend and to also realize that there is an informal boys' club where the men are all looking out for each other and promoting their junior kin while the women are being left out in the cold and eventually leave.
>
> I kept a journal for an Equal Opportunities claim for six to twelve months but in the end decided it would be better to just move on. They can just crush you. People couldn't believe that I'd actually leave—they thought I'd just take it. On my very last day, I found out that myself and another woman in my group were both told that we performed at one level and were paid below that level. She decided to stay. Women are made to feel like it is their own shortcomings holding them back—you think it's you!
>
> There was one woman who started to sue. She had three kids. She left and went to work at Cantor Fitzgerald and started to bring a case. But she was working for Cantor on 9/11 and was killed in the World Trade Center. We all said the company had killed her—because she wouldn't have been at Cantor except for the way they'd treated her.

When Pamela went to her next job, she was asked whether she intended to have any more children. This is illegal—and it continues to happen all the time. She answered "no." She is now pregnant with her second child and it is hard to imagine a more joyless pregnancy.

> *Pamela Matthews*
>
> I know I can do this job with two kids. I know I can. I'm working my ass off right now. I was up 'til 4 a.m. last night—my doctor couldn't believe what great shape I was in! I wish my pregnancy would never

> show, that my boss would never have to find out. Because as soon as he knows, his attitude will change. So I'm bringing in as much revenue as possible right now.
>
> I know when I tell him he'll say "it's great" but he won't mean it. At a Christmas party last year, he misheard something and thought I'd said I was pregnant—and instantly asked me about it. I had to reassure him by pointing out that I was drinking beer!
>
> For him, he'll just think that having a baby means checking out. I'll take a hit. I probably won't get a bonus and I won't get a promotion. This year will be a shit year. It just sucks. I wish my husband could have the baby.

If she doesn't lose her job, she'll probably come back to work fast. So many women do. Ten days after my daughter was born, I flew to New York to address an industry conference. Why? Why can't Pamela show off her pregnancy, rather than try to hide it? Why do women so often comment that, like the heroine of *I Don't Know How She Does It,* they *never* mention their children at work? Because our motherhood makes us obvious outsiders—definitely not members of the old boys' club. And so our motherhood is used to patronize, belittle, demote, and exclude us—all in the most caring tones. What should be regarded as a strength, an achievement, will be turned into a weakness so that the men can get back in charge.

Strategies for Survival

When you have to fight so hard at work, when you are underpaid, excluded, and harassed, what do you do? David Bohnett, founder and CEO of GeoCities, one of the really good guys, once asked me, "You're so prepared to go balls to the wall with David [Wetherell]—why do you stay?"

You can only do it out of love; any other motive is too corrosive. I loved my business and I loved my team. I had assembled, eventually, hundreds of the brightest, smartest, and most creative and dedicated people in the world. Americans, Russians, Argentinians, Irish, Chinese. Every age, every discipline, every conceivable hair style. And I loved defending them and giving them the space and opportunity to do great things. Being able to protect others from hostility can be a fantastic feeling.

Kate Shaw

I used to work in this office with 2 other brokers—guys. And we had an admin who was perfectly nice and perfectly competent. But she was fat. The guys came to me, "You have to fire her." Why? "She's too fat." I pointed out to them that being fat was not a reason to fire a person but they said that, if I didn't fire her, they would—and since I'd do it nicer, it was up to me to do it.

The guys kept pushing me. "She's too fat. If you don't fire her, we will." They were testing me to see: was I one of them? How tough could I be? But I couldn't fire her—it was the wrong thing to do, it was disgusting. So I called a friend up at a big bank across the street and I found this woman another job—a better job. I set it all up, sent her over for the interview and she got the job! Better position, much better pay—'cause she was really good. So she quit to go to the new job. When I told the guys, they thought it was great—I'd caved and fired her. They were just *amazed* when I told 'em the truth. Like: oh shit, what did we just do?

I stayed in a toxic environment, too, because I had enough autonomy and enough space to build a different culture and to protect it. We were a separate business. Our investors had dozens of other companies to think about. And I built a lot of support. I spent a great deal of time finding and then working closely with outside directors who kept everyone honest. I identified corporate relationships that were critical to my business, and nurturing those was my project. Finally, by not being at corporate headquarters, being away from micromanagement and daily oversight, we could build our own culture and play a very different game.

Crucial to my survival was being able to think about my work relationships as work—even projects. They weren't personal and I could stay strong if I never let them get personal. But I was never as smart as Betsy Cohen, who has figured out how to stay in control of her working relationships.

Betsy Cohen

I don't take disagreement personally so maybe that is a good coping mechanism. If there is opposition that I don't understand at first, I can circle back to the person and open up with something like "I wasn't satisfied with how we ended that discussion yesterday and maybe there was something else getting in the way. Were we really talking about the same issue or was there something else in your head?"

Betsy stays in control of her relationships and operates by always assuming benign intent. She's more often right than wrong and assumptions do influence outcomes; even where the intent was not benign, drawing it out can make it look—and behave—that way.

Lots of women get tired of the effort that this takes and despair of anything fundamental changing. The work is hard enough without having to retrain every colleague. They may want to leave but sometimes that just isn't an option. Then the challenge is to find a way of living that keeps your soul intact.

Clare Scriven

It's really tough where I am right now. My boss is really sexist and there's a lot of harassment. I feel like I'm selling out just by staying but I can't afford to leave—there's just me and my daughter and I have to keep us going. I've been keeping a journal of all the stuff he does but I'm a partner in the firm and I can't go back to the life I had before I joined. So I've got really involved in legislative issues. I've testified at the State Capitol, I do a lot of stuff for women and I am politically very active to try to make myself feel better. I'm totally aware of what's happening and I'm just trying to find a way to keep going so I don't feel I'm selling out.

You have to determine whether there are ways that you can make a difference. Are you destined to beat your head against a brick wall—or are there subtle things you can do that really change things?

Yvonne Strachan

I think there are lots of things you can do that are kind of symbolic but do change the culture. I've always worked with unions and had to spend a lot of time in works canteens—with everybody eating big, macho, greasy, fatty meals. Burgers, eggs, fries, bacon, the whole heart attack hotel. So I started bringing in my lunch—fruit, salad—which caused quite a stir. Then the guys started doing it! The fact that I was willing to be different *gave them permission to be themselves too.* From such small things big behaviors are changed.

Though it's tempting, making direct attacks on toxic bosses just doesn't work. The odds are severely stacked against you, and your job is to survive on your terms, not theirs. Often, a detailed analysis of what you are up against is a lot more powerful than any attack.

Melodie Reagan

Guys can be just so rude: yelling, cussing, screaming. I try to keep these guys away from my team. The one thing you can *never* do is be straight with them. Do not EVER go full frontal. Instead, I think you have to figure out what the guy's hot buttons are. Like my boss, the Amityville Horror—I figured out that his hot button was loyalty. What he needed to hear from you was that you were loyal to HIM. If you could demonstrate that, you were in the clear. You can control the flow. I always think you just have to focus: control the controllable. I cannot change other people; I can change myself. I could be loyal to the guy—and I could get the work done the right way.

The challenge is to find ways to do this—to control the controllable—in ways that leave you feeling yourself—ways that don't force you to work like a guy, abandon your values, sell your soul. When you find those strategies, you find power.

Chris Carosella

I had no response when the guy, Joe, made the comment about me being the cunt at the table. He said it and walked on. I was stunned someone would say something like that to me and it caught me off my guard.

I didn't run around telling everyone what he said, even though I really wanted to. I knew he would use every opportunity he could to disparage me, sabotage me, and try to hurt my credibility. So when he made good suggestions in other meetings, I endorsed them. If my department was doing something that helped his, I let him know. And if I disagreed with him, I still let him know that too. Gradually, he saw I was good at what I did: he saw that I deserved to be there and he saw that my department made his look good. He became an ally and supported my group.

Women are usually shocked when I say this. They tell me they don't want to be nice to jerks, they would have told everyone else about the comment and some say they'd retaliate. But people say stupid

> things out of fear and their own insecurities. If that person continues that way, they can do a lot of damage behind your back. But if you show them they have nothing to fear, they can become neutral or supportive.
>
> A few years later, he left to become president of another company. He called to ask me to be his COO. No, I didn't even consider it for a moment . . . but I did take great satisfaction in that he made the offer.
>
> It's really important to recognize that insulting/degrading/ridiculous comments aren't about you—they're about the person saying them. Don't take the remarks personally but do take them seriously because you need to learn what's really going on.

Don't take it personally but do take it seriously—that could be our mantra when we encounter toxic bosses and macho environments. What saved Chris was that she stayed in control of the relationship. The guy might have been a bully—but she was not bullied. She stood on moral high ground and insisted that he meet her there. She did not stoop to his level but remained true to herself. When he left, she was still there and her values were still intact.

Harassment and discrimination are illegal but women face them daily. Sometimes we go to court, sometimes we go "to the wall," sometimes we develop very strong techniques to ensure that we never feel powerless and therefore can never be bullied. And sometimes we walk out. Although the harassment and discrimination are not our fault, we regularly take responsibility for dealing with it—just another chore while we're climbing to the top. On top of trying to evade stereotyping, it strikes me that women have a lot to do before they even start tackling their work.

I would like to think that the days of management by humiliation are over, that we've all learned that there are better ways to run companies. That never again will epithets like "Neutron Jack" and "Chainsaw Al Dunlop" be sported with pride. I look around and see lots of managers—male and female—who manage differently, generously, openly. Many men hate macho management styles as much as we do, and yearn (usually in silence) for a new, different paradigm of power. But the old paradigms, reinforced by tradition and a love of homogeneity, run deep. People like people who are just like them; difference is unsettling. But being gatecrashers means we can see things that some men never will.

Travel Thoughts

- Do you feel afraid or threatened at work? By whom? Who knows about it?
- How much do people in your company respect women? How can you tell?
- What conversations do you feel excluded from? What conversations or events do you feel you want to exclude yourself from?
- What's the problem: a peer, a boss, or the whole culture?
- How much visibility and power do mothers have in your business?
- How can you change things?

Chapter Four

The Emperor's New Clothes

> *The question is not, as for Hamlet, to be or not to be, but to belong or not to belong.*
> —Hannah Arendt

Margaret Consentino

I am sitting here at my desk as a VP/GM in a Fortune 100 company and trying not to cry. I am an anomaly here. I tell the truth to the folks that work for me; I tell the truth to the COO that I work for. (He and his colleagues would prefer to make decisions based on anecdote than fact, and solid business results are less valued than being a part of the club.)

I will probably be leaving soon in search of a place that values values, truthfulness and allows me to be the person that I have come to like. After years of feeling that for some reason I was not innately good enough to be valued in business, I am beginning to see that maybe the problem is not me.

The problem is not me. The fear, anger, aggression, discomfort that we seem to provoke in men makes it easy for us to start thinking that we are the problem. Men often suggest as much: when it's harassment, "She can't take a joke"; discrimination, "She should have fought harder"; stereotyping, "She should have toned it down." We blame ourselves because we are alone—who is there to tell us that the treatment we're subjected to is par for the course? We blame ourselves because women take responsibility for themselves.

We blame ourselves because the business world we've wandered into looks so exceptionally weird that surely we must have gotten something wrong. There is an anomaly somewhere—is it us?

After successfully navigating the shoals of stereotypes, and surviving any number of toxic and hostile environments, it would take a psychopath not to start having some self-doubt. Our experience and interpretation of what we see feels so out of step with what we are being told that we start to doubt our sense of reality. The analogy that most repeatedly comes up when women describe their experience in business is "The Emperor's New Clothes." Why? Because what they see in the business world looks so different from what their male peers seem to see. The discrepancies between how we see the world, and how men see it, are too profound for us to ignore. That doesn't mean that we are wrong.

There are some historical reasons why our perspective at work is so different from men's. The Industrial Revolution bifurcated our lives. For the first time, men went out to their work. Men started to develop cultures around their workplace—with their own language, rituals, and symbols. Over time, this became increasingly divergent from home life. Offices developed their own furniture, colors, and styles. Men evolved business jargon with its own acronyms and shorthand. As the world of work became more specialized, it looked, felt, and behaved less and less like home. Men learned to behave differently too—to compartmentalize, to develop work-specific personae. Their work selves and their home selves became as separate as the architectural styles of workplace and home. In the world of work, rules, values, behaviors, and codes of conduct were developed that made it strikingly distinct from home life. Over time, the split has become more and more pronounced.

As gatecrashers, women have come late to this picture and, furthermore, have not been able to abandon our home lives as comprehensively as men did. Sometimes there is no one left to delegate our home lives to—so we have to bring them with us. As mothers, women have been considered the traditional carriers and teachers of values, and that's a tough role to throw away, even if we wanted to do so. Or perhaps we just haven't been in business long enough to have adapted our mental habits. Whatever the reason, the split between work and home makes us very, very uncomfortable. Time and time again women tell me "I don't want to be two people—I want to be the same person, doing different things but with the same values, the same style." We want integrated, not delegated, lives.

We come in and we see things differently. What others may regard as the cornerstones of the normal business world look to us like bizarre fantasies: assumptions that men developed as their work became more separate from the rest of their lives. These fantasies underpin much of the way that business is done. They make no sense to us but we see them in action every day. They challenge our sense of reality and make us wonder whether we want to, or can, ever truly fit in. But I think our perspective, rather than making us feel bad, should instead be seen as our strength, in that it heightens our sense of values and shows us exactly where one of our most valuable contributions to business may lie. Rather than colluding in these fantasies, we need to have the courage of our convictions.

Fantasy #1: Business Is Not Emotional

The look and style of offices signals clearly: this is not home. We enter offices that encourage us to adopt a different style, one that purports to be unemotional. From business schools to board rooms, emphasis is placed on the rational, logical, numerical language of business. To be considered "emotional" is regarded as a debilitating weakness. Business is supposed to be unemotional, just an objective transaction for the economic development of nations.

And yet we invest the most precious thing we have in it: time. We are asked to "take ownership" in projects, to "be invested" in strategies, to "enlist" in teams. We are asked to sacrifice children, loved ones, parents, vacations, weekends for it. How can we devote so much of ourselves to an activity and expect it to be—or even want it to be—devoid of emotion? Where would we find satisfaction if we couldn't cheer our triumphs and applaud the promotions and achievements of others? I think that, contrary to the received wisdom, business is highly emotional—always has been and always will be. And I think that our awareness of this emotion, and our comfort in handling it, is not a weakness but a tremendous strength. Emotional competence makes us far stronger than denial.

The best leaders I've seen in action are those who aren't afraid of emotion, who don't avoid it, but embrace it. Leaders like Carol Vallone, who, when she acquired a company, didn't come out with the routine lie that this was a merger, nothing would change, and everyone would be happy. Instead, she thought through the business issues carefully and made it very clear that one of the product lines and one of the brands would have to go. Products that employees had devoted themselves to, brands that felt like their children, would be killed off. Instead of denying the emotion, Carol surfaced it and knew that she had to deal with it. She did not ask her team to button up and take it like a man. She acknowledged the huge emotions of the situation—and threw a funeral.

Carol Vallone

> We actually put the product in a vault. We literally stood around and had readings about the product, remembered it, had a eulogy! And it was kinda fun. We remembered it fondly for what it had done for us. And what it had meant for the company. And then it was put into a vault. We didn't cremate it (*laughs*). It was a death. There's no question. I joke about it but it was a bereavement and I felt that we had to acknowledge it just like in any death.

Mergers are always emotional and the standard lies that accompany them fool no one. The lies just reveal how frightening those feelings can be. What gives Carol the wisdom and the nerve to buck this tradition? She says that she just treats people at work the way she'd treat people at home. Far from crippling us, bringing our home selves to work turns out to be a big advantage. Although we may feel the gravitational pull to conform, resisting it is our salvation. Assimilation to something false helps no one.

Business is emotional. Knowing that means we don't have to run scared of it. Far from making us sentimental—weepy wilting violets—this makes us strong. Emotional intelligence is a great asset—so too is emotional competence.

Diane Jacobsen works with large organizations, often building the new products and systems that result from mergers. That means she is at the eye of the emotional storm that these reorganizations produce.

Diane Jacobsen

> You are dealing with emotion. You are dealing with cultural change and transformation and a lot of ego and a lot of fear because every merger deals with lots of layoffs. Throw that into solving a problem!
>
> But it doesn't frighten me. I think it is kind of fascinating. And my boss says "If you aren't worried about this, I'm worried about you!" *(laughs)* I say "don't sweat the little shit Bill—one step at a time, we will get there." My mantra is "deep cleansing breath." If you can't let it go, you will go crazy or go home and hurt someone or small animals. I think women are better at that than men are. Because we will take a big problem and verbalize it to someone and talk it through, solve it and apply it—and men internalize it and don't talk to anyone because they don't want anybody to think they don't know and they can't figure it out and they get all knotted and take some decision and it is "what are you thinking?" and then they have to defend it! So I think it is harder for them.

Women expect to conduct emotional conversations. We're used to it and we're good at it. Gather any group of women—at a conference, in a meeting—and ask direct questions; the candor and passion of the responses contain enough energy to power a city. This is often derided as foolish or naïve—but it is a vital strength that business needs now more than ever. Our comfort with emotion means that we would rather confront conflict and emotion than suppress it.

Fantasy #2: Silence Is Golden

Women often ask me impatiently, "Why can't they just get on with it?" as they watch men not daring to come clean, wanting to avoid conflict or unpleasantness at all costs. The fantasy that business is unemotional means that emotional issues can't be dealt with head-on; it is deemed more professional to pass over them in silence. It looks good—but it isn't.

The costs of silence can be high indeed. I remember a fellow CEO coming to discuss a problem during the Christmas holiday period. Bob was scared. He was worried that, in the run-up to the IPO, his investors would want to replace him with a more glamorous, or more experienced, leader—this had happened before and he was right to be worried.

"Go and ask," I advised. "What's the worst that can happen? Either you're told no, they don't want to replace you—in which case you can stop worrying—or you're told yes and you can decide what you want to do: stay and be part of the process or decide to leave. But don't wait to be told. You'll be the last to know and you'll have no room for maneuver at all."

He never did ask. It was an emotional issue for him and he didn't want to confront it. As it happened, it was emotional for his boss too—who also didn't want to upset him. That's a mutually assured stalemate. In the end, he was notified of his replacement just a few days before the new CEO arrived.

He could have been involved instead of excluded. Asking the unaskable question, having the confidence that you can deal with emotion, is a tremendous source of power. It plays to our directness and emotional confidence. Women connect emotional honesty with integrity; it doesn't seem feasible to us to separate them.

Joan Silver

Integrity is not just not stealing from clients. It is about telling the truth. I was working once with a CEO on succession planning. One candidate was very smart but a pain in the ass, a terrible communicator, an awful manager and probably the smartest person in the organization. He saw himself as heir apparent. But in my conversation with the CEO, I learned he was 6th or 7th in line. So I said, "You know, Rob's perception is that he's heir apparent."

"Oh yeah, I know—but he has all these problems."

"So how are we going to help him be successful? How are we going to tell him these are impediments to his success here?"

"We can't have that conversation. He might get upset and leave."

"But if you don't have that conversation, he still won't get the job and then he WILL leave. Why can't we be honest with this guy? You can't say you value integrity if you cannot have this conversation."

When we insist on integrity, it can be painful—but without it, we just get another mutually assured stalemate. The boss won't talk to the manager and the manager won't ask about succession. No one can move forward, no one can succeed. It's just like the way fear of women crying produces a stalemate that no one can win. Such stalemates result from forgetting that integrity is about telling the truth at every level. The worst thing about these stalemates is that they look harmonious: on the surface everything continues as normal. But underneath the surface, we start to lose momentum.

By contrast, when we insist on speaking out, we can get things moving. At a meeting to discuss a potential new magazine, many senior people had contributed thoughts and ideas. The brainstorming was over and everyone looked to the man who would make the decision. Silence. We had run out of time and run out of steam. The air was pregnant with unasked questions. Harriet jumped in. "So what happens next? How do you make your decision?" Now the conversation got really interesting. Now we could learn something. That single question turned Harriet into the most powerful person in the room.

Every time you find yourself being the Harriet in the room, you will find yourself stared at with an odd mixture of pity, nervousness, and respect. Pity, that you didn't play according to the rules, and perhaps didn't know them. Nervousness, because suddenly people start to wonder what your motive is; do you know something they don't? Respect, on the part of those people who wanted to ask, thought about it—but chickened out. We have to get used to this role, however uncomfortable it may be, because it gets things done.

We've all witnessed the paralysis that sets in when there are no Harriets in the room—when people are afraid to ask for or tell each other the truth. For all their macho posing, many successful men are conflict averse—afraid of the emotion inherent in disagreement. It isn't just Agnes's tears they're scared of—they're scared of their own feelings too. And so they dodge each other, play turf games, engage in endless rounds of infighting and shadowboxing—anything to avoid sitting down with each other and telling each other the truth. I've known CEOs who are unwilling to ask questions because they're uncertain of the answers. CEOs who are unwilling to announce decisions face-to-face because they're immobilized by the fear of bare emotions, terrified of unscripted conflict. Women quickly grow frustrated when men won't be honest, because they then can't move forward. In avoiding conflict, men stop progress. They make a desert and call it peace.

I've seen deals hang in mid-air because no one had the honesty to say out loud what everyone was thinking privately: This is really stupid, and it'll never work. And so millions of dollars and countless hours of work hover somewhere between intent and execution, with insiders hoping that the whole mess will simply go away—but not willing to address the problem head-on.

Such moments are great opportunities for us. Several years ago, my boss had met with Michael Ovitz. Everybody wanted to do some deal but nobody could figure out what it was. Nobody dared to say no. And so it stalled. Eventually, I was asked to see if I could get something moving. We met in the Burbank airport, a tiny, ugly place whose only redeeming virtue is that it's so small it's fast. Nowhere to sit, so we went outside under the roar of air conditioners as jets screamed overhead. The Ovitz folks made vague promises about Leonardo DiCaprio and Robin Williams and Brad Pitt until finally I couldn't stand it any longer. It was hot and noisy and I was grumpy; what they were talking about just made no sense.

"Look, for those people to be of any value to me, they'd have to be available full time to do anything and everything. Personal appearances, interviews, TV spots, you name it. It just can't be worth it for them. I'm not going to give them ten million dollars for it because I can't make ten million dollars out of them—and they're not going to do it for stock when they can get millions for any movie—which you would be *nuts* to tell them to turn down. If anybody could make something like this work, maybe you guys could—but you can't. You just can't. It's just a dumb deal and I don't do dumb deals."

They loved it. The air was clear. For a while, I became almost notorious for my frankness; it did me good and it did the company good.

Our honesty makes us stand out. That may make everyone a little uncomfortable—hence the nervous little laughs we all get used to—but it's a core competence.

Everyone I've spoken to on this matter—men and women alike—knows exactly what I'm talking about when I describe the awkward silence that sets in at corporate meetings when it becomes obvious that the emperor has no clothes. The problem isn't that people don't know the truth; the problem is being afraid to tell the truth. The truth is that women are much more likely than men to be truth-tellers and that women's urge to honesty is a fantastic business asset. Our instinct to speak out is a good instinct. Trust it. Have the courage of your convictions. However alienated it makes us feel, I am convinced that women's urge to honesty is a vital talent. We should not let ourselves become so assimilated that we lose confidence in it. It makes good deals happen; it builds trust.

The managing director of a leading Hollywood talent agency commented that she and her colleagues are regularly described as "cows and bitches" but that hasn't stopped her one bit; it is key to her success. She loves getting deals done and understands that people love working with her because they always know where they stand. And she can tap the energy that comes from being straightforward and clear. It is a fantastic by-product of being gatecrashers.

Fantasy #3: You're Too Honest

Dee Copelan

Many people think it's just easier to hide out, keep your head down until something changes. That may be true, that may be the easier path, but there's a little word—integrity—that keeps nagging at me, personally.

I'll never forget the time I received a performance review that included the feedback "You're too honest." I was shocked! I was raised in the Midwestern United States. I was always taught, "honesty was the best policy." How about George Washington "I cannot tell a lie"? My basic foundational beliefs were shaken. Now I had written proof that honesty was not valued at this company and, furthermore, was considered a fault to be corrected. My experience had already shown me that honesty wasn't valued there, as in most large corporations. So why was I so surprised?

This was one of those "defining moments" where you can no longer pretend the emperor is grandly clothed when he is, in fact, strutting around stark naked. I could no longer pretend that I fit in at my company, that my values matched the company's values. And that required taking action, because honesty, integrity and standing up for my beliefs are values too important for me to give up. So I had to decide what to do. Now I was conscious. Now I was aware. I couldn't go back to pretending I didn't notice. I had to go forward—either move on or make a full-out commitment to try to change things in the company.

Almost every woman in business will, at various points in her career, encounter situations like Susan's defining "emperor's new clothes" moment—in which what is being said, and what she sees as the truth, are contradictory. Some of these discrepancies may involve politics, subtexts, that we aren't aware of. But some of them will be deep-down dishonesties. It's enough to make anyone think that they must be wrong—and so it is at just such moments that it is more important than ever to hang on to our self-respect, our belief in who we are. We have to remember, as Margaret Consentino did, that we are not the problem. At that moment, we need the courage of our conviction that what we see is true and what we are is honest.

Small things may prepare you for this. My first experience filing expenses featured a boss who patiently explained to me that I could not claim only for the cab fare I'd incurred—I had to pad it out with a few more things he invented. Producers would come in on days off and go through program records to help them fabricate their expenses. They laughed nervously as they did this, in full view of their colleagues—but after all, everyone did it. I kept the form he filled in for me, but I didn't claim for the cab. I needed the money—but not that much. This wasn't an especially tough decision but it made me see that how I worked, and how others worked, might not be the same.

Everywhere I go, I hear from women in jobs, or who've left jobs, where they couldn't help seeing dishonesty all around them: kickbacks to contractors, compliance issues fudged, expenses inflated, and suppliers cheated. The comment about being "too honest" occurs with such monotonous regularity in the careers of women that it can't just be personal. Many commentators observe that women are more likely to be whistle-blowers because, as outsiders, we have less to lose. With no real stake in the game, we lose less when we're expelled.

But I think it goes deeper than that—and back to history. I think we've watched men at work and observed that they change. Over time, they have developed ways of working that make honesty hard to define and maintain. A salesman who worked for me described his previous work life as utterly split between home and work: "It's as if I leave my true self locked in the car, go up in the elevator and emerge as Work Self. My true self only comes back to life as I drive home." Psychologists call this splitting, and it has a bad track record because it enables people to do things they'd otherwise find repugnant. WorldCom's Bernie Ebbers can stand up in church, tears streaming down his face, proclaiming "I am not a crook" because he isn't a crook in church. Men can be lovey-dovey dads at home and unemotional, dishonest executives at work because they are two different people. Compassionate, ethical, fair Dad gets left at home, while at work, Corporate Dad breaks laws on equal pay, discrimination, and sexual harassment. This kind of dishonesty is not occasional and it can't be regulated by the SEC. It is systemic, deep, and ingrained. It doesn't make us very comfortable and it doesn't inspire us.

When we don't conform to this norm, we're deemed to be "too honest." Our insistence on bringing our values to work can become troublesome when it brings us into conflict with others who have gotten comfortable leaving their values at home.

Susan Ellis

> We had one brand—the way it was marketed, there were supposed to be no animal ingredients in it but—it turns out there are!! In Customer Affairs, we are all just in shellshock. And this guy, he's pretty high up in the organization, and he says "why can't we just lie?" I was looking around the room thinking: does anyone else have a problem with this? I can't believe what I'm hearing. So I start: "From a risk perspective, this is a big problem. There are people with fatal allergies to particular ingredients. Some will die or have major scarring on their face. Why can't we lie? Because that is not the right thing to do! We have already made the mistake of misrepresenting ourselves to the public—do we want to further that?"
>
> Later they told me that this guy is buddies with the CEO and he just says things like that. But you have to wonder what else he has said. Why not lie? There are so many reasons I don't know where to start.

Like Margaret Consentino, Susan is astonished that what she takes seriously—values, honesty—vanishes so quickly from the business where she works. She can see the ethical problem and the business problem at once. They are connected in her mind, not separated. After years of working for the same company, she is still entirely clear about her values.

We are honest in part because we haven't learned to be otherwise and in part because we won't give up in our struggle to align our private values with our business values. We know it is better that way because honesty is the basis of all relationships—and business is all about relationships. We're used to caring about these things and we know that they make our businesses thrive. However much men may fear that honesty will spark conflict and disagreement, we know that telling the truth is the only way to make people feel valued, respected as adults.

Suzanne Fontaine ran all of the telecommunications for one of my companies. She was one of those driven people, wanting everything to be perfect, the systems to purr. She seemed to know how to get a lot of satisfaction out of anything she did. When the market tanked and CMGI had to decide whether to sell or close, Suzanne attended contingency planning meetings: what to do in the event of a sale, what to do in the event of a closure. Suzanne wasn't happy about it, but anything she did, she was determined to do flawlessly.

"I couldn't believe it. All these corporate guys, sitting around with their pagers and Blackberries, talking about *our* company and saying 'whatever happens, don't tell Margaret. We will make these plans, but don't tell Margaret.' When I asked why, they said that they were afraid: 'Margaret's so honest. She'll tell the truth.'"

Suzanne told me this story, she said, because the episode had shown her why she'd loved working for the company. "I realized I'd never worked somewhere before where I could trust what I was being told. Where I was respected enough to be told the truth." I was shocked by her story—shocked that my honesty had been so contentious and frightening, and shocked too that her experience with the company had been so novel.

Organizations have telltale signs of dishonesty. These aren't big headlines or guys behind bars. They are small, institutionalized habits that tell you the culture isn't straightforward and may have difficulty with your frankness. The recurrent symptoms are hoarding of information, secrecy, and procrastination. Hoarding of information betrays the fakeness of any lip service paid to teamwork. Secrecy is the requisite tool of discrimination. Procrastination is emotional hiding—putting off small confrontations until they spiral out of control.

Joan Silver

> Being honest and building honest relationships are sometimes seen as making women problematic. Some of the difficulty arises from procrastination. Men don't want to deal with problems when they are small—so they get repeated and then the manager feels guilty for not dealing with it. The manager gets all wound up. Until now the problem is about the manager, not the business issue. You just want to tell them: this problem isn't about you—its about the business! You wish they'd just learn the lesson that you have to deal with problems when they're still small—like cancer.

When the emperor strode around naked, he was not the one who felt uncomfortable—it was the truth-teller who suffered. Drawing attention to the discrepancies between how we see the world and how many corporate men see the world can be painful and frightening. This is when our rich life outside of business comes to our rescue. We need the sanity checks that others can provide. Your friends, your family are more important than ever to keep you grounded in reality. Use them and don't let them go. Far from competing with work values, they are essential for maintaining work ethics. You may be derided, undermined. You will need outsiders to support you, encourage you. Many women talk about how their children help them—because we want to be able to explain things to them in ways that make sense. Our children and families bring us down to earth, keep us grounded. Women's networks help here too, because they can confirm your sense that what you are watching is not your fault. That outside context is a lifeline.

The ethics and honesty of an organization start at the top. That means you may not be able to change as much as you'd like. And you probably won't be thanked for your efforts. Many women feel that their honesty costs them promotions, raises—for many, it's the reason they leave. I'm not sure that can be avoided. But I am sure that assimilating, learning to admire the emperor's clothes, is no way forward for us or for business as a whole. However uncomfortable our difference makes us feel, losing our penchant for honesty would make us feel far worse.

The honesty that women bring to work paves the way for a different way of working in an environment that acknowledges and is not afraid of emotion. This does not mean that women are intrinsically saintlike or should be held to impossibly high standards of virtue. But in our attempt to make a place for ourselves in the world of work, we should trust, not silence, the voices and observations that give us a different outlook, different perspectives, different sense of right and wrong. Given the chaos and destruction wreaked by old male habits of denial and stalemates, it's time for women to embrace their urge for honesty with pride.

> *Karen Price*
>
> I can play the games, the politics, that's not the issue. But I wanted us to be more straightforward, simplistic, and realistic. Instead, our company and its direction were becoming more convoluted, the logic of decisions becoming more circular and obtuse. I had had enough. The stress of trying to be true to what I believed was literally destroying my health. I was so tired of trying to tell people that the emperor had no clothes, with no one listening. I resigned about a month later.
>
> We've started a new business and called it Verity. We want the truth, reality and good principles to be the foundation of all our decisions. We want to find a new way of building homes—a way that is completely open and honest.

Many men might call Karen naïve, but she's learned to start as she means to go on. She's been down the assimilation road and found it gave her nothing she could truly value. Assimilation, playing the game makes for a temporary truce at a high price. On an individual basis, it leaves us feeling that our work persona is fake and this is so uncomfortable that, for many of us, it means we have to leave. For business itself, the long-term consequences of conforming to systemic fakery are serious and destructive. Many of the women I've talked to place this old, conflict-averse, truth-silencing way of doing business at the heart of business failure today.

I don't think I've met anyone quite as smart or tough or focused as Dominique Senequier. She is CEO of AXA Private Equity and she manages billions of dollars around the world. Her forthright style has sometimes made her male peers very uncomfortable as she's held out against investments she doesn't believe in. She laughs when she talks about the way men have conducted business—but her laughter is in deadly earnest.

Dominique Senequier

> You have to be willing to say "no." But men are just frozen! Men like opacity—and that's the first sign of dysfunction. You have to be willing to say "no." Given the state business is in today, it's no longer a matter of politeness—it is a matter of survival.

I like to think that we can do better than survival; that embracing our native honesty creates a better way of doing business. One that is sustainable, effective, and unafraid, that can carry us, whole and indivisible, from home to work and back home again. Telling the truth can be disruptive—how could it be otherwise?—but it also creates a way of working that plays to our deepest instincts and deepest needs.

Michelle Turchin

> My new boss is unabashedly, refreshingly honest. This scares her male counterparts on the executive management team. But I am learning so much from her. I am realizing how powerful honesty can be. And I am learning how to be honest with myself about my perspectives—and then say it like it is to my colleagues. This is new for me! Generally it's been very familiar to speak in consulting jargon and not really commit or say anything at all. This is just one of the fun things I am learning now.

The choice is not between masculine power and feminine kindness, between macho behavior and sainthood. Being true to yourself, having the nerve and the self-knowledge to cut through mythologies, is the only way ahead for women—and for business. This sounds obvious; it should be obvious. But no one ever told me I could work this way. Like so many women, I spent years feeling strange, anomalous, like Margaret Consentino. Only as I abandoned my guy behavior and gathered the courage to be frank, open, honest did I stop feeling strange. It wasn't easy—there were lots of bad habits to break—but it was a lot more fun.

I sometimes think that the way women perceive business is so different from the way men do, the perspectives so divergent, that it is as though we inhabit a parallel universe in which we do many of the same things, but with a different perspective, style, and motivation, and for different rewards. In that parallel universe, our personal values are well integrated with work values; being true to ourselves is seen as a requirement, not a difficulty; and telling the truth is required, not reprimanded. I can see that, in that universe, those hundred thousand hours need not be a grind. They could be great.

Travel Thoughts

- Where are the emotions focused in your business? How honest can you and your colleagues be about them?
- What is everyone not talking about? Why?
- What are your biggest concerns at work? How, where, when are these discussed? If not, why not? How can you raise this subject?
- How far are people in your organization rewarded for truth-telling? How can you tell?
- What are the issues you, or your organization, are not confronting?
- What are the taboo issues within your group?

Chapter Five

Power and Where It Comes From

It is ignoble to give birth to nothing but ourselves.
—PICO DELLA MIRANDOLA

Power is the ability to do things. With power, we can achieve goals. With power, we can make choices. With power, we can do things for ourselves, we can do things for other people. With power, we can change the game.

Many women, when asked, say that they don't like power and don't want it. They'll wrinkle up their noses as if something obnoxious has entered the conversation. But when asked if they want to get things done, want to change things, the answer is, of course, a resounding "Yes!" What we object to in discussions about power is what I've come to see as an old-fashioned, masculine concept of power, which focuses on dominance and aggression. The power that defines itself by how far it can crush, belittle, destroy others. Dominant concepts of power feel like a hangover from the command-and-control era when robber barons and military leaders crushed opponents on their way to controlling industries and states. This kind of aggressive power is all about ego and is routinely celebrated on the covers of business magazines that promote—and then demolish—business supermen who promise total command over enterprises of super-human proportions.

Perhaps the best example of the masculine concept of power is The Limited's internal motivational campaign, which they called WAR (Winning at Retail). In an attempt to inspire commitment and dedication, the company issued "battle briefings" and held "battle summits." Managers attending the summit were seated in order of their store's performance so everyone could spot the winners and losers. Video clips of bloody battle scenes incited managers to lead their missions in deadly earnest; it was, they were told, a matter of life and death.[1]

Not surprisingly, many women quit. To us, this kind of power feels both infantile and anachronistic. Infantile because it doesn't seem very far removed from action-hero toys—Masters of the Universe or Action Man—and anachronistic because it implies a simplicity and order to business that, like the emperor's new clothes, we can see simply isn't there any more.

As long ago as 1997, Peter Senge, author of *The Fifth Discipline,* stated, "Almost everyone agrees that the command-and-control corporate model will not carry us into the 21st century. It is no longer possible to figure it out from the top."[2] Almost everyone—but not quite everyone. We've all had our share of bosses who still believe in command-and-control styles of leadership, and research shows that men are more likely to adopt its autocratic styles. Some writers even put forward the notion that this kind of macho, competitive power makes men "natural" leaders because they are the result of thousands of years of evolutionary development. None of this bears much scrutiny—and, of course, no one ever dares to use the word *caveman* in this context—but we still work in a world where such ugly paradigms persist. That's why we say we don't like power: because we don't like *this kind* of power. It's macho, egocentric, and fundamentally out of sync with who we are and what business now requires.

But that doesn't mean we don't like power. We just see it differently. Chris Carosella, who had the power to cancel strip clubs, understands that power can achieve a great deal of good. But crucially, she also understands that it is never just about herself. Her notion of power is not about dominance but about connection.

Chris Carosella

I believe power comes from within who we are and how we use it in the world. I can have a strong sense of self, but if I don't share it with others, there's no power with it. Power includes healthy self-esteem, confidence and a connection with other people. Good is when power is shared for mutual benefits to make a positive difference.

Female concepts of power focus on sharing, on making connections. They aren't self-centered; they are not about heroic egos. Powerful women do not talk about dramatic rescues or single-handed triumphs. Instead, the ideas of power that we enjoy are nonhierarchical and highly participatory. They are about *us,* not *me.* When we replace the word *power* with *leadership,* women find it easy to embrace.

> *Kathleen Holmgren*
>
> Leadership is not just about leading from the front but also about leading from the rear. Making sure to help those that needed additional encouragement or assistance to reach the goal. It's not about individually coming in first, but ensuring the whole team comes in first.

When we start thinking about power as helping and encouraging others, providing resources that someone needs to get a job done, providing the support a team needs to do better work, then power looks very attractive. Marty Johnson, who runs the American Red Cross, sees power as removing the barriers to others' success. It should come as no surprise to hear female leaders regularly defined as more "transformational" than male leaders—we are more democratic, supportive, and encouraging.[3] In a constantly transforming world, this means we are better suited than any command-and-control maven to the business environment we now face in the twenty-first century. The way we like to work is now the way we need to lead. The writer and actress Anna Deveare Smith says that "power is orchestration" and this power paradigm is one we have no trouble accepting.

Where power comes from is complex and where female power comes from is even harder for many to see. Power doesn't come from bosses. The idea of face time is insulting, banal propaganda. Pandering to anyone who will be pandered to is the sure road to ruin for you and for them. Sure, you can find bosses like that and you can rise with them, but you won't have power—you'll just have dependency. Never mistake dependency for power.

Many authors of textbooks on power believe that it comes from such things as titles and the control of resources. There's no doubt that these indicate power. But they don't, in and of themselves, generate power. Kings and presidents—from Richard II to Richard Nixon—have had plenty of both and yet been powerless, because such things can be taken away. For women—and, I'd argue, for men too—the most important power is portable: not power that is given, but power that is intrinsic to the person you are. This is the kind of power that you can take with you wherever you want to go. And it comes from many, many sources.

Skills, Competence, Confidence

All power begins with skills and competence, the bedrocks of confidence. Once, at a conference in San Francisco, a young woman asked me where I got my confidence from. A simple question—but it stopped me in my tracks. Like all good questions, it made me think hard. "Doing stuff," was my eventual reply.

Like many women, I didn't feel particularly confident and, also like most women, I felt I had less confidence than most of my male colleagues. But I had reached a stage in my life where I knew I had certain skills because these skills had led to palpable accomplishments—and it was those accomplishments that gave me confidence. Skills create competence, which leads to achievement, which builds confidence. While this seems very obvious, I'm often struck that women seek confidence in inappropriate places—in others, in religion, in clothes, in institutions, in titles. Although all of these can contribute to confidence, nothing replaces the rock-solid knowledge of having confronted obstacles and cleared them successfully. Skills are the absolute prerequisite of confidence. Because skills can be acquired, confidence can be acquired—but both must be worked at over time.

When I worked as a producer, I once hired a secretary, Janice, who held a Ph.D.—an achievement I was in awe of. But I'd come into the office to find her weeping over her typewriter. "What's wrong?" I had to ask. She really wanted to be a script editor and found her job frustrating, demeaning, dull. I'd been a secretary; I was sympathetic. But how could I urge her promotion to script editor? She had no relevant skills—and she didn't do her current job well. "I can't," I explained, "promote you for doing your job badly." Had she finished her work early, I could have given her scripts to read—and, if she'd done that well, she'd have demonstrated a skill

I could use to argue her case. But she never made the effort to develop her abilities. Wanting opportunity is not enough; there is no substitute for demonstrable skills.

By contrast, Daphne Kuo worked for me as a vice president of finance. In a negotiation with News Corp., her counterpart was a young woman with a lot of style and presence and a very much bigger company behind her. Yet Daphne had more power in the negotiation because she understood every single number she presented. She had the competence to reject a bad deal. Her counterpart couldn't tell the difference; all she had was dependence on a boss who liked her.

Melodie Reagan has worked in high-tech marketing for years. It's a tough environment for women and she's had to learn a lot about gaining, and retaining, power. She's in no doubt that it starts inside herself.

Melodie Reagan

Where does power come from? Competence. Pure intellect is power.

Many women talk about the confidence they gain through academic credentials—accounting, the law. In some industries, like financial services, they prove you have skills; they are the price of admission. Many women, especially in financial services, see an MBA as an essential credential—it gives you permission to be there, in your own eyes and in the guys' eyes.

The MBA, law degrees, accounting qualifications: these make a big difference to women because they are portable—they belong to you. Increasingly, women gravitate to these skills because they'll provide the flexibility and authority our careers demand. Degrees and qualifications also matter to women because we often find it so hard to internalize and take credit for our accomplishments.

Chris Carosella

I spoke last week at a national meeting for a company that was recognizing its top salespeople. I asked the top two salespeople, both women (each earned over $600,000) to talk about their experiences. They said they didn't have any answers, it was a team effort, they just worked hard. They barely spoke above a whisper and seemed embarrassed to express an opinion. That led to a discussion about humility and how women are taught at an early age to be nice, share credit, wait for people to give us recognition. I like to hear women proudly talking about their accomplishments, not denying themselves for anyone. It's not about arrogance; it's about confidence, self-acceptance, power and strength.

Confidence derives from being able to internalize and own our experiences and achievements. When I had to close my last company, all the employees had months to search for new jobs. Their regular comment, coming back from interviews, was "I didn't know how much I'd achieved here until I started talking about it. I could see how impressed people were and I realized just how much I'd learned." Internalizing and valuing our skills and accomplishments is a fundamental aspect of power. You are much more powerful when you aren't afraid to articulate how much you contribute to the business's success.

Women often thrive in sales because just like qualifications, sales numbers provide impersonal proof of talent. Those numbers, objective in black and white, persuade us to be confident. Others say that it is only in job interviews or polishing résumés that they realize how much they've achieved. If you've been keeping that journal of your achievements, this gets easier and easier.

Established norms of femininity make us feel uncomfortable dwelling on our successes; I still resist my husband's cues to discuss great reviews I've had or new opportunities I've been invited to get involved in. Fearing the envy or competitiveness of others, I forget that everyone loves competence. This isn't vanity or boasting: it is about developing the inner strength to make things happen.

Jane Saddler

In May 2003 I was working as a Project Manager when I decided to interview for a Manager position over nine Project Managers. The company requires eighteen months in one position—so I didn't think I had any chance since I'd only been here five months. I considered the interviews to be strategic—putting my name out for the future. So I decided to change my interview style to be a more assertive one. I told everyone I interviewed with that I was the best candidate for the job and here's why (then I'd provide a short verbal list of qualities I thought I was strong in). Well, I did get the job, I'm now managing nine project managers since May and I'm really enjoying it. It was also the best interview experience I've ever had.[4]

For most women, the hardest thing we do is negotiate our pay. Because we trivialize our achievements, we forget our value and feel powerless. But the more we value our skills, the easier it is to make sure that others value them too. Negotiating our pay has a significant ripple effect: more pay says to others that we are worth more. Being worth more means we get better assignments. Better assignments lead to promotions. In this way, molehills become mountains. Owning your skills lets you negotiate from strength: a dialogue, not combat. Internalizing your worth allows you to enter these negotiations not as a petitioner but as an asset.

Cindy Solomon

I have a dear friend, a psychiatrist, who went to medical school when she was thirty. She believes that she is one of the best child psychiatrists out there. She isn't arrogant but she knows she is one of the best. So every six months, she will go to her boss and ask for more money. "I know I'm the best, I want to be paid the best, here's what I want." And every six months she gets a raise.

So what is it about her? She has confidence, she knows she is important to the organization, that they are better off with her there and she knows that, whatever happens, she will land on her feet.

Institutions can sap our confidence, persuading us that our power derives from them rather than from ourselves. Large, established companies often loom so large in our minds that they deskill us, making us feel it is the company—not us—that bestows value.

Susan Ellis

I was talking to my mother the other day about my new boss and I just felt so disheartened. "If he doesn't like me and I lose my job, what will I do? I will have nothing!" And it was my mother who reminded me: "Yes you will. You will have yourself. You have you."

Susan's mother is right: what makes Susan great at her job is Susan, and she carries that power with her wherever she goes. While companies may reeingineer, bosses may come and go, you always have your skills, your experience, your accomplishments.

Cindy Solomon

> I've talked to women who were treated like crap—worked hard, were underpaid—and sat there for years because they didn't believe in their own value. It's like learning a sport. You have to practice. Analyze what you did right. If you trivialize your achievements, you don't learn confidence. It's just another skill.

High-achieving women regularly set themselves goals that are a bit of a stretch. Then, when they reach those goals, they have a solid achievement they can look at and point to, knowing their strength. I repeat: Skills lead to competence, which leads to achievement, which builds confidence. And then we have the power to support, encourage, lead.

Inside Out

The great thing about confidence is that once you have it, you can stop thinking about yourself and start thinking about other people. Real power derives from being able to see other people as other people and figure out what they need from us to succeed. This applies as much to bosses as to subordinates. Power doesn't come from dominating or infantilizing those around us, but from making them powerful too. Confidence allows us to more easily see the world through others' eyes. Freed of the recurrent need to revalidate our place at the table, we can start seeing how it looks and feels to others.

This goes beyond empathy. As an executive, it requires listening and observing acutely enough to understand what's needed to make everyone succeed.

Cindy Solomon

> Women are so intuitive that we think this will just come to us. But it has to be a conscious effort. What do I need to know about that person's personal agenda to get done what I need to get done? I know, because she pulled out an org chart, that she's probably visual; she will probably appreciate the visual representation of data. She had the file ready for the meeting and, at the start of the meeting, had it all laid out. So she wants information clearly organized. She's not a brainstormer. You need to think all the time: what am I learning about the people I'm working with? What sells to them?

One of the smartest women I ever worked with was a lawyer and accountant named Nancy Braid. She had a great reputation for being fair and for being a blast to work with. She spent her life in negotiations and was exceptionally good at seeing what the other side needed to succeed. The other side, however, was not always so imaginative. So she'd teach them how to negotiate effectively with her. "I just keep saying to these guys—give me a reason. Give me a reason why agreeing to your terms will make the deal better for me, or my life better, or the product better. Please is not an argument. I can help you if you can show me how it helps me."

She tries to teach people about what others have called "the hidden iceberg of needs." She tries to teach them to stand outside themselves and find the win-win. She's developed an outstanding reputation because everyone comes away from her knowing more than when they began. It's a startling and inspiring contrast to the negotiations my father used to describe, in which his chief triumph required the humiliation of the other parties.

Everyone needs things from meeting, negotiations, or relationships. You are more powerful when you understand what those needs are. For some it may be clarity, reassurance, details; for others it may be new ideas, speed, raw data. Power accrues by understanding those needs and deciding how you want to address them.

Jane Saddler

Women tend to work hard and expect their effort to be noticed—I know because I did this for years. When I learned to "read" my management, determine what they valued and focused on that, I started receiving bigger raises and bonuses. Reading management includes (a) learning what they want from you (this varies—some want you to run the department budget, other's don't); (b) figuring out whether they want you to take the lead on hot issues and inform them later or tell them up front before you take any action; (c) determine if they are downward-facing (more interested in their employees) or upward-facing (more interested in their upper managers) because this determines how they will view things. One manager may want a weekly report and not want to hear anything else from you (meaning you put out all the fires alone). Other managers may want you to consult them before you go firefighting. Some managers want you to come up with initiatives.

> I figured this out by observation, then trial and error. Interestingly, I did have more than one person give me this advice, but it was after I'd learned it myself!

Observing and listening aren't thought of as traditionally powerful activities. But they are. We begin to understand who we are dealing with, what their unstated (maybe even unknown) needs are. That knowledge puts us in a position to build mutual successes.

The paradox of this kind of power is that it looks like the opposite of power: it looks like service. Because it isn't about serving our own, egotistical needs—but identifying the needs of others and serving those.

Bonnie Reitz was part of the management team that turned around Continental Airways from the worst airline in America to the success it is today. For her, the most powerful position is one in which you can support the needs of others.

> *Bonnie Reitz*
>
> I would have never described myself as leading from behind but it is exactly what we did. We had a monthly officer meeting. We would have presentations from the core elements of the business. And after the first few years, I never did them any more. I rotated them among the VPs that worked in my division because each of them needed a platform to show the different view points and talents in the division. It gave them a platform. One of the guys said to me, "Don't you worry that it makes you look like you don't do anything?" *(laughs)* Everyone wants to contribute. Why should I speak on the things that they are doing? I have plenty of opportunities. The guys were afraid to give up a platform. My whole division shined. The caliber of executives shone. You can't win without everyone doing their best.

Bonnie calls this the Inside/Out way of thinking: you get power by giving it, your company becomes powerful by serving. It is a far cry from autocratic gurus and Bonnie sums it up with a great paradox: if you listen, you will be heard.

The more we share, the more we have. It's obvious to us—it is not always obvious to men. A senior banker once told Sandra Kiely, "You should be looking out for yourself, not your people." Sandra was managing director and chief administrative officer of National

City Investment Management—but apparently her male colleague didn't think she knew how to manage. He was stuck in the old paradigm. By seeing through the eyes of others (employees, investors, stakeholders), we can make much smarter decisions. Jackie Streeter, Apple Computer's VP of engineering, regularly moved people out of her department to jobs where she thought they'd be a better fit. This flew in the face of all the old measures of power. But she didn't link her status with headcount; she focused on results. She could see the company through the eyes of her senior management, directors, investors. She could see beyond herself.[5]

"It isn't personal." That single comment has been repeated to me as advice by almost every woman I have ever talked to. None of them means that work isn't personal. What they mean when they say "Don't take it personally" is that powerful people stand back. They observe the patterns and needs of their colleagues and can address those without feeling subservient. Powerful people are confident enough to look beyond ego to the success of the project and to serve that. Because the project can be an accomplishment. It takes a lot of ego to have so little ego—but it is very powerful.

Relationships

All business is relationships. That insight seems very simple—and it is. But the world is divided between those who understand and embrace it and those who don't. In a business environment characterized by constant change and transition, we know that our paths will cross our colleagues' all the time. Building good relationships wherever we can is the bedrock of our careers. Indicating how powerful this can be, psychologists refer to relationships and connectedness as "social capital," and they're serious in inferring that these skills grow, compound, and create real value. Nevertheless, women's skills in this area are often undervalued—"people skills" are often accorded less respect than number or code crunching. But without strong relationships, and the trust they develop, no business can function.

Perhaps we shouldn't be surprised that our skills are often undervalued—we've developed them to very high standards. In research studies, women score better than men on motivating others, fostering communication, and listening to others—all relationship skills. We do this so well that men dismiss this as a "natural" skill, but it isn't that. Relationship building takes time, effort, discipline. Great relationship builders are polite, reliable, punctual, respectful of others' time and attention. They always ask lots of questions. I am always struck that it is among the most senior leaders that I encounter the greatest courtesy: leaders of gigantic companies are infallibly responsive and on time—often far more so than their underlings. This isn't a coincidence.

Great relationship builders don't care about status. You can have relationship power or social capital in any job, at any level, at any time in your career. Because social power derives from who you know and who they know. Likewise, those at the tops of organizations often have social power not because they're at the top, but because they keep in touch with those at every level. We all know people with legendary abilities to remember names—I envy and admire them, but I don't think that's as important as being able to see who people really are. When I was a very junior researcher, I worked with an eminent television and radio presenter, Joan Bakewell. She taught me an enormous amount—not because of high intelligence or a dazzling Rolodex. But every single conversation Joan had with someone seemed to count. She gave the conversation time. She thought about what was said. Her responses weren't automatic. She never, ever gave the impression of being in a hurry and she never changed her style: it was the same whether she was talking to a receptionist or a CEO. And she always scheduled her own appointments. People called it charm—and it was charming. But it was very much more powerful than that: the attention she gave made people want to help her. Successful women accrue social capital at every level because they know that making connections between people is at the heart of creativity, innovation, and leadership. Established leaders keep in touch with young talent. Technical leaders make a point of connecting with artists and thinkers. Everything hinges on the quality of the relationship.

By contrast, I've worked with men who operated with a slash-and-burn attitude to relationships. What they cared about was the deal, the deal above all else. No time for small talk, no interest in individuals. Deals got done, fast and furious. And then thrown to others to implement. When, as invariably happened, aspects of the deal started to come apart, or needed retuning, there was no relationship to fall back on. These executives could close deals but they couldn't implement them—because implementation requires relationships. And when business got rough, no one moved to help these guys. They were on their own because they always had been. This kind of deal maker inspires no trust and fails to understand that trust is the basis on which solid business has to be done.

Jeffrey Pfeffer of the Stanford Business School argues that business success depends not so much on having a strategy as on implementing it well. And implementation, he says, depends on people: how they are treated, their skills and competencies, and their efforts on behalf of the organization. In other words, business success depends on relationships. Not on brilliant individuals, but on outstanding dialogues, connections, and, crucially, trust. Women with great relationships have the power they need to make strategies work.

Reputation

Excellent relationships build your reputation: the public sense of who you are. A reputation for honesty, directness, integrity means that you may find it easier to be believed, to get good deals done, to be taken seriously. A reputation for keeping promises may save you a lot of time, providing guarantees, references, contingency plans. Your reputation, built up with every relationship you have, determines who people see and what they expect even before they meet you.

Some of your reputation may be out of your control. If you went to a school that others see as great or awful, that will inform how you are perceived. But every contact you have will improve that reputation—or make it worse. Every meeting or phone call represents an opportunity to build a great reputation—or lose it.

Chris Carosella

Good reputations make it much easier to reach higher levels of achievement. People like to work for someone they trust, in fact I think most would rather take less money to work for someone they trust than to make more money and work for someone who has a bad reputation. Bad reputations prevent good work from getting done.

> Those with good reputations are generally women who put others first but those with bad reputations are very self-focused. One woman, Mimi comes to mind. I first met her when we were both sales executives in Chicago. Mimi would do things like call on loan processors (who made about $15,000 a year) while wearing a fur coat; they hated her. She supervised a sales rep and he complained that she'd make him do her personal errands. She'd call our boss at home after 11 p.m. because she had a question about her commission check. People would send her memos addressed to "Me-Me."

It's hard to overestimate the invisible power of reputation. When people hear that you are honest, reliable, or successful, it changes the way they receive what you say and what you want. Understanding your own reputation also reinforces what you are trying to achieve. I remember a friend once telling me about a conversation he'd had about me with a colleague. "Margaret," the colleague had told him, "was fearless. She just argued and argued her case until they agreed." I'd had no concept that that was what I was doing, or that it was admired—but once I heard this, I made an effort to reinforce that reputation. I want to be seen as a valiant champion of good work. And once people knew I was tireless, they were less inclined to initiate trivial debates.

Reputations develop when you're not even there. Someone with a great experience of working with you tells a colleague who's heard similar praise elsewhere. Suddenly, people you've never met think well of you, want to work with you. When you need them, this prefabricated support is invaluable. Being associated with exciting products, breakthrough technologies, successful campaigns—all of these associations with your name build a fabric that can support and develop your standing in the community. It's an extraordinary experience to walk into a meeting room full of strangers, everyone of whom already thinks well of you.

Credibility is worth its weight in gold. When you introduce someone, you vouch for them—that is, you put the weight of your reputation behind them. You only want to do that when you mean it. A friend once introduced me to John, who ran a film distribution company. It wasn't a bad little company and John was right that it needed investment to capture some immediate, big opportunities. I thought the business had a real chance. The problem was that I didn't believe in John. I thought he wanted a lifestyle—not a commercial company. I didn't believe he would honor his investors. For me to introduce him to banks and investors would mean that I vouched for him. And I couldn't vouch for him without risking my reputation.

Bad reputations rub off. If you work for someone with a reputation for dishonesty, cruelty, or any kind of sleaziness, you may start to be thought of in the same terms. Our reputations are built every day by the accretion of small things: the acts of colleagues, the tirades of bosses, meetings we scarcely remember, phone calls we forgot to return. It's important to think about what kind of reputation you would like to precede you. What do you want to be—and what do you want people to think of you? A great reputation can work like a genie, dispelling opposition before it arrives, creating enthusiasm before you get started. And a bad reputation takes forever to shake off.

Alliances and Networks

Lex Crossett was a big tech bully. He'd just come from CompuServe; he thought Microsoft made the only and the best software in the world and that everyone else was just stupid. At the time, I was moving heaven and earth to launch a piece of software we had bought from BBN, the Internet engineering firm. Our investors, CMGI, had paid a lot of money for it and my company was predicated on it. But Lex was convinced it didn't work. Finally, it came to a showdown—Lex brought his concerns to a meeting and I had to defend myself against them.

That morning, I told my husband that I might be home by lunchtime—the business could be closed. That's how bad Lex had made things.

I brought three people to the meeting: a senior software architect, the VC who had bought the software in the first place, and another CEO who had hired me. Lex came alone. We won. It was the business's first near-death experience and we survived. In retrospect, the funny thing is that Lex was right—the software didn't work. But I had allies and Lex had none.

Unilateralism looks tough and panders to traditional, macho notions of adventure heroes who single-handedly save the day. In myth, that is. In business, you are never alone. The higher the quality and breadth of your alliances, the more powerful you will be. Even the most exceptional businesspeople, who've inherited their empires, have watched them teeter without allies.

Just after their merger was announced, we decided to challenge AOL Time Warner on their Instant Messaging policy. Since the merger needed approval from the FCC and FTC, we saw an opportunity to force their hand. It was no small challenge for a start-up, less than a year old. My SVP of Marketing knew Blair Levin: ex-chief of staff at the FCC, urbane lawyer, and elegant tactician. Blair, of course, knew everyone at the FCC along with many of the companies that had an axe to grind with Time Warner or AOL: Microsoft, Excite, AT&T, Disney. AT&T supplied economists; Microsoft paid for some extra legal advice. Excite supplied technology effort. Other start-ups joined together, even with their competitors: Odigo and Tribal Voice, for example.

AOL had sixty full-time lobbyists. We had none. AOL had Colin Powell on their board, Time Warner had General Al Haig; we had no recognizable supporters. AOL had infinite resources; we had no headquarters, no office, no point person. We just had allies—and we were able to force the only concessions agreed to in the largest merger in history at the time.

Allies aren't friends—they may even, as in the AOL case, be competitors. Although friendships may come out of them, that isn't their purpose, and many alliances break apart as soon as their goal is achieved. Inside a company, allies may be outsiders whose stature or support can reinforce or validate a strategy you're promoting—outsiders often have more influence on an organization than insiders. Alliances always enable us to achieve together what we can never achieve alone.

Networks are similar but not the same. Strong networks aren't built overnight and they serve no specific program. Networks are so powerful because individual people and events can't break them. They grow when you are asleep, exhausted, distracted. They are powerful precisely because they are beyond your control. At first you may think of your network simply as all the girls you went to school with, that you meet for drinks or gossip. And make no mistake—that is a powerful network. But then it will start to grow: a network is all the people you know and work with, and all the people that they know and work with, and so on. More formal networks within organizations are valuable too; one investment banker told me that, when layoffs began, it was the women with networks who survived. Networks provide knowledge—by its very nature, a network can always know more than you can.

To be effective, networks need a lot of love and attention. Building a network is not about building a huge Rolodex but about storytelling—knowing people well, knowing who's really good at what, remembering who needs what. Networks thrive in exponential proportion to the effort and attention to detail that you put into them. Networking has become such a buzzword, some people seem to think that, like speed dating, it replaces relationships. It doesn't. Networks *are* relationships—and, like all relationships, they require paying attention to who people are, what their needs are (the hidden iceberg again), and not wasting people's time with introductions that don't reflect those needs.

Networks triumph in job hunting; no other tool is proven to be as effective or powerful. Up to 80 percent of jobs are filled by people using their network contacts; as such, they far outweigh the effectiveness of headhunters, Internet searches, or newspaper ads.[6] Similarly, ask any sales director and she will tell you that networks are the most powerful sales engine she can devise. Whether you are in a thirty-person design firm or a twenty-five-thousand-strong software company, networks can drive your visibility, your reputation, your revenue.

Benjamin Franklin is reported to have said, "If you want to make a friend, let someone do you a favor." He clearly understood that asking for help is a privilege for the helper—and he must have been a great networker. Networks work best when they are generous and reciprocal. I'll help anyone I can, assuming they will do likewise when they can. I don't keep score and will give a lot before I give up. I'd rather err on the generous side, and I realize that the consequences of my help may be random, beyond my control.

I'd always rather give more than I get from a network—but everyone has their limits, because without reciprocity, networks wither. When I came to Boston, I knew only two people. One of them was a Harvard College and Harvard Business School grad. Tim had lived in Boston forever and was—or so he claimed—an ace networker. He would always call me when he was looking for a job and, out of ancient family loyalties, I'd always help him if I could. But it seemed a little odd that I was helping him—I, who knew no one, helping someone who had lived in the town his entire life. After many years, I realized that, as much as I helped him, he never, ever helped me, never introduced me to a single person. He was a network user, not a network builder. In the end, I gave up on him.

You can never know who will help you—which is why developing the habit of great relationships is so important. I got my first CEO position through a woman in my network. We weren't friends; we didn't know each other very well. In making an introduction for me, of course she helped herself—but that wasn't her only motive. She understands the power of networks and we keep in touch for that reason. She's smart, she never wastes anyone's time, and I wait for the opportunity to repay her. Similarly, I got my first magazine column through a friend of a friend who made an introduction that led to another introduction that eventually generated the column. Small amounts of attention to relationships pay huge dividends when they are part of a network. The compound interest built by social capital is truly staggering.

To be productive, networks must be positive.

Karen Price

> I started a group at our company that held brown-bag lunches once a month. We brought women leaders, role models, in to speak to the group about issues they had faced in their careers. I did this because, while I was successful professionally, I was looking for role models who balance life overall better than me. I did this group for several months and then came to a stark conclusion. Most of the women who attended the lunches only wanted to sit and complain. They didn't care what the women speakers said to boost them and teach them. The women in our company who were doing well, advancing, getting along with their male peers, rarely attended. So I quit doing the lunches.

Many women avoid women-only networks, especially those within corporations, feeling that these organizations build dissatisfaction, rather than power. And they worry about being singled out as a malcontent. Personally, I love the company of women and often find these groups blazingly honest, refreshingly funny, and energetically supportive. The advice and insight of other women combats your sense of isolation, providing context and perspective and helping you to see that many of the things that happen to you are not about you. But your networks should not be limited to women, nor should they be limited to formal, organized groups. By their very nature, networks should be organic—grown by your skills, interests, needs. Networks shouldn't be full of people you're trying to impress or suck up to; neither should they be full of people trying to impress you. The best networks feature people at all levels; are positive; are defined by your values; and reach beyond your industry.

Networks provide perspective, context, objectivity. And not just for work—but for life.

> *Holly Godwin*
>
> Networks are ABSOLUTELY CRITICAL for moving up. If you do not know the right people, the right way to behave, the right places to go and be seen, then you cannot rise to the top. The people in your personal network are not only useful for helping you move up, they are also helpful in correcting you when you need a sanity check. EVERYONE should have a Personal Board of Directors (PBOD). People from your work, faith/spiritual life, personal relationships, family, etc. Those people whose judgment you value and whose opinions matter to you. Those are the people who should be on your PBOD. If you don't have a network like this, GET ONE. You will go nuts without it.
>
> I believe the key to the PBOD is to make sure it is balanced . . . if it is all work and no family, then guess where your advice will be skewed? If you neglect one area of your PBOD, you will neglect that area of your life.

Janet Hanson lives and breathes the power of networks. Since her experience of leaving Goldman Sachs on maternity leave, she and her husband have spent more than a million dollars building 85 Broads, a network and website for Wall Street women. She has seen the power of networks to help women find jobs—but, even more important, helped them hear their own voice, given them the courage to think for themselves. Within 85 Broads, ex-Goldman Sachs employees can advise current ones and give them the support, encouragement, and connection men have enjoyed for years. She sees no reason why women's confidence shouldn't match their demonstrable intellect.

Institutions can cripple that confidence—and networks can rebuild it. They push women up the learning curve faster by making it clear that our talent and ability are not the function of the institutions we attach to—they are ours, to take with us wherever we go.

Women are great networkers because we understand that power depends as much on supporting others as on being supported ourselves. No one runs a network; no one can command it, control it, or issue orders. When I talked to Janet about the network she's built, and what it has taught her about the power of networks, she used an analogy that cut to the heart of what really good networks offer. She called them our underground railroad.

Mentors

Paige Arnof-Fenn

I have benefited tremendously throughout my career from mentors. They can be colleagues, professors, bosses, and senior people in organizations. You need that Sherpa in your life to learn the ropes. People who are generous with their wisdom, knowledge, and contacts have been vital. Not just in corporate America but as an entrepreneur.

Research into men's careers is unequivocal: mentors make all the difference in career advancement. Virtually all executives will tell you that mentoring is an important part of their development. Likewise, for women, having a mentor is seen as an essential ingredient to success and not having at least one is seen as a serious detriment. The lack of mentors for women is one of the reasons given for women not making their way to the top.

A mentor is someone who believes in you more than you believe in yourself and who will help you not to accept the status quo. They should give you support and keep you ambitious. True mentors make you more powerful not because they loan you some of their power but because they help you to develop your own. For that reason, you may find them at any level of an organization.

Paige Arnof-Fenn

My assistant when I ran the Olympic Coin Program, Beverly Spears, was also a mentor to me. Beverly and I are very different in many ways—she is a black woman, one of 20 children, 25 years my senior.

> Her only child is my age. She has had a tough life. I learned more watching Bev handle people and situations than you can imagine. She always takes the high road and never compromises her integrity ever. She is such a good judge of character and has an amazing instinct. So street smart it is scary. She is truly a survivor.

Most of my mentors have been men—not surprisingly, since I've worked primarily with men most of my life. Some, like Gordon Clough, kept my soul strong when I worked in toxic environments; he gave me interesting work and respect when others around me were mocking and derisive. Others, like Piers Plowright, taught me never to consider a project finished if I had the time and resources to improve it. He also taught me to take big creative risks, something he did himself all the time. Peter Armstrong first ignited my ambition when he asked me what he could do to get me "to the top table faster"—that question alone changed my thinking. None of these men thought of themselves formally as mentors and I didn't think of them as such either. But that's what they were. They taught me a lot, they felt invested in my success, and they pointed out areas of improvement.

Andrea Jung, CEO of Avon, said, "Some people just wait for someone to take them under their wing. I've always advised that they shouldn't wait. They should find someone's wing to grab onto."[7] This is another case where asking for help is a gift to the helper—and most people will say yes if they can. Mentors can offer protection, exposure, and visibility. Perhaps most important, they can be your champion when bad things start to happen. Women find it hard to fight for themselves without feeling brash or selfish. But we all need advocates.

> *Pamela Matthews*
>
> I started my career in banking and left when things went wrong and I took it personally—I thought an attack was about me, not just politics. I thought I was taking a stand and really I should have kept my cool. I didn't network, I just didn't really understand what was happening to me. At my going away party, a guy came up to me and said "why didn't you come and talk to me?" and it just hadn't occurred to me to get supporters.
>
> Then, I had a baby in 2000 and my career was derailed shortly thereafter by management who 'mommy tracked' me. I thought

> people could SEE that I did a great job. But I didn't have advocates, I didn't have people who would go to the mat for me. I assumed the MDs would support me. You have to solicit people who will go to the mat for you.

As a CEO, I've watched mentors bring immense value to my company. Sue Aman, a brilliant young engineer, felt she needed a change and began job hunting. She was fortunate in her mentor, Robin Colodzin, who absolutely went to the mat for her, demanding that the company provide a role that would stretch and stimulate her. In forcing the company to find ways to keep Sue, Robin didn't just do a great job as a mentor—she did a great job for the company as a whole.

As a mentor, I often find the most useful thing I can provide is context—a different perspective from the one that comes with the job. So often, the only visible goals are the ones on the org chart: the next job, the bigger title, the better department. In that quest, of course, corporate mentors are invaluable. But the best mentors, like the Personal Board of Directors, are Life Mentors. I remember once talking to a young employee of mine who was in a rather dreary job and wanted—quite reasonably—to move on. Soon after this discussion, I woke up in the middle of the night with a shock: no one had explained to Mike about his stock options. Should he stay to the end of the year, they would be worth more money than he would ever be able to accumulate through savings. The career decision to move on might be sound but no one had considered the financial ramifications. In the end, Mike stayed, bought his house without a mortgage—and redefined his job.

Choices are never between this job and that job but between this job and all jobs. This company and all industries. Internal mentors are invaluable in helping you navigate murky corporate waters, but Life Mentors show wider horizons, richer choices. You have to have both.

The Power of the New

Expectations cramp our style. Step into an existing job and, whether anyone tells you so or not, you will be surrounded by silent expectations. Your colleagues will expect or hope that you will do the job as well as or better than your predecessor. That you too will serve cookies, hold short meetings, or take Fridays off. You'll pick these up by osmosis and, perhaps unwittingly, start to mold yourself around them—or against them. Without a single direct conversation, the fences of other peoples' hopes and fears grow around your power.

Think of it in marketing terms. If you launch a new brand of cereal, what does everyone want to know? Is it cheaper than corn flakes? Sweeter than Lucky Charms? Healthier than Special K? In product markets, an effective strategy is often to go where the competition isn't. In power markets, exactly the same strategy can apply.

Which is why new jobs offer such promise. New positions are created in response to a need—a crisis that needs systemic prevention, a new market segment that needs specialized attention. But beyond the immediate, functional need, the expectation skies are clear. You have the power to create the job according to your skills, your style, your needs.

Risa Edelstein

> Ziff-Davis was a good experience for me in that I was working in a "new" department that was trying to use the Internet to create an online education business. This made it very entrepreneurial since our department was small and limber. I learned a tremendous amount and was able to exceed sales expectations by being highly creative. I also was able to leverage the assets I had within the corporation (i.e. I knew the President of my division very well) to attain my goals yet not piss too many people off including my boss—whom I made look good since we achieved our sales goals.

The power of new jobs is so great that the job itself may not matter. My third job at the BBC had the title Features Copyright Assistant. Created in the wake of a major copyright fiasco, I was required to ensure we had copyright clearance on all material in programs prior to broadcast. Once I had a few systems in place, this was pretty easy. But the systems required that I was involved in every stage of the editorial process: devising and commissioning programs, working with directors, producers, and authors, researching materials, clearing the final program before transmission. Before long, I produced my first program and it was nominated for a prize. Two years later, I was running part of the department and had more than doubled its output.

Political analysts would describe what I did as building a power base in a niche that is largely uncontested. Robert Caro writes tellingly of the immense power Lyndon Johnson built from the hitherto powerless position of leader of the Senate. The absence of opposition can be immensely liberating. On a blank slate, we can design ways of working that play to our strengths and values. Instead of playing the game, we change it.

The same applies, on an even bigger scale, to new companies—where, again, the absence of precedent can be inspiring and empowering. New companies, usually starved of resources, live for the creative, interstitial player who seizes initiatives and builds momentum. The earlier in the life of a company you join, the more opportunity there is to have power and influence on the development of the business and its organization. Here there are no footsteps in the sand; the paths and achievements you choose can be your own.

Time and Place

Controlling time and place challenges the wiliest politicians. But just because you can't control them is no reason not to appreciate their power. We could never have gained the visibility we did, during the Instant Messaging war, without the perfect timing of the AOL Time Warner merger approval.

Timing can make all the difference in pay negotiation. While I'm not advocating that you devote your entire career to negotiating pay raises, this remains the area in which women feel most powerless and in which we demonstrably fail—so it's a good area to look at when seeking ways of increasing your power.

> *Jane Saddler*
>
> A few years ago, I was working as a Project Manager on a PC hardware platform. I learned that I was making $10K–$13K less per year than all my peers, although my management frequently gave me 2–3 platforms to manage while my peers had one platform. I was told that this was because I did better work, etc.
>
> So I waited until I was in the middle of a project—not at the end or beginning—which made it much harder to replace me. I got an offer for a similar position at a smaller company and wrote my

> resignation letter to my boss. By the end of the day, he called me in my office and offered me a 16 percent increase and a promise to start grooming me for management if I stayed.

To replace Jane, mid-project, would have cost her company a lot of money (which they had) and time (which they did not have). Jane did many smart things in this negotiation, but perhaps the most important thing she did was to choose her moment.

Traditional analysts of power make much of proximity: the importance of being physically in close range of the boss, CEO, president. And we're all familiar with the legendary power of personal assistants whose power is always wildly greater than their salaries. I find myself less impressed by this kind of power, because it isn't portable, it cannot be internalized, and it rarely results in concrete, owned achievements. Nevertheless, the interstices of office geography obsess many—I once returned from a meeting to find John Garrett, a senior executive from an affiliated company, trying to preempt my move into a new office, so keen was he to be near our chairman! I was flabbergasted by such infantile behavior by an otherwise sane adult; clearly these things matter a lot to some people. I tend to regard this as another aspect of dependency and not a source of power. I think the same about "face time"—the notion that your progress and achievement may be enhanced by the amount of time you spend in front of your boss. Valuing face time means any power you gain is a discretionary gift, liable to be withdrawn on a whim.

Real power may be found by pursuing an opposite course of action. When I joined CMGI, I found I'd entered a very complicated and very political organization. Some twenty-two operating businesses, over forty-five venture investments. Corporate structures and company structures, boards within boards. It made the Medicis look like a Scout troop. Soon after I arrived to start my own company, the VC who had recruited me, Guy Bradley, said, "Get an office somewhere else. Get out of headquarters." He wasn't being unfriendly—it was the best piece of advice I ever got. Escaping the politics of the place meant escaping a million distractions. My job was to hit my schedules and my revenue targets. Did I care if AdSmart outsourced their web hosting? Did I care if everyone hated Engage's CTO? Focus is everything. On hearing corporate gossip, my mantra became "It's not my problem." I found an office location that made recruitment easier, allowed a different culture to develop, and gave everyone a great deal more freedom. And I outlasted most of my peers. Your own space says more about you, and does more for you, than proximity to someone else's.

F.U. Money and the Parallel Universe

The last, ultimate source of power is the willingness and ability to walk away. I used to dine with a guy who was immensely charming but sometimes drank too much. When he did, he became tyrannical and abusive. He'd made many friends with his charm and lost them with his bullying. But we got on fine. Why? Because I always took my coat and cab fare. He knew that I was quite prepared simply to walk away.

Nothing quite beats having your own "storming off in a huff" money. So often, when I ask women why they've put up with bad pay, poor jobs, toxic bosses, and values they abhorred, the response is that they could not afford to leave the job. I am never quite sure whether this is an excuse or the true explanation—but I do know that the best way to ensure that we don't get trapped is to be able to leave.

> *Pamela Matthews*
>
> I live so if I lose my job it is okay. I didn't over buy on my house or our cars. We drive a 92 Honda. Our "Fuck off money" is cash for one or two years. [The bank] thought I wouldn't leave but I knew I could. We live modestly—we don't belong to country clubs, we don't send my daughter to fancy private schools. We keep our expenses low.
>
> My parents were teachers and, when I went into Wall Street, I just thought "Let's see if I can do this." They didn't have any connections, we didn't know anyone and so everything I have achieved, I've had to achieve with my own skills. I did it all myself and so I want to make sure that whatever I do next is my choice.

Knowing that you can walk away doesn't mean that you will. But knowing that you can changes the way you feel about your decision. Portable power is important because it causes us to remember that the ability to change things doesn't come from bosses or titles or corner offices: it comes from within ourselves and grows when we share it. This is a very far cry from traditional, masculine notions of power because it doesn't hurt anyone.

As I watch my female friends and colleagues lead teams and companies in a style that is so far removed from The Limited's WAR, it strikes me that they are building a parallel business universe where power has a very difference face. There's a gathering mountain of evidence that suggests that this concept of power is more effective, more efficient, more appropriate to the business environment we face today.[8] Our win-win style of doing business produces better long-term gains, and female managers outshine their male counterparts by almost every measure.[9] We are powerfully effective—while remaining true to who we are.

When newspaper articles repeatedly ask why we don't want power, they seem to me to miss the point. We don't aspire to powerlessness—god forbid—but to a different kind of power. What successful women demonstrate, and young women yearn for, is an alternative model of power that grows with sharing, that enlarges rather than belittles, that attaches to ideas and teams and values instead of institutions and gurus. Power that is self-perpetuating, not limited and rationed. Power that is measured not by how much brutality we can endure but by how much we can eradicate. Power that is not about putting others down, but about building others up. We get glimpses of it and these dissuade us from accepting second best. We feel like gatecrashers in the old command-and-control world, but in a parallel universe—a different world of female power—we could have a real party.

Travel Thoughts

- What are the achievements that give you confidence?
- What's below your colleagues' iceberg of needs?
- Who can you help?
- What kind of reputation do you have—and what kind do you want?
- What have you done to build your network lately?
- Who is on your Personal Board of Directors? Is there anything you value that isn't represented?
- Who's your mentor?
- Can you afford to walk away?

Chapter Six

Sex, Love, and a Vision for Life

Question: Tell me how you feel about this
Try to control me, boy, you get dismissed
Pay my own fun, oh and I pay my own bills
Always 50-50 in relationships
—DESTINY'S CHILD, "INDEPENDENT WOMEN"

We work for many reasons: to pay the rent, to develop our talents, to build self-esteem, to find friends, to be independent, to make a contribution to the world, to have financial security for our retirement, to have a purpose. Even at its most average, work develops and articulates who we are, what we care about, how we relate to the world. At its best, work makes us feel whole, engaged in a dynamic relationship with the world.

But it isn't everything. Work is not our only relationship or contribution to the world; it is just part of a whole skein of relationships that make our lives. No woman I've known has sought or felt comfortable with a life that is work and work alone. But every woman I know struggles to find a way of integrating all the different demands on her time, loyalty, love. And this is no vague, sentimental desire: it is fiercely felt and has to be fought for.

Since women began to go out to work, we've faced the challenge of how to combine our personal lives with our work lives. We haven't wanted to follow the male example of compartmentalization—and, anyway, there usually isn't anyone left at home to look after us. Instead, we have a more ambitious goal: we want to be one whole person, with different tasks and responsibilities but with consistent values and styles. Everything else feels dishonest—at best a performance, at worst a lie.

The standard term *work-life balance* suggests that the key to these issues is to find some perfect equilibrium and then preserve it. I think it's more complicated than that. Balance is certainly *not* half and half; many of us want more intense engagement in our work *and* in our relationships than that bland formula implies. Moreover, while these issues most often present themselves as time conflicts, they are more than that: they are value conflicts. Which values will we allow to dominate our lives: the values of the corporation or the values of the individual? Who defines us: our employer or ourselves?

In the past, the corporation largely called the tune, determining who moved where and when, what the working day, night, and year looked like. But that's all changing. Women don't want to work that way, families can't—and as we struggle with these issues, we are beginning to find a whole different way of looking at them. We know we can't trust our employers to make big life choices for us. We make decisions according to our own ethics and needs, not according to org charts and corporate career plans. We want to escape the old paradigm—in which work dominates and our private lives are subordinate—and replace it with a new one in which work and personal lives can be treated with mutual respect. And so we struggle mightily to wrench men and their corporations into a different way of looking at life. It's worth the struggle, because putting values first is better for business, better for women *and* men, and significantly more sustainable.

But we have a long way to go. From the very start of a career, we're confronted with highly polarized choices. This is the beginning of an epic struggle between work life and private life. They struggle for dominance, they resist cooperation. Work demands one thing—total devotion—and we want another: a total life. This presents itself mainly as a logistics problem, but it is more than that—it is a battle over who comes first.

Lynne Kingsbury

I make it a policy *never* to go out with anyone from work. I just don't like to mix these things. On the other hand, I'm here *all* the time. I hardly ever have time for anyone. One guy phoned me up

> recently—he was really sweet but there wasn't really any chemistry between us—and asked me out for dinner that night. I said I couldn't because I was working late. "What about tomorrow night?" I said I had to work, I had to get five hours' sleep, I just didn't know. And he said, "I don't know if this relationship's going to work if you can't even accommodate me for dinner." And I just told him to stop whining!

What I hear in Lynne's story is a very familiar voice. It is the voice of the corporation saying, "You will have no love before me. You will love me alone." Translated into daily life, this means that women often feel that they can't take time away from work to find a partner and they can't find that partner at work. Why? Because either of these activities takes time, effort, loyalty, love away from the business. And companies get jealous.

According to various studies, between one-third and two-thirds of employees have affairs with their coworkers, so having relationships at work can't really be deemed exceptional behavior any more. More strikingly, nearly half of those said that their relationship led to marriage. Not surprisingly, work turns out to be a good place to find someone who shares your interests, aims, ambitions.[1] Yet some women feel that they should not go out with a work colleague. They feel there is an inherent conflict between their work lives and their private lives, and this conflict makes them very uncomfortable. But when they attempt to resolve this conflict the way the men always have—by keeping work life and personal life separate—they discover that however hard we may try to keep the two lives separate, life doesn't cooperate. The workplace is full of people who are exceptionally compatible with who we are: they have chosen the same area of work, they share many of our interests, they're often a similar age and driven by similar hopes and goals. And we're spending those hundred thousand hours with these people! It's little wonder, then, that office affairs and marriages are so common.

In our quest for an integrated whole life, I don't think we do ourselves or our companies any real favors by trying to bifurcate our lives. I see a lot of stress and unease on the part of women trying to separate roles, and I see an impoverishment of the business culture in companies whose employees are asked to leave their true selves—often their most vital selves—at the door. If we want a business world in which values are valued and integrity is systemic, not optional, we have no choice but to insist on bringing our whole emotional, sexual selves to work every day.

No, of course it isn't easy. And I should know. In my very first job, I went out with one of my coworkers, Gordon, who was both older and more senior than I was. Everyone knew about it and the affair itself didn't bother anyone. What really pissed them off was the fact that on his days off he loaned me his parking pass. Because he was a presenter and I was just a production assistant, the relationship shattered the office hierarchy. The hierarchy, not the relationship, was the problem. But Gordon was an absolutely wonderful guy, kind, generous, knowledgeable, a serious thinker. I learned a lot from him. In retrospect, I don't think I did the wrong thing. The relationship wasn't an idle flirtation but a serious friendship that outlasted the affair by years. I wanted a relationship, I spent all my time at work—where else would I find someone?

Perhaps some people thought I was trying to sleep my way to the top. It's an accusation often hurled at women, and, very occasionally, it does happen—though it isn't a very successful career strategy. But more often, these slurs merely betray a discomfort with women's power and a determination to undermine it. In any event, it seems to me absurd to abjure intensely important personal relationships just because bystanders might misconstrue them. It is, after all, your life and not theirs.

Cathy Aston

I met my husband at the office. I don't think it was as difficult to develop the relationship as one might imagine. Yes, there were clandestine meetings and we did keep it quiet for many months. We worked in two different departments that often interacted, but there was no conflict or reporting issue. Because of the hours that we work, you'd be surprised at the number of couples that come out of that work environment. Many couples within my circle of friends are the result of this.

For many, the biggest challenge is privacy. When I worked in television, two colleagues, Jon and Anna, announced they were getting married. I'd known Jon for five years, Anna for two. But so successful had they been in hiding their relationship that no one had even suspected they were going out together. Each morning, they drove together to a nearby car park where they separated into different cars so no one saw them arriving together. What was most discomfiting was that they both turned out to be such exquisite liars.

An easier approach was used by Ben and Cristen. When they started going out together, everybody knew it. You could see it in Cristen's face; you could hear it in their conversations. It was, perhaps, mildly distracting for everyone, but both were outstanding employees. Nothing in their relationship jeopardized their work—and that is what kept onlookers comfortable. They were smart and never let their professional standards drop. Their openness—even after they split up—put everyone at their ease.

Office marriages and relationships can disturb the balance of relationships in offices and they require a lot of diplomacy. Nepotism raises its ugly head—is your relationship influencing work decisions? Many company policies are designed to deal with these issues—many prohibit anyone from being (or becoming) the boss of their partner and some even have what are jovially called *love contracts:* these aim to protect companies from subsequent harassment suits.[2] But no policy has ever been invented that appropriately curtains the private from the public. Office relationships just force you to think about boundaries. How much do you want your colleagues to know about you?

Some will say that women's affairs are judged more harshly than men's. My own experience is that the bright guy who worked for me and dated every single woman in the office did *his* reputation damage—he so clearly didn't know what he wanted. Gender isn't the issue; the quality of the relationship is. Offices are poor settings for frivolous affairs, but no job, no company should cost you the really important partnerships. As I listen to women talk about their desires for a full, integrated life, it strikes me that blocking personal relationships off from work is what men have always done—and it's a far cry from what we seek.

I'm biased, perhaps, because I met my first husband at work. He was a brilliant, funny producer, and I fell madly in love with him. The public development of our relationship was agonizing: everyone could see us having lunch together, making plans together, leaving together. I'm convinced that the whole department knew the day after we first slept together. They knew when we split up and when we came back together again. When we decided to get married, I felt like I had to invite the whole department. But I felt then, and I still feel, that it was worth it. Who was the company to tell me I should not do this?

Of course, work is not the only place in which you can find a partner—it simply shouldn't be ruled out. What's important is to ensure that you save for yourself the time and energy needed to have a full personal life. I remember discussing this once at a partner's offsite, run by a large investment bank. As I was arguing the immense value to business of whole, rounded employees, one of them asked: "Can't we just ask the singletons to do the long hours?" The implication, of course, was that life issues were relevant only to married couples and, more particularly, married couples with children. He had clearly missed the point. Yes, your relationship with your partner needs and deserves time and attention—but so too does your relationship with yourself. My first husband died when I was thirty and I did not remarry for six years. For a time it suited me to work immensely long hours. But then I stopped and instead spent time with friends, time at the gym, time at the theatre, time alone. People thought I was lonely—and of course, for some of that time I was. But I gained a sense of self, an enjoyment of my own company, a comfort in my own skin, that gave me a lot of confidence. Private lives aren't just for families and couples—everyone needs a life. For our parents, our communities, our pets, our selves.

But it is hard to protect that life. Work will take and take and take, if we let it. You need a very strong sense of self to manage work's jealousy. It is, in a way, a fight for life—your life. Inhabiting corporate structures that were not designed for us or for the way we want to live, we face a struggle that is incessant and, if anything, intensifies with marriage. A marriage, after all, is a very powerful loyalty statement, and managers, however much they appear to celebrate the event, often act like spurned lovers.

Combining careers with love also challenges bosses, often beyond their ability to manage very well. Gone are the days when women had to quit their jobs on getting married. And most companies have policies in place to ensure equal treatment of employees who are married to each other. The problem women face when married to a colleague tends to come more often from their immediate colleagues than from policies. Managers and coworkers can feel threatened by the solidarity a married couple represents.

Jennifer Herron

I love to work with my husband, we make a great team. I think it is other people who are intimidated by the situation. It makes managers very nervous. They tend to think we are conspiring against them, which is generally the complete opposite. We tend to solve problems at home.

Lately it has been good and bad to work together. We have a nightmare for a new division manager and he has been playing us off one another. He announced in a staff meeting that he was very concerned about my coverage, hinting that I might be laid off. Then later that week, he informed my husband that he had found coverage for me and I was fine. Never did he speak to me or even send an email!

Partnerships challenge loyalties, and work wants to win. Those 4 A.M. emails intrude to ask, who do you love more? As reengineering and downsizing continue, loyalty seems to be a one-way transaction in which you give and they get. You have to be very determined—and very confident—to be loyal to your own life. Alison Knight recognized that her company would take from her as much as it could—unless she was confident and thoughtful enough to know where to draw the line.

Alison Knight

Before, I was afraid to demand balance because the company I was at wanted "total" commitment as a condition of moving up—live in a company neighborhood, socialize with other company employees etc. Husband-wife teams were not uncommon.

You have to decide what your limits are and live by them. I say that from a vantage point of knowing what it is that I bring my employer and being able to demonstrate value. It could mean risking your job but I've found that as long as you don't make a big public deal about what you "will and won't do" you can organize your own life.

The most common struggle is over time. I remember watching the senior partner in a law firm stay at work past 10 P.M. on his daughter's birthday to gain the five minutes of face time during a document sign-off. He was making a value statement: work was more important than his daughter. (His boss, of course, never noticed him and never knew what he'd sacrificed to be there. All his sacrifice bought him was absence of criticism.) Time is the oxygen of relationships, and companies are greedy. The increasingly prevalent sixty-hour week spells out clearly who's in charge—and that's before all those extras: the client dinner, the weekend golf, the weekend offsite. All these supposed perks and privileges of success are, in effect, a test of values.

This struggle is made more painful because work's enticements are significant. We want to be paid well. We want the thrill and satisfaction of excelling at something difficult. Our achievements makes us love work more because they confirm our skills and sense of competence. Women can be reluctant to confess how much we love work, what a buzz it gives us, what pride, what self-esteem. We offer up other reasons—"Somebody has to pay the mortgage"—because we don't want to provoke more jealousy, but in our heart of hearts we know we do it because we love it.

Nancy Frank worked for a boss whom she describes as tough—but she also says that she was a great boss because she demanded (and got) more and more out of Nancy. Nancy's love of her work brought her into conflict with her love of her family—and she wasn't really willing to sacrifice either. This is a painful place to be: between two stubborn loves.

Nancy Frank

> At home, my husband would often say I was not there enough for dinner, I was traveling too much. I got a lot of pressure at home to do less and less. I can remember walking into the office, saying to my (female) boss, "I have to cut back my travel or it could cost my marriage." She said, "This will put us both in a tough place, won't it?" Here I was, head of Marketing for a firm with clients all over the U.S.! She said, "Let's do our best to make it work" but I felt pulled on both ends. I felt like Solomon's child, cut in the middle. My husband would say, "No one's doing this to you but you."

The paradigm of male dominance is so ancient and still so prevalent that many men feel challenged and jealous when they see their partner at work, competent, confident—and in charge.

Lynne Kingsbury

> It's hard to have a relationship when a lot of my job, in sales, involves entertaining. Sometimes I've said to a guy I'm dating, "Why don't you come along?" But then he got all offended because I'd spend the evening talking business. He said he felt like a wife! And I was talking business all night because that's what I was there for.

Corporate entertainment—and every company does it—can be brutal to the ego. No matter how glamorous the event, it casts one half of a couple into the spotlight and the other half into oblivion. When I remarried, I hated attending Lindsay's medical events and he hated attending my media events. Almost the only row we ever had was at the London Film Festival. I had to be there, schmoozing with producers and directors who worked with my company. But not a soul spoke to Lindsay, nobody cared who he was or what he did—not being in the business, he was no use to them. He had come out for an evening with me and found himself spending the evening alone. So he started to sulk—and I started getting grumpy because he was sulking.

After this episode, we just stopped going to each other's work events, but sometimes this felt childish to me; I felt we ought to be able to negotiate these things better. Now we are much more explicit (and experienced) in identifying what the event will be and therefore in understanding, if we go together, what we have signed up for. When I go to Lindsay's work events, I go to support him and to understand his work environment and colleagues better. When he comes to mine, it's for the same reasons. We don't take each other's participation for granted, we don't do these things too often, and we acknowledge that they aren't time together.

However hard it is—and it is hard—we can't achieve the kind of integrated life we seek if we erect immoveable walls between work and home. Negotiating those boundaries, determining how flexible or sturdy we want them to be, requires a lot of trial and error and humility—on both sides. Nancy Frank's husband may have been jealous, but it didn't mean he was unsupportive.

Nancy Frank

> As much as he resented the intrusion my career had on the family, he benefited from it greatly. He would do things that were very helpful for a corporate spouse. Like he went to one of the functions, met

> the CEO and later wrote to the CEO to say how impressed he was by the company, that he could understand why his wife was so dedicated and committed. He sends this beautiful letter to the CEO and the CEO stops me in the hallway one day and says he appreciates the letter—so I ask [my husband] "What did you do?" "Oh, I just wrote a little letter. . . ."

Relocations pose all the same challenges, writ large. Who is most important: the husband, the wife, the company? Someone, something has to give—how do you decide?

> *Karen Price*
>
> I worked for the largest engineering company in the world. It was a badge of honor and corporate dedication to have moved a dozen times in 15 years. It showed how valuable you are to the company if they want to keep you and continue to move you. The men would brag about how they'd get notice they were being moved to a new location, or new country even, and the lovely wife would pack up the kids, sell the house, and move the family to catch up with the husband. My girlfriends and I would wonder how that would work for us. We wouldn't have a "little man" at home to just pack up and move us. We wanted husbands who had their own careers. So, how were we going to move every other year with our husbands who also had careers?

Many large corporations make a fetish of relocations, using them as the ultimate test—and in doing so they continue to lose large numbers of smart women who want to do great work, just not at the expense of the rest of their lives. Men often interpret this as a lack of seriousness, a lack of commitment, and that's what it is—a lack of seriousness and commitment on the part of the employer, who still fails to understand that dominance is not the name of our game.

If relocation is a test, women increasingly reject the test. "The problem with women," said Peter Wright, VP of global HR for Estée Lauder, "is that I just can't get them to relocate. We're a global company and we have to have senior people all around the world. And they just won't move!"[3] To keep his best women, he needed to redefine his problem: to look at local workforces that could be trained, and to look at executives who wanted travel and to groom them.[4] But Wright didn't want to *serve* his workforce—he demanded that they serve him. *His* problem with women was that he didn't appreciate that we don't want our relationship to work to be defined by servitude or domination, win or lose. That polarization implies we must choose between work and life, and we reject that choice.

When women—and couples—confront choices like relocation, they don't measure success according to whose career wins and whose career loses, but according to how well the joint project—the marriage—thrives. It's about mutual understanding.

Paige Arnof-Fenn

> I was offered the job at Coke so he stayed in Washington D.C. and I moved to Atlanta. We were both on the fast track and knew that if one of us "gave in" we would end up regretting it, so we commuted. It was an important experience for both of us. We really missed being together so we both resigned from our jobs and picked a new city where we could both get good jobs. It was a joint decision where we both felt we made the right call. Since then it has never been hard for us at all to decide. I think we will move again one day and the decision will be a joint one and right for both of us. Our marriage is very important to both of us and our preferences are very much in sync. We've both built great résumés and really value our time together and quality of life. It is about so much more than the job itself.

Marriages force us to confront hard questions. Not just "Which is more important—work or home?" but "What are the values that define our lives: corporate values or individual values?" Companies with traditional power structures are about dominance, not equality. How far are you willing to allow those corporate values to invade your private life? Do you really want a married life in which one of you is dominant and the other subordinate? These questions collide incessantly in time management, travel, corporate events, relocation, career planning. Ad hoc decisions don't work, because the choice is too important—an existential, life-defining choice. If fairness is crucial to us at work, then as we seek integrated, consistent lives, fairness at home is just as important. If we want to get out of the old win-lose ethos at work, it is absolutely essential to keep it out of our homes. And so we find ourselves inventing and demanding new behaviors and expectations *in both places.* This is pioneering territory for most companies and many couples. Like all pioneering work, it is long, hard, and pretty messy.

Cathy Aston's story is one in which, at the outset, work values—specifically, corporate values—dominated. She knew this at the outset; she'd met her husband at work and they were both very committed to their careers. But after several years and four relocations, she found that corporate values had undermined her marriage and her sense of her own value.

Cathy Aston

My husband and I met when I was transferred to Detroit from Chicago. It hasn't always been easy. He is part of that ancient male dominated culture who generally take the side of the company; I always used to kid him that I knew I was third on his list when we got married. His first love was the company, then his children by his first marriage, then me. We were both driven individuals and both very focused on reaching our career goals. When a promotional opportunity was offered to me which required us to live apart, neither of us thought twice about it. The company had been downsizing for six years and we knew there would be very few opportunities for advancement under the more traditional means. We lived apart for twenty-two months, the last five of which I was pregnant. His perspective would be that we'd live apart before he would let me leave the company (not quit working or switch jobs but leave *this* company). He is very loyal to this company, which did not bode well for our relationship.

Cathy spent years working for a toxic boss, in an environment in which the guys talked to each other about golf—and to the women about nothing. Loyal and dedicated, determined to deliver her usual 200 percent, Cathy kept proving herself (to the company, the boss, and her husband) until she became ill.

Cathy Aston

I needed to heal and the only way I could see being able to accomplish that was to leave the company. My husband made it perfectly clear that if I left the company, he'd leave me. Many of my female friends were quick to point out that this was abusive and while I didn't disagree with them, I couldn't or wouldn't let my marriage end because of some misdirected loyalty on my husband's part.

My point in all of this is that couples, but particularly women, need to understand how each will react in certain situations. If faced with this type of issue, I would have expected 1000 percent support from

> my husband and yet I got none. It was a real eye-opener for me. If men and women don't fully understand one another, their beliefs, their support structure and their ability to trust and compromise, then the stress to a marriage (especially a dual-career marriage) can be overwhelming.

In the end, Cathy seized control of her life and, by hiring a discrimination lawyer, eventually wrenched her relationship with the company and her husband into some kind of proportion. Her experience may be extreme, but it is a salutary warning about how profound the struggle between company and partner can be—whether spouses work for the same company or separate companies. The marriage based on work doesn't work.

But even in marriages in which work itself doesn't dominate, work values easily intrude. In companies, money generally equates to power. The more you are paid, the more power you have—and the less dirty work you have to do. This equation doesn't work at home because there isn't, or shouldn't be, a boss. You're in this together—right? Yet sometimes it's hard to keep those corporate values at bay.

> *Ruth Cohen*
>
> He earns three, four times my salary. He pays for all the vacations and the apartment. So of course I feel I have to make it up somehow. So I do the ironing. I do all the cooking. I broke my arm once and, after it was set, I was told not to use it for three days. So I asked Bill to do all the weekend cooking. On Sunday evening, when I asked him what he was planning for dinner he barked, "I've already cooked six meals this weekend!"

I know Ruth's husband and doubt he'd be comfortable with the idea that he has purchased his dominance. But he is so imbued with work values he probably hasn't noticed. Glenda Roberts, on the other hand, has worked out a different approach. Everyone works for the whole.

> *Glenda Roberts*
>
> When my husband makes a bed, I don't say thank you to him—because he hasn't done it for me. I say "Good job!" because he's done it for us, he's done it for the household. We all benefit from the work that we *all* do.

I'm sure Glenda and her husband don't think of it this way, but they run their household according to female concepts of power: the power is in the collaboration, not in the dominance of one person. It all hinges, crucially, on values.

> *Mary Giery Smith*
>
> The night before he proposed to me, my husband asked me what I thought about money. I replied that it was a tool, not a goal. Luckily, he felt the same way. That was the clincher question for us in a lot of ways. While we are both professionals and, frankly, very good at what we do, we have both made conscious career decisions not to pursue positions that would unduly strain the fabric of our marriage or our family. Money, position and power are just not worth it to us. But I think we are closer to "having it all"—if "all" means a comfortable life, a good marriage, happy children and time to spend with them—than many people I know. We don't have everything there is to have, but we have everything that is important to us.

What's so important here is the *us*: money, position and power are just not worth it to *us*. This is not a drama of dominance or self-sacrifice. This is a marriage that is about fairness and commitment to the whole. About deciding and making life choices *together.* That solidarity, of course, makes us feel far stronger when we confront the jealous company: our commitment to our whole lives isn't selfish, it is for *us*.

To protect that solidarity, fairness is fundamental. When I remarried, my husband Lindsay was totally committed to medical research and I knew that it would probably never pay as well as the work that I did. That doesn't matter. He does the work he loves; I do the work I love. We live within whatever means we generate. Neither of us is the designated breadwinner; together we share responsibility for the way we live. Domestic life is not delegated—and neither is it means tested. We both do the dirty work. The value of our work isn't reflected in pay. Has running my companies been ten times more important that my husband's research into multiple sclerosis? The question doesn't even make sense. Only corporate values equate importance with salary, and the goal of the whole life is to live by our own values—not to surrender to the company's.

I sometimes joke that it's a lot easier to be fair when you pay someone else to do the dirty work. Quarrels over ironing, cleaning, and putting the dishes away resolve easily when a cleaner makes them vanish. But that's not always possible—nor is it what everyone wants. I make a point now of telling Lindsay when I feel the balance is wrong, and I try to do so before I get steamed up about it. Our contributions to the household are quite different: I do daily stuff and food, he does infrastructure and wine, we both do finance. When we have really obnoxious chores, we make a point of doing them together; it's the only way they can be fun. But what matters to us both above all is that neither feels exploited or subservient.

Almost everyone, at some point in their lives, feels very tempted to quit—or to ask their partner to quit. We all nurture the 1950s fantasy of coming home to dinner in the oven, a fire in the grate. When I was running two companies and making a lot of money, I used to think how great it would be if Lindsay were at home and I could just work all the time. Then I'd think about it seriously and wonder how I could ever have the right to ask him to sacrifice his scientific career. Would I want that responsibility? No. Did I really want to work *all* the time? What for? Would the mutual respect of our marriage be enhanced? Hardly. I could not ask him to do something I was not prepared to do myself.

To be fair, a marriage has to recognize and embrace the difference and *independence* of both people; this seems to be the only way to escape the masculine model in which one serves and the other dominates. But sometimes this is so hard, requires so much time and effort and talking, that it is tempting just to give up and go home.

Cathy Aston

I wouldn't have been any good staying at home. I love my husband and I've forgiven him for his lack of support but I can never trust him to truly take care of me. Maybe that will change some day but for now I know it's up to me, which is why I'm creating a world for myself that will allow me the challenge of an interesting job and the ability to balance my personal life better. I am a woman who needs the challenge of an interesting job to go to every day—but it is not my life. Recognizing the distinction can make all the difference in the world to survival and ability to change the world.

Fiona Wilson

I meet these women that I went to school with and they say "I'm supporting my husband" and I just think—what? What happened to your education? What happened to your individuality? And I also think: what happens as you get older? So many of these women reach their 50s and 60s, get divorced or their husbands die and they discover that they don't have enough to live on. So there they are, going out to work for the first time in maybe 30 years. It's terrifying.

It *is* terrifying. I don't claim to understand where women today get the idea that they don't have to pay their way, that someone else will look after them. I appreciate the centuries of tradition that combine to make women fear their own power and worry that commitment to their careers is selfish or unfeminine. But, especially in an age of layoffs, restructuring, and divorce, their dependency and lack of self-support leaves me worried for their self-esteem and their futures. Poverty is a real issue that women have to face—not just because of having babies but also because of divorce. Although the divorce rate hovers around 50 percent, only 15 percent of women receive alimony. The average age at which marriages fail is around thirty-nine—a point at which starting a career is very difficult. After a divorce, the wife's standard of living is estimated to fall by 73 percent. Dependency has huge costs: American women over sixty-five are more than twice as likely to be poor as men of the same age.

Alison Knight

My having a career is good risk management for us as a family because we don't have to rely on just one job for our livelihood. I watch the ladies in my neighborhood whose husbands are the breadwinners and think it would be nice to have their flexibility, but they are just one layoff (or heart attack) away from a very precarious situation.

Either-or doesn't work because, again, it makes one part of life dominant, the other subservient. Sometimes dangerously so. More inspiring is building, crafting, refining a unified image of life defined by values, in which decisions retain a dynamic relationship to the whole.

Linda Alepin

You have to have a vision—not just in work but for your life. Know what you are in pursuit of. Instead of looking at life as a series of tradeoffs between work, family, love, etc., I try to view life as a "whole". I look at what it is about spending time with the kids that is fun, or what it is that I love to do at work.

We walk around with so many unexamined paradigms that it is a wonder that we have any freedom at all. As women came into the work world, we jumped feetfirst into the dominant male paradigms—money, power, and title. It is only in the last ten to fifteen years that women have started to create their own paradigms. We are challenging paradigms every day. We are questioning whether it is all about "you work hard and then you die." We take on more "but it's always been that way" issues. Since we are not the incumbents, this is the game to play. It is through this exploration and challenging of fundamental truths that we are having some of the most profound effects.

The parallel universe rejects the notion that the old, traditional business values—hierarchies, the value of money, the measurement of effort by time—have a role in whole lives. Instead, we start with a vision for a whole life in which work has a role: a role that undergoes many changes, but that is not the solo or dominant role. This is hard for companies to accept; it means that they must start to rethink issues like relocation, schedules, and measurement of effort by time rather than results. It also means that they must change traditional notions of when careers accelerate and when they taper off, and they must find ways to make these more closely map to the ways we want to lead our lives.

We accept that the onus is on us to make our values coherent and compatible, but we would like to see companies adapt to the insistent individuality of their workforce. Where they don't, it is increasingly the case that couples leave the corporation to set up their own; they become *copreneurs,* managing businesses, employees, and schedules together.[5] Their pursuit of the whole life, far from compartmentalizing work and life, career, and family, boldly brings them together.

Cindy Wilson

I have an amazing husband who is so supportive and calm. He helps me through the stressful times. We now work together. When

David joined the business, we melded our talents to create a space where we could both work, knowing that our ultimate goal was the quality of life for our family. We rarely lose sight of this goal.

Karla Diehl

My husband is the visionary, strategic force and he handles all the capital concerns. I provide the operations and systems direction and all the Corporate Culture initiatives. The advantages of working together are that we both respect the other's abilities in the arena in which he/she plays; we can pinch hit for each other when one of us can't be in two places at the same time, we are working shoulder to shoulder in moving our business forward. The disadvantages are that, when we take vacation, half our senior management team is gone at the same time! The best part is creating an environment where our values and ethics are reinforced every day.

Ultimately, each marriage is unique and the way in which each succeeds is generally invisible to the naked eye. Each is somewhere on a continuum between couples running businesses together and couples who (like Lindsay and me) pursue entirely separate careers, protected by boundaries but integrated with shared values. Across that whole spectrum, what prevails is women's insistent search for innovative ways to keep their lives, their selves, whole.

Cathy Aston

I've also started my own part-time business. While I don't have the time to dedicate to the business that I'd like, it has given me something else to focus on, something positive. And it brought me into a circle of women who shared some of my problems and experiences and who helped me regain my perspective. It saved me, nearly literally, to have a few nights a month talking about something that was not related to that horrible work environment. It helped repair the self-esteem and confidence that I have always had and that had been ripped away from me by circumstances that were well beyond my control. . . . Everyone is given the same twenty-four hours; it's how we use them that sets us apart.

The arrival of women in the workplace changed the workplace; it is still trying to figure out how, where, if we fit in—and learning how it has to change to get the best from both men and women. The same galvanic changes have occurred in our personal lives:

however hard the old models try to reassert themselves, they don't work, and we search for new ones. I am struck that the most satisfied women I talk to place fairness, equality, at the heart of what they do. Their private lives are defined by mutual support, respect—and patience. No one expects it be easy, so when things go wrong, no one's terribly surprised. Blame is irrelevant. We only blame those who don't try. No one wins if anyone loses.

What gives me hope is watching couples—straight and gay, young, old, copreneurs and corporate executives—develop a language for discussing their choices and decisions that is about values and contributions, not about hierarchies. They all look pretty puzzled when asked, "Who is the head of the household?" Like most people who make hard choices, they haven't chosen this path because it is easy, but because no other path seems viable. At times, they all wish they could surrender to something easier; they just can't see what that would be.

Many women ask me whether or not the struggle to be fair to two individual careers doesn't mean that both parties get second best; since none is given priority, does it mean both suffer from a compromise? I haven't found that to be true—in fact, quite the opposite. Smart women seek smart partners; successful women enjoy their partner's success. One life makes the other life richer. Having a life makes work more sustainable, and it keeps us anchored in a reality in which we care passionately about right and wrong, honesty, fairness—all those values that business so badly needs. Companies may be jealous. But women are not. We know that in unity lies strength.

Travel Thoughts

- What are the values that define your life: corporate values or individual values? How much time do they get?
- What sacrifices does your work demand?
- What do you love more: your work or your life?
- How fairly do you divide the chores and logistics of life?
- How secure are you in the event of illness, divorce, layoffs? Do you feel safe?
- What is your vision for your life? Is it shared?

Chapter Seven

The Whole Life

Life, strife, these two are one,
Naught can ye win but by faith and daring.
On, on that ye have done,
But for the work of today preparing.
Firm in reliance, laugh a defiance
(Laugh in hope, for sure is the end),
March, march, many as one,
Shoulder to shoulder and friend to friend.
—Dame Ethel Smyth, "March of Women"

Gatecrashers aren't catered to. At no point in our careers is this more obvious than when we confront the decision about whether to have children. For all the lip service that society and business pay to motherhood, little is done to make our decision (or its consequences) easy or even rational. For many women, whether and when to have children is the hardest and the most radical decision we will make in our lives.

You can't absolutely decide that you will have children; you just decide to try. But you can decide not to have them, and many women do—for almost as many reasons as there are women.

Paige Arnof-Fenn

I'm not interested in the experience at all, never have been. I had a great aunt who is in her 90s now and she was the first woman editor at Macmillan. She and my grandfather's brother never had kids by choice and they had a great life together. They were very happy, had a strong marriage, traveled all over the world, lived in a great place, had interesting friends. I remember visiting them when I was young, maybe eight years old and thinking they had a great life together. I have plenty of wonderful children in my life—nieces, nephews, goddaughters. I hope we will spend many great times together and that I will always be remembered as a great influence in their lives. I don't think you have to be blood related to someone to have a strong impact on their lives.

Sharon Tunstall

I'm not sure why I never wanted children but I just never have. I've never felt that desire. It's not that I don't like children. I'm very close to my two nieces and nephews. But I just wanted to be an adult with a career and a meaningful relationship. I don't feel that I missed out or am not "whole" because of this. For me, it wasn't a choice—it was just what I wanted.

I have many friends who either decided not to have children or who were never in the position where children were a possibility. Their lives are full of rich relationships and commitment. They've been great friends and great colleagues, and their choice fits them perfectly. Not having children has not been a career move and it hasn't turned them into workaholics either. That they lead fulfilled lives is obvious from everything they do and everything they say. These women have chosen not to have children for good reasons.

I also have friends who chose not to have children for bad reasons. Too many trips, too many promotions, too much to do. And I am haunted by one of them. Sally, a fantastic friend, enjoyed a frantic, dazzling career. Starting in executive search, she rose to senior HR positions in a global business. Her colleagues adored her sanity and smart advice, her style, humor, energy. A fun partner, great friends, a fabulous home—her achievements brought justifiable pride and pleasure. Until, in her late forties, she found herself crying every night on the train home. Too late, she realized that she wanted a child. For many years, Sally and I had seen or spoken to each other every week, but when I started my family, this was so painful to her that we lost touch entirely.

Sally's tragedy was not that she didn't have children—but that she didn't have them for the wrong reason. Distracted by the siren song of corporate congratulations, she forgot—forgot to take time to think, to reflect on her values, to imagine she might change. The present was so much more insistent than the future that she forgot the future entirely. She thought she had to choose—so she chose her present lifestyle. The jealous corporation won. What is particularly sad about Sally is that everyone who knew her knew she would be supremely capable of being both a great mother and a great executive at the same time. But she felt she had to choose; she did not believe that she could have both.

Men don't feel that way. Of the MBAs who've risen to within three levels of the CEO position, 84 percent of men have children, whereas only 49 percent of women do.[1] Of 1,600 MBAs surveyed, 70 percent of men accommodate a family—but only 25 percent of women do. Clearly, men feel confident that they can combine a career with a family. Women aren't so sure—and to make matters worse, we are monotonously assailed by voices encouraging us to panic. Time and again we are subjected to stories of formerly high-flying women who've left the corporate world for their families. The focus of these stories is always the individual women—not the companies they've rejected. The implication is that their return to the kitchen is an individual decision, their choice. This flies in the face of statistical data that show that, at corporations that welcome pregnancies—with paid maternity leave, flexible schedules, flexible career planning, and opportunities to work from home—women return to work, and stay there, at a rate very close to 100 percent.[2] When women give up trying to combine a career with a family, we see the companies failing the women—not the other way around. Isn't it curious that the story is never written that way?

Just as Victorian women were told that education would render them sterile, we are told that the only guarantee of early and bountiful fecundity is to abandon our careers.[3] No one bothers to add the data showing that women who have their children later in life have higher lifetime earnings and a wider range of opportunities; that, in contrast, young parents tend to separate and divorce much more frequently than older couples. Instead, press stories about high-flying executive women who've given it all up to bake cakes have become as predictable and repetitive as the annual fashion item about the essential little black dress.[4] These stories exude a triumphalism that hints at the ultimate macho fantasy—the exodus of women from the male domain of business and power. After a nasty little experiment, they infer, we girls have learned our lesson and gone back to the kitchen where we belong. The gatecrashers have finally been thrown out.

Popular culture deifies apocryphal mothers who do nothing but bake cakes, go on field trips, and are available twenty-four hours a day—while our corporate culture delights in breakfast meetings, client dinners, and six-month consulting gigs out of town. Motherhood is romanticized, sentimentalized, and idealized—while professional careers are developed as models of toughness, hard-nosed realism, and macho bravura. Such polarization contains a brutal if simplistic message: you have to choose whose side you are on. Men can have it all but girls can't. Business isn't really our domain and we should give up before we even start.

But the facts tell a very different story. All over the western world, women are combining careers and motherhood. The male breadwinner model is being replaced by the dual-earner model. Half of the workforce is female and the majority of women workers are mothers. Seventy-four percent of working mothers have children between the ages of six and fifteen. Fifty-nine percent of mothers with children six and under, and 55 percent with children one and under, are in paid work. Contrary to conservative scaremongering, there is no clear and consistent evidence that the change in family life has been harmful to children.[5] In fact, parents in United States are spending more, not less, time with their children—who, in surveys, say they get enough time with their mothers.

And the economy now depends on us. Our pay is largely responsible for the rising standard of living enjoyed since the 1970s; economic growth as we know it just isn't possible without women. As much as the guys may hate to admit it, they can't afford to do without us. Fifty-five percent of working women now earn about half or more of the family income, and 18 percent of us provide all of it.[6] Families consisting of breadwinner dads and stay-at-home moms now account for just one-tenth of all households.[7] So the fantasy that somehow we are all going to bow to some kind of genetic inevitability and abandon our quest for independence, fulfillment, and power is just that—a fantasy. We don't want the fantasy, we don't need it—and no one can afford it. Instead of focusing on some kind of 1950s, Ozzie-and-Harriet-style idyll, we would all do better to understand the extraordinary opposition working mothers encounter at work and to learn lessons from the growing number of success stories emanating from creative, committed families.

Lest We Forget

Pregnancy announces loud and clear that we are undeniably female. This is so disturbing to some men that they go into denial: I remember several of my CEO peers being astonished when I told them I was back from my (ten-day) maternity leave. Although I had been demonstrably pregnant for months, they had chosen not to see it.

Companies punish women for getting pregnant. The United States, the richest nation on earth, is one of only six countries that have no statutory paid maternity leave. Only five other countries in the world are so severe: Australia, Papua New Guinea, Swaziland, New Zealand, and Lesotho. Some enlightened American corporations provide maternity leave under short- and long-term disability plans—as though being pregnant were some accidental misfortune. This means that any maternity pay is entirely at the discretion of the employer; we're supposed to be grateful. Although the Family and Medical Leave Act gives fathers the right to take unpaid time off, in practice most firms require that vacation time and sick leave be used up first. Despite overwhelming evidence that both the mother's and newborn's medical outcomes are significantly improved by maternity leave prior to birth, few American women enjoy this privilege, working right up until labor. In this context, all the baby showers, pink-ribboned baskets, and sentimental greeting cards reveal only hypocrisy.

The absence of maternity coverage also means that we are punished financially. The journalist Ann Crittenden estimated that leaving her full-time employment for motherhood and freelance work cost her somewhere between $600,000 and $700,000—not counting the loss of her pension. Even a short break has both financial and career consequences. A survey of two hundred female MBAs found that those who took a break from the job market of an average 8.8 months were less likely to reach upper middle management—and they earned 17 percent less than comparable women who had no gap in their employment.

So we rush back to work (again contravening medical advice), and when we get there the punishment continues—or gets worse. Remember Kate Shaw, who came back to find her male assistant at her desk? Her story is repeated the world over. And Kate knew she was "lucky" her company didn't find an excuse to lay her off. Because it is illegal to terminate women just because they've become mothers, this action is usually buried inside layoffs, restructurings, or reassignments. Not untypical is the case of a business development executive who returned from maternity leave to be given a new territory requiring 100 percent travel. When she resigned, this was presented as "her choice." She wanted, her management said, to spend more time at home. In fact, she wanted nothing of the kind. What the company was telling her, in effect, was that she could stay only if she behaved as though she weren't a mother at all.

Because the business norm is a male norm, motherhood is deemed out of place. Women go through complex logistical contortions to maintain a surface calm. This, in itself, takes a lot of energy and sometimes carries a financial penalty too.

Diane Jacobsen

I was in Toronto with 2 of my colleagues and our flight got delayed. So we went into the Red Carpet lounge. I have a babysitter when I am out of town for the night but my daughter is a latchkey kid so if I am not going to spend the night away, I don't get someone to watch her. And I had not planned to be away for the night. I had planned to come home and take her away for the weekend. So I am on the phone with her and I am trying to decide whether I should call someone to come watch her or is she okay by herself? She and I are talking through it—how do you feel about this? Do you want to go to someone's house for the night? She was about 12. And one of the guys who was sitting next to me has three kids and, after I got off the phone he said, "You have to deal with this every single time you leave town don't you?" And I say "yes." And he said, "God I just walk out of the house. And I hadn't realized before that you can't." And I said no I can't. When you tell me that I am on a gig for 6 months in Pennsylvania, the first thing I do is call the babysitter to make sure that she is available for the next 6 months from Monday night to Thursday night and my per diem pays for her babysitting—not for food, which comes out of my pocket. So it costs me money to go away. And he was like "wow. . . ." He had never thought about it before.

Women learn to keep their family off the radar screen. We learn not to mention our children when guys talk about their weekends full of golf. When we're looking tired, we cite travel rather than flu or birthday parties. We observe, but keep our mouths shut, when men coo in admiration at the Good Dad who left early for his son's soccer practice—and the same men scowl in silent disapproval when women disappear for the same reason. Guys who are good to their kids are heroes, but women leaving for the school run are slackers.

Donna Collins

> If a man goes home at 5 p.m., or to a school play or a child's doctor appointment—he is a family man. If a woman does the same, she isn't giving it her all. I found when I was pregnant I worked so much harder just to prove that I was not going to slack off, that I was committed to my job. I took on more to prove that I was not going to produce less.

The reward for Donna's commitment was to be laid off when her daughter was seven months old. The old jealous fight, between employer and loved ones, is relentless.

Holly Godwin

> I was on a project contract and I stipulated before beginning that I MUST be home for my daughter's birthday. However, part way through the week, we ran into problems. An acquisition location turned out to have really subpar PCs and instead of the location taking 2 days, it was going to take all week. The VP of IT wanted me to stay even though we had agreed at the beginning of the week (as well as at the beginning of the contract) that I would be home Wednesday night for Melissa's party. I offered to fly home in time for dinner, go to the party, and leave in the morning but they said that this was not acceptable. I had to threaten to quit to get home.

Over and over again, our loyalties are challenged—stupidly, unnecessarily, perversely. Is it surprising that women conclude that men want them to fail? We see that our children are being used against us in a macho game of emotional chicken. Yes, it defeats some of us—but mostly it makes us very, very angry.

Pamela Matthews

I feel betrayed! I did everything I was supposed to. I busted my butt to have this career and this happy family and it is damn near impossible. And now all you get is extreme guilt for being a working mother! Society today values stay-at-home mothers and the rest of us be damned! I am definitely on the outside. Either I am neglectful of my kids or my husband clearly can't provide for us because clearly something is "off" if I am not at home with my daughter. My question to Wall Street (Jack Grubman, I mean you) is: Why do you strive so hard to get your daughter into the top nursery school and so on when society and you and everyone really don't want her to have a career or make any impact on the world? Why are we doing this when NO ONE will support us? We are 50 percent of the population, we are YOUR daughter, we are YOUR wife, we are YOUR mother—and you treat me like this?

So why do women like Pamela persevere? When it is so difficult, what keeps us going? Why don't we give up?

Making Work Work

There are many dirty little secrets about working mothers, but the best-hidden one is also the best news: lots of women have great jobs and great families and aren't giving up either of them. How they manage this is personal, because personal values determine the trade-offs we make. Because everyone realizes, sooner or later, that such trade-offs are the key to success. You can't do everything, so you have to decide what really matters—and what just doesn't.

Dee Copelan

First, forget about perfection—it's unattainable. Remember those old TV commercials about the women whose goal in life was to have the cleanest house, the shiniest kitchen floor, and the whitest laundry (actually, I guess those are still on TV . . .)? Get over it; it just gets dirty again immediately. Try for "good enough" and you'll be surprised how much extra time you gain. It's the same in business. Writing a new job description? Think "good enough." Writing a business memo? Good enough. The 80/20 rule really does hold true—that extra 20 percent effort spent trying to make ordinary things "perfect" isn't worth the effort. Save that extra effort for what is really most important to you.

Weeks after my son was born, I remember looking at a pile of laundry and thinking: oh well, I'm going to have to learn not to mind some of this. And I did. For years, we lived in rented apartments where I decided not to care how they were decorated. We had no curtains and absolutely no interior design. I just figured that people would have to take me as they found me and if they disapproved of my domestic minimalism—well, that was their problem. What I discovered, of course, was that the only person who even noticed was me.

I also become the school's deadbeat mom. At Thanksgiving and on Mother's Day, I was the one without painted toenails, who didn't bring handrolled sushi or home-baked cornbread. I just didn't do that stuff. I was also the one without makeup and coordinated seasonal accessories—no autumnal sweaters, no Christmas-tree earrings. I made everyone else feel great. As for my children, all that mattered to them was that I turned up. If they ever noticed the toenails, they didn't care.

Holly Godwin

> You cannot be popular both at home and at work. The trick is to try and keep people at work and at home from getting too unhappy with you. If you always put the one above the other, then the neglected side of your life will most likely disappear. I think finding a "balance" is almost impossible. What I have done is to sometimes let work take precedence and sometimes family does. For instance this weekend, I will be at the office from 6 p.m. Friday through 3 a.m. Monday for an ERP cutover. This will mean that I am not going to be home for Mother's Day or my husband's birthday. Clearly, at this time, work is taking priority over family, because of the magnitude of the situation at work. There is a $14 million project on the line and I must be there. On the other hand, even though I had to threaten to quit—I made my daughter's fourth birthday.

No one finds it easy to miss a husband's birthday or a school play, and we put a lot of effort into making good choices that are consistent. The choice I've struggled with most, and that most women I talk to worry about most, isn't about work time or family time, but about time for me. At times, I've found myself home five—or even ten—minutes early. Instead of rushing through the front door, I'd drive around the block. I had a few minutes to myself—and I savored them. Peace and quiet is a rare commodity.

Betsy Cohen

For me, some of the personal things I like have been put on a back burner—I only exercise once each week and I'd like to do more, I see my friends less often than I'd like, and it is hard to travel to visit family members for fun or if they have needs or health problems. It takes lots of attention and coordination to attend to work and school and community commitments, plus coordinating the work of running our household. By hiring helpers for the lawn, cleaning, some driving of our kids, extra babysitting when the kids were young, and more, sometimes it can feel like the household is a fast whirling circus. So, one cost is loss of a tranquil or calm home environment—at the end of the work week the rest of the weekend is spent catching up!

Sleep and leisure time (or self-time) are among the top things mothers forgo to find the time to spend with their children. We try hard to make the right trade-offs but, in sacrificing our own needs, we can find ourselves making some dangerous decisions. Houses can be mended; the same is not always true of bodies. Especially after becoming a mother, one of the easiest things to ignore is our health, especially exercise. One of the worst ironies of women going into business is that now we can die of all those things that men die of. I still struggle to find the time to get to the gym, to stay healthy.

Fighting for self-time is more important than it looks. I remember a frightening conversation with a girlfriend who had breast cancer. When her friends learned of her condition, many of them acknowledged that, like her, they had kept postponing the checkups, the mammograms. Always too busy, always putting themselves last. Don't do it, she warned me; everyone depends on you staying healthy. Make that appointment, have that smear.

The way we spend our time is a better indicator of our values than how we spend our money. We can make more money; we can't make more time. That means we use it very, very carefully. And are constantly learning how to use it better.

Cindy Wilson

Decide where you want to be. Be flexible. Get help. Schedule your appointments for yourself like you are the client. This took me a long time to figure out! Schedule your school projects like your

> kids are your number one client! Create an honest work life for your colleagues and staff so that they too are able to juggle in a supportive and trusting way.

Many women report that after becoming mothers they become far smarter about their use of time; now that it's precious, we waste none of it. Combining a demanding job with a family requires—and develops—more creativity, flexibility, and sheer ingenuity than you will find inside most corporate boardrooms. We don't just have to work hard, we have to work smart. We have too much to do to waste time on office politics, gossip, or turgid meetings.

Gail Rebuck

> I've always had to be home by six. Once you have a hard exit, there's less time for chatting. Women are often accused of being cold or unapproachable when actually they're just trying to get the job done. We don't waste time just hanging around the office.

Learning to use time effectively doesn't necessarily mean that we always use it efficiently. Sometimes it's quite important not to; importing the efficiency metrics of the office can feel inappropriate at home. One of my colleagues once made a cryptic remark, "When with your children, be there." As I caught myself reading while the kids watched videos, doing email as they painted, or cooking while they created LEGO constructions, I understood. I was in the same room as they were—but I wasn't with them. They'd be pretty blunt about it. "Play with me," they'd insist. The truth is that I didn't know how to. I had the play skills of a two-year-old: I only knew parallel playing. So I had to learn. I've also had to learn the importance of downtime—learning to allow everyone time to do nothing. Scheduling and protecting the Sundays without a project, without guests, without an expedition somewhere. Just time to pay attention to each other when we aren't multitasking—when the only real task is attention. Days like this feel like vacations and probably should be scheduled like vacations too.

Many men—and some women—ask why we do it. Why work so hard? Why struggle? Why not give in gracefully and go home? Everyone has their own answers, but here are mine. I stayed home for nearly nine months after my son was born; it nearly drove me demented. Work expands to fill the time available—so I'd spend the day getting diapers and making dinner, desperate for adult conversation. I struggled (and mostly failed) to make small talk with other mothers I met; their passion for babies was not mine. I loved my child—immensely—but I didn't love babies or the company of babies or mother and toddler groups. And I discovered that even the full-time, stay-at-home mothers were riddled with guilt! Had they breast-fed long enough or too long? Were they spending too much or too little time at their child's school? Should they push harder, or less hard, on violin practice? From that time, I learned a great lesson: no amount of time with your children prevents guilt. The best antidote for guilt is a sense of achievement.

Donna Collins

> I thought I loved both babies and children—until I had a baby! I found it more stressful to be home full time than to work part time with a baby. I think because I am fairly social and there is not much in the way of feedback you get from raising a baby, no one comes around to tell you are doing a great job. And you give and give and give. That is one thing we do get from work—a sense of accomplishment.

My sister once wisely told me that your children need you more as they grow older. As infants, they want food, comfort, warmth, sleep. They can get that from many people. As they get older, their demands grow far more complicated. Exploring emotions and morality, they want your advice—no one else will do. And so I decided that I would work hard, very hard, while my children were still small. I'd work hard to earn the financial freedom, when they were older, to give them more time. And that's how it's worked out. I made money and the money has brought me more choices.

The money isn't trivial. Every year that a woman takes out of work costs her enormously—in reduced income, in reduced savings, pension, and social security. As if earning less than men weren't bad enough, dropping out of the workforce for any substantial period of time makes us, in effect, dependents. We earn less, we save less, we have less to retire on. Six out of ten women have no retirement pension.[8] Those women who do have pensions receive about half the retirement income that men do.[9] Poverty remains a real and imminent threat for women in a system designed for men that is now wholly anachronistic. We dare not think what would happen should our husbands leave, be laid off, become ill, or die. Such vulnerability holds no appeal for me or for many women who are working to ensure that they will not find themselves in so precarious or beholden a position.

The choices we make are the lessons that we pass on to our children. When my children see me working hard, I try to avoid lame excuses. I try not to say that I have to work, that my boss makes me, or that we need the money for toys. I try to explain that the reason I work so hard is because I love what I do and work is a great, ennobling activity. I want my children to grow up with an attitude to work that is not begrudging but is positive and realistic. I want them to see that hard work is the way to earn what we value.

Diane Jacobsen

One of the things my daughter has learned is that she has seen me struggle. She saw me in graduate school. I moved the two of us from a nice house to a group house for women for $500 dollars a month and we were eating beans and rice. I used to call it Mercenary Dating because I would go out with some guy and order the biggest, most expensive thing on the menu—and bring half of it home so we'd all have meat. And I was in my forties and my daughter was old enough to know what was going on. We were living pretty lean and she saw me working really, really hard and staying up really late, but she also saw that I finished it and I got a great job and a nice house and all those things. The whole notion that it is a lot of work to be successful is something that she has grown up with.

Humor helps. It's a way of forgiving yourself—for not being perfect, for not being able to do everything you want to do, the way you want to do it. No mother can survive the first year of parenthood without humor—and working mothers need a double dose. When I found myself pumping milk in a grubby little press room at La Guardia (the only private space Delta could provide), I could have felt sorry for myself. Instead, I just laughed at the inanity of the entire setup. Laughter made me feel better.

Diane Jacobsen

I did Starbucks' corporate prototypes. Howard Schulz hired me himself. Because he was running out of time, he gave me two weeks to come up with a proposal which he'd given firms with 300 people

> a month to do. I came back with a lot of ideas and wrote them all up. And that morning I had a meeting with him.
>
> I used to take my daughter over to the coffee shop near her nanny, drop her off and then go down the street to work. I had a blue wool dress on and I was looking nice. Well I am sitting there with my daughter at the coffee bar—and her diaper leaks! All over my arm. So now I have urine all over my blue dress. So the nanny comes. I have to go back to the house, have a shower—but there's no time.
>
> So I'm in this meeting with Howard Schulz and I am trying to stay far enough away from him so he can't smell the urine on my arm while I'm doing this presentation. I can smell it and I am thinking "I don't want him not to hire me because he thinks I've been sleeping in alleys with bums" and I am going through the whole rigmarole and he ends up hiring me. And I think: I got a job with urine on my arm! I know men who've gotten a pen point on their white shirt and taken the afternoon off to go out and buy a new shirt and have it monogrammed! So I think back to that and think—some of the stuff people get so worked up about!

Extended families help a lot. When Elaine Davis plans trips to any of the many Glaxo headquarters she visits, her first phone call is to her mother. Glenda Roberts can give Microsoft's acquisitions the attention to detail that she does because her mother is at home helping to nurture the entire family. This support cannot be taken for granted; not everyone has parents and in-laws who can or want to help this way. And even when they do, discretion, tact, and gratitude are essential—Glenda's mother saw fit to remind her, when she moved in, that slavery had been abolished! In my own home, my business trips are feasible because my husband, his father and stepmother and/or a nanny and occasional friends provide a complex skein of support that, in itself, takes some managing.

No mother on earth will tell you that she has this all figured out. Our dislike of posturing silences even the occasional pride or comfort we feel. And every woman has a collection of mantras that help her stay on track, stay organized, keep focused:

- Don't put it down, put it away.
- If you bring your kids presents when you return from business trips, buy lots and keep them at home as backup.

- Cook twice as much as you need and freeze the other half.
- Make a space at the office where your kids can do homework.
- Have a time budget for your kids so there's a minimum amount of time you must spend with them every week.
- Don't live for the weekends. Do something fun in the middle of the week.
- Review the coming week with everyone on Sunday.
- Let them do it their way. (When you delegate, really delegate.)
- Put it in the book. Have one message book where all family members enter and leave messages for each other.
- Make a date night: book a regular babysitter so you have to go out for adult conversations.
- Don't let work dominate the dinner conversation.
- Take a walk every day. You can always find fifteen minutes.
- Always put the same things in the same place.
- Get the kids to do some of the work—they learn and feel more involved.
- Books on tape are great for commutes.
- Schedule downtime: time with no arrangements for anyone.
- Buy lots of kids' presents during sales—that way you're ready for anyone's birthday.
- Avoid coincidences—don't toilet train and move to a new house at the same time.

What hurts women is the sense that we are alone, left to face an endless logistical challenge by ourselves. I remember hearing Liz Dolan talking about her sister who was always just slightly undersupplied with child care—and I recognized myself. Our old bad habit—being reluctant to ask for help—comes back to haunt us at the time when we need help most. The challenge from companies is so brutal—you have to choose—that our response wildly overcompensates: I don't have to choose, I can do everything. Consciously or not, we collude in our own oppression. But the truth is, we don't have to do it all to have it all. We can get help.

Men are perfectly capable of doing any domestic work and most do so before they get married. They cook, they clean before marriage—and those skills don't evaporate when marriage or fatherhood arrives. Yet even in households where the wife is the major breadwinner, mothers spend on average thirteen hours a week more than fathers on child care and domestic chores. Fathers contribute no more than 30 percent of the domestic chores and child care—even when they're unemployed! Women spend most of their disposable income and disposable time in housework and child care.[10] The injustice of this is something that we can confront and remedy.

The assumption that men won't contribute, or can't contribute, just creates the conditions in which that becomes true. The very best way to de-skill someone is to do all the work yourself. I watched over the years as one of my best friends did this to her husband. Jean was convinced that her husband wouldn't carry his weight. Men are so useless, she thought—what can you expect? Defensive at the outset, she hoped her anger might shame him into action. So she would cook all the meals. She would change every diaper, attend every midnight terror. She would take the children to their first day of school, she would get to know all their friends, she would organize all the birthday parties. She would, in fact, derive her self-esteem from his incompetence. So what did her husband do? He checked out. How could he offer anything valuable in the face of this whirlwind of competence? Her competence stood between him and his kids. He couldn't do anything with them because he didn't know who they were. Since he was bound to fail, why bother?

In the face of our hypercompetence, many men can become selectively incompetent—that is, they choose not to learn how to help. The fathers who don't know where things are kept, which batteries the toy needs, which is the favorite sweater, or how the iron works—they could learn, but they choose not to. To mothers, it seems so much easier just to do it ourselves—but it is so very much more effective to make Dad competent.

Just like fairness in marriage, fairness in families has to be worked at deliberately and consistently. When we let fairness slip—he's had a hard week, he's been away—fathers lose their engagement with the day-to-day. This can look and feel trivial, but it isn't. Children are such moving targets that, if Dad misses a few weeks of a child's life, he gets behind. He no longer knows the favorite food, toy, or friend, or what the learning issues are. A couple of weeks like that, and before you know it, fairness is gone. So everyone has to keep up all the time. Children can only learn about equality by watching it in action.

We're like many families in that the important currency in our household is time. I used to keep track of how many early starts or late finishes I'd had each week—if too many, I was in debt; if too few, I was owed. I was as worried about being exploited as I was about being the exploiter. We did the same with cooking. If we fell into a pattern in which I cooked too often, I stopped. Lindsay and I are both stubborn people and neither of us is willing to take on everything. I'm vigilant about not letting the wrong patterns get established. I worry that if I take on a task once, I may get stuck with it forever—because it's just human nature to let someone else do the work if they're apparently willing to. This is harder than it sounds, because so much of family life can be a pleasure—cooking, time with the children, entertaining. These things produce great rewards. But if any one person owns them—as privileges or as obligations—they lose all their fun.

In Sweden, a study of fathers has produced some intriguing results. The single most important factor in determining how much time a father spent with his kids was the mother's attitude. The more money and education the woman had, the more she was willing (or the more she needed) to involve the dad. This was true regardless of the culture the father came from—it was true also of Arabs living in Sweden. "Culture was less important than economics."[11] We do not have to work alone; it's better for everyone when we won't.

Linda Alepin

The attitude I always took to my husband was: you get to help! That way, we did just about everything together. And it wasn't a trick—you are a much more important part of the family when you contribute than if you just consume. You get to help.

Robyn Benincasa learned the same lesson as a firefighter, Ironman competitor, and builder of world-class teams. Struggling through a grueling desert race, one of her team mates reached a breaking point and turned to her to ask for help. She learned an important lesson: "Asking for help is a gift to the helper." This is an essential insight for mothers, families—and managers.

Glenda Roberts

> I'm a project manager; I'm used to handing out assignments and making sure they get done. So I don't even ask. Before I go out the door, I just tell my husband, "You need to make the beds and put the laundry in the washing machine." That's his task. We all have tasks.

Parenting, it turns out, is fantastic management training. While companies may insist on polarizing the two activities, women know that they are profoundly symbiotic. Far from detracting from work, motherhood teaches us how to manage better—not just faster, but better. Carol Vallone, CEO of WebCT, learned that telling her son what was happening each day eased his anxiety—and then she realized it was a great management technique too. Jacqueline de Baer has built her business at the same time as raising four children.

Jacqueline de Baer

> It puts you under time constraints so you just have to manage. You have to communicate well. You have to delegate. When you do that, it allows other people the freedom to perform without being hounded all the time. And it goes further. Although employees are certainly not children, you still need to coach and develop and encourage them in many of the same ways. You develop them, their skills. You know they'll probably leave you one day and that you can only keep them if you keep developing them.

Other business owners tell me that having children has made them more focused, more patient, calmer, and less volatile, because they just have to fix the problem and think, *How do we move forward?*

My own mantra—*Don't make promises you can't keep*—has stood me in good stead with my children but perhaps even more so with my business associates. The old model, which bifurcated work and home, looks really moribund as we start to see that far from being polar opposites, work and home inform each other.

Karla Diehl

> My boys are 11.5 and 13. My kids respect me for the work I do and the total love I pour on them. My business associates respect me because I am always there when they need me to make the tough decision or give advice. I find a lot of transferable business/parenting skills, like

- Give information and suggestions but step back and let the person decide.
- Do not dictate how a task must be done . . . just dictate that it must be done.
- Set boundaries for acceptable behavior and enforce penalties swiftly when they are violated.
- Encourage, love and forgive but do not fall into the trap of trying to be their friend.
- Ask what their concerns are and then give information or suggestions to address and correct them.
- Set high expectations and they will find a way to deliver them.
- When they come to you to talk, listen very carefully; this takes courage and they trust you to handle them respectfully.
- No matter what the news, stay calm. As a parent or a manager, you do not have the luxury of panicking in front of the troops. We must instill confidence even in the face of crises.

Every executive mother I've ever spoken to says the same thing: their parenting helps them at work, their work teaches them lessons for home. Is it any wonder that when Volvo experimented with mandatory paternity leave, their executives returned with better management skills?

For years, management visionaries have talked about the relevance of parenting to leadership—but institutions have proved resistant and obtuse. Peter Senge wrote, "I believe that organizations must undo the divisive pressures and demands that make balancing work and family so burdensome today. This is necessary because of their commitment to their members. But it is also necessary to developing the organization's capabilities."[12] He wrote that in 1990—and he's still way in front of the organizations he was writing about. Most corporations pay lip service to families and family values, remaining intransigent in the ways that they think about work, the working day, the working year, and individual career structures. They just can't accommodate themselves to the idea that external activity generates internal value. The split between work and family persists in the minds of anachronistic male managements that lack the imagination and flexibility to overcome their territorial jealousy of our whole lives.

There are, of course, exceptions. Sometimes corporations surprise us by how imaginative they can be—and make us wonder why more companies aren't similarly creative.

Elaine Davis

My husband and I decided to move to California and GlaxoSmith-Kline has no offices there, so I thought I'd have to leave. When I went in to tell them my decision, they said, "Don't leave. Work from home. We'll wire up the house—you can work from there." The only absolute request my boss made was that he should be able to call me on my old phone number!

So that's what happened. We moved to California, the house was wired up, my office phone went through the company switchboard. A few people were skeptical but it has worked. So much of our work as a global company is done electronically—from hotels, airplanes, homes and offices all over the world that it matters less and less where you are, physically. Most of the time when I am on site in London, Philadelphia, or North Carolina, the "residents" of that building are traveling somewhere else! It does scale and I think more and more people are doing this.

Elaine is unusual, and she knows it. That she can be a vice president for a global pharmaceutical giant says a great deal about how much change is possible. More typical are the companies that provide an array of so-called work-life balance programs (flex time, job shares, working from home), only to find that no one takes them up. Why? Because employees perceive that such programs will brand them as losers. Many work-life programs fail because they are merely bolted on, when what is needed is deep, systemic change. Cultures that continue to prize face time and the number of hours worked may pay lip service to whole lives—but they don't mean it. Which is why, in many companies, the programs are designed, promoted, taken up by about 5 percent of the labor force—and abandoned. These programs nibble around the edges; they aren't prepared to look afresh at how work is measured and valued.

Few of the women I talk to who seem most comfortable with their families and careers have been the beneficiaries of corporate work-life balance programs; some didn't even know that their companies had them! They've regularly found that the shape their careers want doesn't match the career structures of traditional corporations and that if they take time out, they can't get back in. Corporate vanity or machismo maintains that business is so fast-paced, mobile, and demanding that once you leave, you can never catch up again; once you leave the party, you can't come back in. Faced with this intransigence, women have wrenched flexibility from the system by changing companies, changing careers, looking for companies that don't make them choose. Very often, the companies they find are young companies, without the cultural baggage of more established institutions. And so our peripatetic careers are searching careers: looking for companies that will allow us, trust us to lead full, whole lives.

Bronwen Hughes

The break—I definitely planned this one. My intentions were to spend more time with Anna and be more involved with her daily life. I signed up with the volunteer literacy program at her school. I also volunteered in the lunch room because I wanted Anna to see me scraping plates as well as teaching literature. Life was much less hectic and I found myself really slowing down and enjoying myself. It gave me the ability to set rules for my next job and to do it on my terms.

I began my current position as a part time consultant. I wanted to ease back in and see if this was what I wanted. I found that it was a great fit—very flexible, a chairman whose wife works and who has two small children. I can pretty much do what I want, including working from home whenever it suits me and picking Anna up from the school bus (I wanted to preserve some of that unstructured time with her). I travel quite a bit but I limit it to one night stays. I really don't like being away and I find the travel very tiring. I also have the attitude that if it doesn't work out or I stop enjoying it I will leave. I suppose I've finally got to the point where I realize that I hold the cards and the choices are mine to make (took me a while!).

When women fail to find the companies that fit, many just give up the gatecrasher role and conclude that their only recourse is to start a business of their own. To start from scratch, building a parallel universe where the old battles are not even a memory. Women are leaving traditional organizations not to bake cakes[13]—but to build for themselves the organizations they can't find anywhere else.

Nancy Frank

I highly recommend it. I am having fun—it has been a wonderful thing. It is a trend that is really taking off, a groundswell I don't think will be reversed. It is the 21st century thing because it fits with life. The old corporate "go to the office every day and treat people like machinery"—people won't put up with it any more. My husband loves it. At first he couldn't believe it and he was quite nervous: will it work? Can she pull it off? Is this just trying to put a fancy face on becoming a home maker? I remember the day I moved the office furniture in. My husband was, like: "whoa! This is for real!"

In the parallel universe that women build, there is no grand canyon between work and home. Why? Because both are based on, and serve, the same values, needs, hopes, and ambitions. We don't want lives that are compartmentalized, destined always to be at war with one another, jostling for attention and rewards. We want lives that are integrated and consistent—in which we undertake different responsibilities but with consistent, coherent, and substantial values. There is no magic template that we all fit into, in which we all find satisfaction—there's just learning, all day, everywhere. Honesty becomes normal when mothers and fathers don't have to lie, pretending that doctor appointments are client meetings and school plays are sales calls. In that world, children see that work is ennobling, inspiring, and fun and that making a contribution far exceeds the excitement of consumption. And in that world, we're all a lot less tired, because we aren't at war with ourselves and our loved ones.

People often ask me why I'm so sure the parallel universe exists. They are so beaten down by the insistent screeching of a polarized, mechanistic culture that they've lost the ability to identify anything different. They see failure, pain, defeat, exhaustion—and they're helped in this by women's modesty and privacy, which keeps our success stories silent. But I see and hear those stories everywhere—more and more of them, gathering momentum.

Teresa Spangler

I have a 13-year-old daughter, I and my husband have both had careers that took everything we had. I play guitar and am playing better than I ever had, I'm working on a book, have a recording studio in my home and have my own business and yes, you can have it all if you can define it all and plan around having it all. There are sacrifices but I feel I have had it all and will continue to do so.

Donna Collins

Yes, I have it all right now: a job that challenges me and keeps my skills sharp—3 days a week. A delightful daughter who amazes me every single day. A social life that includes civic work, recreation time, plain old girl time and a supportive husband and loving family. What more could I ask?

Suzy Hurt

Balance is very hard to achieve. As my career has progressed, so have the amount of hours and travel. That said—I protect my weekends. I do not work weekends or typically even at home at night. I do work long hours but when I walk out the door—work is behind me. When I am home, I am free of work and focus on my home and personal life. Do I wish I had more free time? YES. Would I be willing to give up my responsibilities or challenges in my career? NO WAY!

Mary Giery Smith

I have a wonderful husband and happy, healthy children. We have a nice house in a nice neighborhood and we have a small circle of good friends. We have enough money to enjoy ourselves, not enough for large extravagances. I have a job that I deeply, truly enjoy in a field that I love and I work for a relatively young, independently owned company that is far and away the best managed company I have ever had the privilege of working for. I don't plan too far into the future and I think that leaves me open to change. I've changed careers with more frequency than Elizabeth Taylor changed husbands and, like hers, my changes generally have worked out to my benefit. "All" for me is having everything in balance, and I think I am as close to having it as I ever will be.

We all have bad days, of course. Sick kids on board meeting days. School starts while we are out of town. Days when we feel there just isn't enough of us to go round. And just when we've got the hang of things, our children change and it feels like we have to start afresh. But why would we exchange such richness for anything less?

I look at my children and feel proud that their sense of the possible is so broad, fair, and inclusive. They have something that my traditional upbringing never gave me: real time and engagement from their father. I look at my husband and admire the fairness he practices and the rich relationship that he sustains with our children. In the parallel universe, millions of women experience and stretch the full range of their capabilities, talents, and passions. It's exhilarating, exhausting, and deeply rewarding. It's hard to beat the thrill of doing something you've been told can't be done.

Travel Thoughts

- Do you want a family? Why—or why not? Are those reasons compatible with your values?
- If you are a mother, do you want to keep working? How safe would you be if you quit? Are you comfortable with the professional and financial consequences if you leave—and are those consequences shared equally with your partner?
- What chores and obligations can you throw away?
- Who can help?
- Where is self-time? Where can you find it?
- When you are with your kids, are you really there?
- What do your kids learn from the way you live?
- Do you collude in your partner's helplessness?
- Does your organization understand that parenting makes you a better manager?

Chapter Eight

How High Can You Go?

We can, do the impossible
We have the power in our hands
And we won't stop 'cause we've got
To make a difference in this life
With one voice, one heart, two hands, we can.
—LEANN RIMES, "WE CAN"

The short answer to the question "how high can you go?" is "as high as you want." Yes, that means you will enter uncharted territory. Though women are 46 percent of the American workforce, we hold only 8 percent of executive titles and 9.9 percent of line positions—so getting to the top can be a lonely climb. But all over the world, women are running companies, dominating industries, on a scale never seen before. In a business world in which discontinuity is the order of the day, being the first in a company, a job, or an industry is perfectly feasible. Cindy Solomon was told that there would never be a female VP of marketing for Playtex. But she got the job *and* she upped the ante—becoming the first female VP of sales and marketing. You can do it.

So what's the catch? Well, the hard part has two parts. First, you have to know what you want. And second, you may have to make some changes to get it. Change companies, change locations. If you really want it, you can do it. So what do you want?

On Top of the World

In 2002, women held one out of every thirteen top positions (executive vice president or above) in the five hundred largest American companies—up from one in forty in 1995. Back then, only one of the Fortune 500 companies had a female CEO; now seven do. Some estimate that, by 2020, one in five of these positions will be held by a woman.[1] In Europe, British firms lead the way in promoting women—seven out of the top fifty most powerful European women work in the United Kingdom. Perhaps more interestingly, in the United Kingdom women dominate the media. Running networks, newspapers, and publishing houses, their famed peripheral vision seems to have given them a solid, commercial sense of the zeitgeist. Similarly, in the United States, concentrations of women can be found in advertising and entertainment. Three of the world's top agencies and half the world's major movie studios are headed by women. This is getting serious.

Sales and marketing seem the most propitious places to start, but few of the world's most powerful women have stereotyped careers. In fact, what is so striking about them is how different they are: long hair, short hair, lawyers, accountants, entrepreneurs, saleswomen. They manage huge numbers of people and vast amounts of wealth. These women are not just window dressing. They're appointed because they've proved they can do hard things well.

In smaller and private companies, it's almost impossible to trace the number of women. The C200, a strangely secretive organization of female CEOs managing companies worth over ten million dollars, claims over 440 members—but that group is by no means comprehensive. All over the world, women are running businesses, as CEOs and in top, profit-and-loss positions.

And they're having fun. I remember when I ran my first company in the United Kingdom and wondered out loud what the company policy was on a particular issue. "It's what you say it is," my assistant informed me. Wow, I thought, this could be interesting. And a lot of the time it has been. I've been able, in different companies, to build cultures that respected employees and customers, that offered flexible working for parents, that reflected my passion for fairness and innovation. In my own small universe, I've been able to promote the commercial and personal values I believe in and to give the men and women working for me different kinds of learning and experience. In doing so, I've made my own small contribution to changing the game.

When Gail Rebuck became CEO of Random House, the predominant British workplace culture was one of "jacket on the chair": being seen to stay late was so important that, even if you went out, you left your jacket on the back of your chair to indicate you might be coming back. But because she herself had young children, she had to leave work by 6 P.M. Her example helped to change the culture. "My personal view was that it was wrong to reward people for staying very late on a consistent basis. Either management was putting too great a burden on the individual—or the individual was failing to cope with his or her workload and needed some help." One of the many great things about top positions is that you can effect cultural changes—and change people's lives. It's a wonderful experience.

Betsy Cohen

> Being a top woman means that within your company you have a voice at the table. When important business and personnel issues are discussed and decided, I have an important role. Sometimes being a woman means you hear or see some things that others don't see, and you can bring that up in a positive way. You can help set strategy, give input on key plans for the business and people, and take on leadership roles that need doing. For a person who sees herself as a leader, who sees herself making a difference, being higher in the organization is definitely more satisfying.
>
> Becoming high level means that you have access to other top people from whom you can learn. And you get to be a role model and make a difference in the lives of those coming behind you in your company or in the community. When you start to lead internally, you can also begin to get involved in leadership roles in community groups or associations. In doing so, you learn new skills and make connections with other talented people in your community. You might even meet others in a national scope. All these activities add to one's continual learning and growth, which is key to having a successful career and a successful life, in my opinion.

It's an experience that more and more women want. A Catalyst survey showed that 55 percent of American women and 52 percent of British women who were not in senior positions wanted to be.[2]

This dispels the notion that women aren't ambitious or don't have a desire for responsibility, power, or public success. So there's a huge congruence of interest: women want these jobs and companies need women to take them. Almost all senior appointments are made—or should be made—in the company's own self interest, and it makes sense to appoint women. We keep outscoring men in management skills and ethical decision making. In most industries, she is the customer, she pays the bills, she determines the success or failure of new products, new strategies, new markets. In a consumer market determined by the decisions of women, it is ruthless self-interest to put smart women in positions of real power. This is so obvious that a huge amount of research has been done, trying to explain why it didn't happen earlier—and why it doesn't happen more.

Because as we know, it doesn't happen as often as, logically, it should. Only 9.9 percent of women hold line positions—those carrying P&L responsibility and that lead to top jobs. Only 11.9 percent of corporate officers are women and 5.1 percent are in the roles of chairman, CEO, COO, SVP, EVP, and vice chairman. Women occupy only a shocking 12 percent of board seats in large companies—and only 5 percent in smaller companies. In the years from 1987 to 1997, the percentage of women sitting as directors on corporate boards actually went down—from ten to eight—reminding us that there are no guarantees that these numbers will keep rising. In the same period, the number of women serving as CEOs in the Inc. 100 did increase—from zero to one—while the number of those firms with female board representation actually declined. Body Shop founder Anita Roddick has estimated that to reach parity with men we will need approximately five hundred years—and it will take another five hundred years to replace them in today's proportions!

Clearly, getting to the top takes courage. But women have courage; that isn't the problem. When asked to explain these numbers, men and women come up with strikingly different answers. Men maintain that the absence of women at the top is due to lack of experience and the absence of women in the pipeline. This is patently absurd. Plenty of educated women are packing the pipeline. In the United States, women earn 57 percent of bachelor's degrees and 58 percent of master's degree. We make up

46 percent of the workforce. "Large numbers of women are thus well educated, engaged in managerial careers and not greatly burdened by domestic responsibilities. These women are available to ascend to positions of high-level leadership."[3] Women, on the other hand, point to "male stereotyping and preconceptions" (the geisha, bitch, guy syndrome), "exclusion from informal networks" (the old boys' club), and an "inhospitable corporate culture" (toxic bosses and alien environments) as fundamental roadblocks to their advancement. In other words, we can't come in because we aren't men. And men prefer to work with men.[4]

We are still gatecrashers.

Is it worth it? Of the 55 percent of women who said that they would like to be in senior positions, only 19 percent said that they hadn't ruled it out.[5] The other 35 percent have gotten dressed, gone to the party, looked around—and turned back. And 45 percent have decided not to go at all.

Going for It

For every one of the brave 19 percent, a lot has to happen to make success feasible. She will need every power tool she can lay her hands on—skills, networks, mentors, opportunities, timing, raw nerve. She will have to let people know that she is ambitious. This may sound absurd and be uncomfortable—but men rarely assume ambition in a woman. They do assume that she wants to get married and have kids. They do assume that she isn't the breadwinner and therefore isn't ambitious because, after all, she's just a girl. Visibility is fundamental to success and part of visibility is making people aware of how good you are and how serious you are about your career.

The ambitious woman will be better prepared if she has the chance to work for a company that takes appraisals seriously—so she can gain an honest assessment of how she's doing and keep her career plan and her progress in sync. (If she's fobbed off with conflict-averse niceties, she will lack the data she needs for her career planning—which is why her mentors will be so important.) If the company means what it says about diversity, her appraisals will measure and reward her female values as well as all the traditional, male ones. This means she will be rewarded for building great relationships inside and outside the company, she will be rewarded for recruiting and supporting talent, for telling the truth, and for managing conflict effectively. She will receive more kudos for averting crises than for coping with them. She will receive quality projects with ample resources, which allow her to shine and lead. None of this will obviate the old P&L measures—but all of these criteria will be taken, and judged, seriously.

She will work many long nights, and weekends and holidays may become vague memories—but she won't accept that success requires total self-sacrifice. She will have a family; it will develop her as a person as well as a manager, and she'll get a lot of support from as much of her extended family as she can. She will have lots of child care from nannies, grannies, or friends. Her success will be deliberate and planned in order to ensure that it doesn't cost her her life. Getting to the top requires being as businesslike and strategic about the career as we would be about managing a company.

Cindy Solomon

If we begin to work smarter about what we want and what we are willing to do for it, I think the proposition gets much easier. In looking at the women that I believe have had amazing accomplishments and yet have found a way to have a life, they have always been very proactive and businesslike (versus personal) in their dealings with their career. The minute they have achieved their goals in a specific situation or realize that the company is not set up for them to be successful, they move to their next position, usually within a different company. Moving doesn't mean they are not good enough, not smart enough and rarely if ever are they "hurt" by the companies' inability to recognize their worth. They just move somewhere they can more effectively contribute. During my years at Playtex, I was seeking to achieve the only way I knew how which was to out-work everyone else. If I were to do it again, I would out-think the organizations and opportunities rather than out-work them. That would have allowed me to have some life while I was achieving my work goals.

No success comes without costs. Personal and professional trade-offs have to be made, because high-level careers require a lot of time, focused attention, and drive.

Betsy Cohen

> One cost is loss of a tranquil or calm home environment—at the end of the work week the rest of the weekend is spent catching up! Another cost is the stress of pursuing a high level position unto itself. Anyone, man or woman, who has high aspirations faces the fact that opportunities and luck don't happen on the plan you create. Patience is difficult and can be stressful. There are few senior positions and more candidates than positions, so that can both motivate and wear on a person. On a more minor note, one cost is lack of sleep, lack of time to take personal care, time to really enjoy planning or preparing meals at home—some of the small pleasures of life get cut in the need to do the bigger, more pressing work and home needs.

Opposition is inevitable—toxic bosses, toxic colleagues, stereotyping, and alien environments—but the determined woman will, as Gail Rebuck once described it, "slug it out." She will do so because she loves her work and her team. Their support, enthusiasm, commitment, and success are profoundly rewarding—often even more rewarding than the official recognition of title and salary. Through missed vacations and weekends, through perhaps the failure of a relationship or a missed family event, she will keep working because she passionately loves what she does and derives from it a rich and profound sense of being strong, smart, and alive. And she has the substantial satisfaction of looking after, and providing for, those she loves.

Betsy Cohen

> Being a top woman can provide excellent financial rewards, which is motivating to me. We have raised wonderful teenage sons who are school leaders and highly motivated to succeed and give to others. Part of having good kids is good parenting, regardless of income. But some is due to the experiences our boys have had that financial success brings—exposure to other cultures, travel, volunteering and meeting lots of diverse, high level people at our home. And financial success has also given me satisfaction that I have the ability to set aside money for the kind of retirement that I dream of having down the road.

Women are often reluctant to talk about the pleasure of having money; we've seen men use it to explain and excuse too much. But knowing you are financially secure, that your loved ones are secure, is a great feeling. Not being dependent on others is a great freedom; giving to others is a meaningful pleasure.

Of course, not everyone achieves the positions they'd like. Even after a lot of sacrifices and discipline, some may lack the support, the structure, the opportunities, and the luck to get to the top. Then the really hard thing is to sit down and ask why. Did I not pay attention? Did I misread the signals? Was it too early, too late, too fast, too slow? Do I work at a toxic company that will never take me seriously? Did I work hard enough? Too hard? Smart enough? Not every failed promotion is discrimination. Some rejections tell you things you need to learn—about yourself, about your company. Do you need to change your department or your company? Is it a matter of tactics—or do you need to rethink your strategy? When all the emotional dust has settled, try very hard to ask the right questions in order to understand what has happened.

I twice failed to get jobs I wanted. In retrospect, I don't think I prepared well enough for either of them. I didn't take the time to research who I would be speaking to and what their values, issues, concerns were. Because I felt I could do the job, I thought that was enough. I made the mistake of thinking the interview was about me. It wasn't—it was about them. What did they need? What could I bring to make their business better? I reapplied for one of the jobs I'd been rejected for—and got it the second time around. So I'd learned something.

Rejections, like mistakes, are powerful lessons—and, like mistakes, they teach us a lot. However painful they are (and they can be very painful), try to learn from them. Learn about yourself, your colleagues, your company, your industry. Don't lick your wounds; get feedback. Many male managers are reluctant to provide this; they are afraid of being sued, of being hurtful, of telling the truth. Make them talk to you. Listen to what they say—and what they don't say. Use your personal board of directors and ask their advice. Only you can decide whether you should keep trying. Whatever you do, keep thinking about what you've seen, heard, learned. Keep refining your plan.

Although not all rejections are discrimination, some are. You can, and should, seek legal advice if you believe this to be the case. Seeking legal advice does not commit you to a fight, but you must inform yourself. You must understand what has taken place. Only then can you decide: do you stay and slug it out some more, do you leave, or do you sue?

Holly Godwin

> There is always an element of SECRECY in promotions, salary decisions, which I did not find in my previous company (which was a start-up headed by a woman.) The secrecy here, for me, leads me to wonder what else I am not being told. One of the biggest issues I have with my job currently is that I was at Director level before. But when I got here, I ended up back at the "individual contributor" level. I have a lot more to offer than I am being allowed to give and that rankles. I think a lot of it has to do with attitudes about women here.

In many cases, exactly what is going on isn't obvious. Jobs are still filled without interviews by guys who make other guys feel comfortable. How else to explain the fact that so many chairmen of Fortune 500 companies are sons of former chairmen?[6]

Sue Priestley ran HR for CMGI from its early days as an Internet incubator. Over the course of three years she had recruited and advised dozens of new CEOs and executives, who had hired thousands of new employees. Like any software company, CMGI's growth was entirely a function of its ability to attract talent; the company could not have enjoyed its explosive growth without Sue's oversight and insight. She was eventually given a VP title, years after everyone thought she already had one. And then one morning she was informed that a new senior VP of HR—the CEO's golfing buddy—had been appointed above her. Henceforth, she would report to him. Of course, she was expected to be a trooper, a loyal soldier. Instead, she left.

Companies should not let such events occur, but they do, around the world, constantly. No discussion, no interview—sometimes not even a vacancy. The message is clear: we don't want you—we want a man.

I had a similar experience when I worked for the BBC. I didn't argue with the decision; although they didn't appoint me, they appointed an excellent guy. What shocked me was the assumption that I wouldn't mind. Had a man been so thwarted in his career, his bosses would have recognized that they'd have a problem and offered some consolation prize—more money, a juicy project. But nobody thinks about a woman's ambition. Buy her dinner and she'll play nice. What, I wondered, did they think I'd stay for?

Pamela Matthews

> My takeaway is that you aren't fooling anyone but yourself if you think your career success is based on merit because it is all about whether your boss likes/supports you. And, sadly, most bosses are male and they like/support junior people who are in their own image and whom they can relate to most easily. This may be subconscious but if you think about it, most men will only support/prefer you if you are "cute," "sexy" or appealing to their libido. Otherwise, they are going to buddy up with someone they feel comfortable with—it's human nature. And of course, add all the golf, sports events, networking events that cement these ties and leave women in the cold. (I dream of a corporate world where most are women and we are very powerful and very wealthy and when we entertain clients, we have a day at the spa. I've had enough golf and strip clubs.)

When confronting their own ambitions, the question women face throughout their career is: is it worth it? Should I slug it out? I don't believe that it is our mission to be the cannon fodder for the new world order and I'm not in favor of women sacrificing their lives, their health, their womanhood to wrench a male world, not of their making, into their own image. Like many women, I think the cost may be too high. But the rewards are high too—and if this is what you want, I firmly believe you should try. But have a strategy, make plans, be disciplined. Don't expect it just to happen. And take stock all along the way; check the signals. Don't trust to luck.

The philosopher Elizabeth Anscombe argued that the decision to go to war cannot be moral if, from the outset, you know it cannot be won. Don't fight losing battles—save your life. In a real as well as in a spiritual sense, you have to be prepared to say you're mad as hell and won't take it anymore. Why? Because taking it destroys your soul. If you continue to work for people who think little of you, it is only a matter of time before you start to share that low opinion. Because if they were wrong, you'd be gone by now.

How Ambitious Are You?

Over a third of women say that they want senior positions but have ruled out going for them. Why? First of all, ambition, with its overtones of wicked witches and conniving stepmothers, carries few positive female connotations. The masculine model of career success—back stabbing, ruthlessly treading on friend and foe in the climb to the top—feels ugly and uncomfortable. How many women are comfortable announcing in public that they want to run the company one day? It doesn't feel feminine. You'll be labeled a bitch.

Even if we can persuade ourselves that ambition per se is not a bad thing, we must also persuade ourselves that we can win. We don't take that for granted. When producers for a highly intellectual talk show, *The Brains Trust,* invited women to take part, they regularly found that the women—no matter how exceptionally distinguished—felt that they lacked the qualifications to take part in so distinguished a debate. The men, however lowly, never felt the same compunction.[7]

To succeed, we first have to believe we are worthy. That's hard to do in a culture that, year after year, tells you that you don't fit in, that you aren't welcome. Why do women rule out the promotions they seek? Because they read the signs that tell them they won't win. We might be able to overcome the stigma attached to female ambition if we could point to scores of whole women at the top of organizations—but we can't. It is impossible to overestimate the powerful statement that is made when companies have no women at the top. How better to tell women that they won't succeed? Companies can have all the diversity policies they like; none of us believe them when we see the usual array of men filling the top table. Companies either mean it or they don't, and mostly, they don't.

Ann Day worked for a global electronics corporation. She had years of international experience and is incredibly loyal to her employer. But she knows just how far she can get.

Ann Day

> I had taken over for my boss on an "ad interim" basis. My new boss who was selected to hire the new head of the department had once said to me, "We try to hire more women but they either have affairs with the men, or get pregnant and then aren't much use to me." He is also the one who told me that I should "smile more" in response to a heated business discussion.
>
> Anyway, in the process of creating a short list for the position, my "boss" asked me "do you want to be on it?" in the same breath as "there are 8 candidates already there." The mood of the overture was very much "if I don't want a lawsuit, I have to ask you, but you don't stand a chance, sweetie, even if you have been doing the job for 6 months."
>
> So in the face of all of this, working like crazy as we were moving into budget season, trying to manage my own health and a possible future move, I actually took myself out of the running. I probably knew deep down that I was not going to get it anyway, and as it seemed wisest to cut my losses. I should mention that this position and the other heads of corporate staff (some 30) have never been held by a woman . . . to the point that, at the first corporate heads staff meeting I attended, the chair addressed the group as "gentlemen." I was not even acknowledged.

In the end Ann stayed with the company but moved into a different division in a different country. Fighting for the top job in that company was probably futile—and she wanted a life. No one but you can determine how hard to push, what trade-offs to make. There are moments in your life when the career is not your priority or when trade-offs favor work less and life more. But make sure that the choices you make are truly your own.

My mother, a very talented businesswoman, spent a great deal of time talking about the things she might have done. "I could have done this, I could have done that," we heard throughout our childhood. Now, on reflection, I think she was right: she could have done many of those things. But she never tried. If you want the top job enough, you owe it to yourself to try. Don't underestimate the costs, don't be intimidated by the risk. Think hard about how much that job might—or might not—mean to you. That way you can feel, as my mother never felt, that you gave yourself the chance. If you don't give yourself a chance, no one else will.

Many women don't try because they believe the sacrifice required will simply be too great. They believe the scaremongering stories that tell them they can have a family or a career, not both. Worse, they're told that their ambition may leave them sterile, single, unhappy, and disappointed. Many of these stories remind me of nineteenth-century "science" that "proved" cycling would shrink our wombs and education would make our brains so heavy we couldn't conceive. But however ludicrous many of these claims may be, their demoralizing refrain suggests that to get to the top we must expect to abandon our hopes of a secure, happy relationship. We may have to sacrifice thoughts of having a family. For many, many women, that is too high a price to pay. When women are faced by a brutal either-or choice, we reject it.

That price is determined by what economist Shoshana Zuboff has labeled *career taxidermy.* Using the image of a dead stuffed animal, she sees modern corporate career structures as fundamentally moribund. They fail to fit the life cycles of women, and although they may look alive and well, they fail women so spectacularly that companies lose any chance of keeping them. The career taxidermy she's describing is both predictable and inflexible: in your twenties and thirties, you rise within the corporate hierarchy, achieving a senior position in your forties before your career starts to level off in your fifties. On a graph, the pattern looks like an inverted U. "The first casualties of career taxidermy are the more than 60 percent of all women who work, the 78.3 percent of women with children between the ages of six and seventeen who work, and the 63.9 percent of all women with children under the age of six who work."[8] For them, this career shape just doesn't work at all. For many women, the most productive years may be after their children are grown. A woman's natural career, Zuboff argues, might look more like an M—but that's rarely on offer in large, traditional corporations, which value youth over wisdom.

Chris Carosella

I was a senior vice president at the age of 30. It was important to be young in that culture because career decisions were made early on as to where one could go and what their next promotion would be. I've since learned that a lot of promotions in rapid succession builds breadth but not depth. Intelligence can occur at any age but wisdom comes with age and depth of experience. I prefer being wise.

This is not just about relationships and children. Often, women decide not to pursue a route to the top because they know that doing so requires too great a sacrifice of their values. It requires that they adopt behaviors they simply can't stomach.

Diane Jacobsen

I am a single mom and, after work, I'm home. They don't know anything about my private life. I don't fraternize. My head's clear. I don't have to play the game. I think that if getting promoted means I have to suck up to so and so—I'd rather quit. I'm serious. I don't want to have to do that. It shouldn't be a prerequisite. It should be good work, selling work, the work itself that counts—not endearing myself to some person falsely. And that's scary because everyone's doing it!

Men and women alike face these challenges—but when women face them, they usually do so alone. Moreover, they feel that success fundamentally requires a deep degree of assimilation, a sacrifice of womanhood and female values, that they cannot help but reject.

Joan Silver

Being honest and building honest relationships has been seen by companies as problematic. Often women are too straight with clients and realize that more importance is placed on politics than on results. I remember one woman said to me, "I looked at the people being promoted and the things I saw that were necessary and I just didn't want to do those things. So I knew I would never get any further."

We look at some of the figurehead CEOs—Carly and Anne and Martha—and it doesn't look like they are having any fun. Hard faces and firm jaws framed by sharp cropped hair stare out from the covers of business magazines, exuding an air of corporate homogeneity that's unappealing. Yes, we want power, and yes, we will work hard—I've never met a woman who wouldn't work all the hours of the day and night on work she loved and identified with. But we don't want to pay with our lives.

Chris Carosella

I had no life outside of work. To progress higher in the company would have required me to completely turn my life over . . . many more relocations, unbelievable hours, and no time for other interests.

> I met a woman who ran one of the other businesses. She had no life, talked about how she never saw her children, how her marriage was falling apart. I also knew a lot of the wives of the men who ran the businesses. They constantly complained about never seeing their husbands and about always having to move. No thanks . . . there's more to life for me than just this company.

Many men argue that they dislike this culture too—that they would rather be home for their children's birthdays, would prefer an environment in which they needn't leave their better selves locked in their car. The cultural artifacts of a workplace that still operates like a 1950s old-boy network is as frustrating for them as for women. And some of these men suffer ostracism and career setbacks because they insist on being fair to their families. But men rarely suffer financially and politically the way that women do. And many other men compartmentalize these things: home values for home, work values for work. Women reject both of these options. If the price of corporate advancement is to lock my better self up in a box and bring it out only on special occasions, I won't do it. I may want it—but not that much. I'd rather have a life.

Changing the Game

If 19 percent of women want top jobs and will go for them, and 35 percent want them but won't, that leaves a whopping 46 percent of women who say they don't want the top jobs anyway. These women are often dismissed as unambitious, but to see them as such is to misread who they are and what they want. Many of these women are intensely ambitious—but their definition of success is not determined by what traditional corporations have to offer. It isn't about hierarchies and dominance. Instead, they define success in their own terms.

> *Donna Collins*
>
> My work ambitions are to have a challenging career where I can contribute what I've learned based on my past experiences as well as learn new skills to keep me sharp. I would like the opportunity to share what I have learned with a younger colleague (being able to mentor someone) and be fulfilled enough to be a good mother.

Meena Naidu

What is my idea of success? It's about achievement and fulfillment. Well, before I was obsessed with promotion, with money. If I didn't have a promotion every six months, I thought there was something wrong. I worked my arse off and knew exactly where I wanted to go. Now, I don't really know at all where I want to go.

To be quite honest, there is no fulfillment in just working for the sake of earning more and getting higher. I think what I do now has a lot of purpose. Last week I went to lunch with the transport minister of Kenya and was trying to explain to him how he needs to be more engaged in development process, otherwise organizations like the World Bank will just take over and will leave Kenya with something it doesn't want or need. It was a hugely fulfilling meeting. Now did I need to be the MD of the company to have this conversation with him? No.

The fundamental premise of hierarchical organizations leaves women like Donna and Meena cold; dominance per se has never been what we are about. We're skeptical about what the price of reaching the top will be (we know there will be one), and we don't get excited just by the idea of being on top. It never really occurred to me that just being boss was intrinsically appealing until I had an employee who desperately wanted just that. He ached to be a CEO. It was a tricky situation because I didn't think he had what it took. I talked to him about it and asked him why he wanted the job. What I discovered was he didn't want the job because of what it would enable him to do, he didn't want it for the money and he certainly didn't want it to do the work. He wanted something that singled him out as Top Dog. In all my years as a CEO, this had never occurred to me. I don't think I'm particularly humble or saintly; I have never found women inspired by the idea of lording it over others.

Many women see in career advancement the law of diminishing returns.

Holly Godwin

The higher you grow, the higher the bar gets raised. When you make VP, you want to be CEO, when you make CEO of this company, you want to be CEO of that larger company. When you have a

> jet, you want a bigger one. And so it goes on. There is sacrifice in every rung you climb up the ladder. What is the point at which the sacrifice is no longer worth the monetary or prestige gains? That is the question we need to answer.
>
> It is a moving target, there is no ultimate destination. I think people need to sit back, decide what is TRULY important to them, decide what the point is at which they have enough, and then stay there. What is the point at which sacrifice is no longer worth the monetary and prestige gains? That is the question each of us should answer before mindlessly putting in more and more hours at work, especially when we are not passionate about what we do.

But traditional organizations are modeled on continuous movement; some even fire you if you fail to rise. Many positions, designated "training" positions, are designed to be moved through. Staying there is not an option. My own mother-in-law was forced, at one point in her career, into a promotion she hated. In many organizations, staying at a certain level that you love can be a quick way of being written of as a no-hoper.

But many women want neither to rise nor to stay put. They want to move across. Remember those ten careers we may expect in our lifetime? By the time I was twenty-nine, I had a senior position in BBC radio, was known and trusted, and had increased our output three- or fourfold. It couldn't be expanded much more. I attended the most important meetings with the most senior people in the organization. At one of these, I looked around the table and saw a dozen men in their mid-forties and thought, I'm going to have to work with these guys, having the same meetings, the same discussions, for the next twenty-five years if I stay here. So I applied for a more junior position in television. I lost a lot of status and a lot of power. But I could learn new things. Six years later, I left television and went into business. Ten years later, I started writing. Although I've held many top jobs, I've been far more driven to learn than to lead.

> *Michelle Turchin*
>
> I would like to continually reinvent myself throughout my professional career, doing different things.
>
> Women are more apt than men to search for meaning in their work. I hear women say "keep your priorities straight" referring to

other people taking care of their health, spending time with their family etc. versus pushing themselves endlessly at work. Also I am not motivated by the corporate profit race that is dominated by men. This may be a sacrilege but truthfully I don't care about helping companies make more money. Yes, from a human standpoint, I do care about providing job security and positive employment terms to people. And of course, having done an MBA, I intellectually understand the quest for financial returns. But I still don't really care. The whole thing just doesn't engage me, speak to me, or get me excited.

Our whole capitalist society is based on financial returns, but I ask with increasing frequency "what is it all for?" I temporarily ignored my need for meaning when I accepted the "great learning opportunity" and good-paying job here. But I do have a nagging need to do something more meaningful professionally. I try to focus on the parts of my job which are great: I am learning a great deal, I now have a wonderful boss and mentor, I earn a good salary that affords me the lifestyle I want, etc. But the thing about the need for "meaning" in my life is that as much as I try to ignore it, it keeps on pinching me on the arm and reminding me that it's there.

Women like Michelle are profoundly ambitious—not for things, titles, or money, but for meaning. They find it increasingly hard to satisfy that ambition within conventional companies, run to satisfy conventional measures of success. The psychological self-determination of such women challenges corporations and, in increasing numbers, finds them wanting. So distinctive is this trend that U.K. sociologists have defined a group they call the TIREDs—Thirty-something Independent Radical Educated Dropouts—who leave traditional organizations to do something entirely different. The acronym makes them sound burned out, and that is misleading. They aren't at all exhausted; they are just tired of standard success measures, tired of macho organizations run for money alone, tired of old battles over old issues in pursuit of old values. They define success in highly individualistic terms and are strikingly unconcerned about how that success looks to others.

Jana La Sorte

When I left corporate America to strike out on my own, I took a huge pay cut willingly to try to restore my sense of self and regain

> ownership of my time, ideas etc. That is worth more to me than money for money's sake. Plus I believe in the credo "Do what you love and money will follow." And I mean that simply on the "you-will-do-fine" front, not necessarily that you will become a millionaire.

Alison Murdoch had a dream job, working at Sotheby's for five and a half years. "It was immensely fun and exciting—very hedonistic," she recalled. "But having such an interesting life made me realize it wasn't interesting at all. I just burned through it quite quickly. I thought: this is what a lot of people want but there is more to life than this."[9]

Alison now runs a community center in a poor part of central London. Some TIREDs and free agents start their own businesses, many teach, many are driven by a desire to make a serious contribution to their society. They measure success at least as much by what they give as what they get. The business manager who leaves to run a homeless shelter, the sales manager who works in a hypnotherapy center, the Big Three accountant who goes into teaching—these are real examples of profoundly ambitious people. They just aren't ambitious in the conventional, masculine sense of getting money, titles, dominance over people.

Psychologists and philosophers distinguish between hedonic happiness, which is the pleasure derived from food, drink, and things, and eudaimonic happiness, "which is not derived from bodily pleasure, nor is it a state that can be chemically induced or attained by any shortcuts. It can only be had by *activity* consonant *with noble purpose*" (my italics).[10] Alison and the rest of the TIREDs are no longer ambitious for hedonic rewards because they found them so unsatisfying. But they are highly ambitious in seeking for work with real purpose. To describe such women as opting out is to miss the point entirely.

Linda Alepin rose to top jobs at IBM and at Amdahl Corporation, was CEO of an Internet start-up, and now is a partner in an international consulting firm. She organizes her life around what she calls her "commitments," and these reveal a strikingly ambitious woman. She just isn't ambitious in the conventional, male sense of the word. These are her commitments:

Linda Alepin

- Being a powerful stand for women as an unstoppable force creating futures where all peoples' dreams can come true
- Exploring new pathways
- Being fully alive in body and spirit
- Building a great company where teamwork produces white lightning and belief in ourselves magnifies our abilities
- Helping my children build their visions
- Making this year the best of my marriage

It is not failure, but success that prompts women to examine the real value of their achievements. What, we ask ourselves, is our success worth to us? Fiona Wilson spent years in advertising and marketing. But she felt alienated by the culture and the products of her employer.

Fiona Wilson

When I was working in various companies over the years, I was very aware that I didn't aspire to be the CEO. I was definitely ambitious, and sought after, but beyond a certain point, I knew I didn't want to go "all the way." I wanted to do whatever I did to the very best of my ability. I wanted to feel proud of what my team and I were creating, and I wanted to be the very best leader I could be. Sadly when I would take stock at the end of each month or year, I didn't feel good about what I was contributing. I think my lack of interest in being a CEO was not about lack of ambition to lead an organization per se, but a lack of interest in running the type of organization I was working for. The funny thing is, I absolutely see myself as running a business school or some other kind of center or related business one day. I am naturally drawn to running things, improving things. But it will be a business or institution that I can believe has value and worth, and is in line with my own ideas about equity and fairness.

When companies excuse the absence of women in their top ranks by saying there aren't enough women in the pipeline, often what they mean is that they have lost women like Linda and Fiona. When the company fails to come up with a mission that is meaningful enough, and methods that are impressive enough, talent like hers walks out the door, never to return. Not (as company management might like to imagine) to have babies, stay at home, and bake cookies—but to find other, more meaningful ways to deploy their skills in a world open to change.

Joan Silver

There's a real misconception that women leave to be with kids. In the last year, we had very few women in senior positions—and we've lost 25 percent of them in the last 6 months. They'd demonstrated that they could compete—they were just doing it in a way the organization didn't value. Loss to the competition might have worried the company but loss away didn't. These women all wanted to be at the top of their game and felt that they could not thrive where they were. They wanted to work in ways that were consistent with their values.

We see companies struggling now to come to terms with this. The "triple bottom line" that aims to measure environmental and social impact reflects companies' growing realization that their stakeholders want them to be doing meaningful, not just profitable, work. In this way, already, women are changing the game. Changing measurements of success, changing how we think about the whole purpose of work.

Paige Arnof-Fenn

I used to think that if I made a lot of money, then I could make a difference later in life. But I've realized that it is more meaningful to make a difference every day with every encounter, every person you touch—because having lots of ripple effects throughout your life is actually a bigger impact than leaving one big check at the end.

Paige has worked in Wall Street, for Procter & Gamble and for Coca-Cola. She wants something different now. As I think about those three groups of women—those trying for the top jobs, those who want them but don't try, and those who don't want them at all—I am struck that, for all their apparent differences, fundamentally they want the same things. They want to do work that is compatible with their values, that they can be proud of, that does not require a sacrifice of self and soul. Some—a minority—find it within traditional organizations (at least for a while), but most—79 percent—do not. That's a very big failure rate. Typically, companies blame us: we don't fit in, we won't make trade-offs, we get pregnant and are "no use." When we won't let the companies dominate us, the companies retaliate with criticism, blame, derision.

Is that stalemate inevitable? To break out of it requires major structural rethinking by corporations. Career norms must change for men and for women. Leaving and returning must be celebrated and rewarded—not grudgingly tolerated. Success must be defined by how it is achieved—not by what is spent and who is flattered. Long-term values must stage a comeback to get the women to come back. Values have to sit at the center of business and determine decisions from the strategic to the trivial. The larger meaning of the business—not just to shareholders, but to customers, employees, and their larger worlds—has to be articulated and has to be credible. Women quickly see through dishonest, disingenuous mission statements, and mission statements like "Kill the competition" are just a total turn-off. Saying things and not meaning them doesn't work, just as paying lip service to women and then not promoting them fools no one.

When we look at all the statistics about where women are and what progress they are making, it is tempting to wring our hands and decry the obstacles and frustrations that still obstruct women in business. They are numerous, counterproductive, wasteful, and unjust. But when I look at the women as a whole—those making it to the top and those challenging and changing the definitions of success—what I see is that, far from being left behind, women are the true trailblazers in business today. Headcounts and salaries may be one benchmark—but, increasingly, we measure our success not in how well we play the game but in how profoundly we change it. In the parallel universe, success is measured by how consistently life maps to values. It is about richness, not riches.

Travel Thoughts

- How high do you want to go? Do you have the skills you need? If not, what is your plan to get them?
- What is the obstacle to your success—is it the company, individuals within the company, yourself? Does your organization know how ambitious you are?

- What makes you think that you are not worthy of success?
- In an ideal world, what would your career look like?
- What is the price of success within your organization?
- What are your commitments?
- What is your success worth to you?

Chapter Nine

Breaking Up Is Hard to Do

I am not afraid of danger. I am afraid of living miserably.
—ROBERT YOUNG PELTON, ADVENTURE TRAVELER

It sounds so simple—no promotion, bad pay, overt discrimination, tacky business practices: of course you should leave. Everyone will—and does—tell you so. So why is it so difficult? Why does nobody say that they left too early and why does everybody say that they should have left months ago? Remind you of anything? Breaking up is hard to do.

What Time Is It?

We all talk about leaving. It's an emotional reflex, as old as we are: I'll leave and *then* you'll be sorry. I've known women who've been talking about leaving throughout their entire careers and never done it. I've also known women who've talked about it for decades—and then suddenly just up and left, to their own amazement as much as everyone else's. How do you know when the time has come?

Cindy Solomon

At the forums that I sometimes address, you will get maybe a thousand people—all corporate women being sent by companies. And I'll ask them: how many of you want to leave to do something else outside of corporate America? And 900 would raise their hands! These were the best and the brightest because at least their companies were

> sending their women to events like this. They are unhappy but they're staying put! Why aren't they picking up and leaving? Why don't they believe they will be successful elsewhere?

Women leave companies when any one of four things occurs: when they see that they cannot change the institution, when they themselves are no longer learning, when they feel ashamed of the standards and values of their employers, or when they feel that, inside themselves, they are dying. Sometimes women can't work up the courage to leave until all four of these conditions are satisfied. I think one's enough.

The realization that your institution isn't going to change is hard to accept. As women, we've had the role of change agent foisted upon us and we don't like to give up. Our own success within the company makes us optimistic—and it makes us loyal. But if people are hard to change, institutions are even harder. Examine your optimism carefully: is it justified—or is it just wishful thinking?

> *C. J. Hathaway*
>
> I left the corporate world ten years ago and started my own business. I was just so tired of the politics and backstabbing in the corporate environment, of spending the majority of hours each week doing what to me were meaningless exercises (reworking budgets ten different ways and justifying every line item; justifying my support staff; etc.) The final straw that gave me the courage and impetus to leave? After spending four years nurturing and building a great team, the company hired a new president who was openly contemptuous of my position and proceeded to systematically tear apart what I'd worked so hard to build. One by one, I was forced to lay off my staff until it was only me left. I'll never forget the words of my boss when I told him I was leaving to be an independent contractor. . . . "Wow, you've got balls!" I know he meant it as a compliment—but how sad is that?

Watching your work being destroyed is a pretty good sign that whatever change you could bring about is doomed. Likewise, most power structures are obvious enough for you to see when your goals and values will be thwarted. After Sharon Tunstall left Nike, she went to work in the music industry, an industry that refreshes its product a lot faster than it updates its management style. All of Sharon's bosses were males who felt threatened by, rather than grateful for, her proactive initiatives.

Sharon Tunstall

Power to them was control and they couldn't control me. To them, HR was just pay checks and benefits. Once, I tried to get them to think about succession planning, and they just said "Why would we want to do that? That's a stupid idea." In the end, I left because I was a threat to my boss, the head of HR. He just couldn't handle me. I used to go around him, to the head of the individual labels. I'd really started getting some traction there and he just couldn't stand it. I had influence and he felt very threatened by that. So when he raised it I said, "Just pay me out" because I reckoned really, life was too short for this.

It takes a lot of experience to be able to distinguish between the fight that can be won and the fight that can't. In Sharon's case, having a boss who shared none of her goals or vision for the job made it inevitable that she would fail; rather than do so, she left. Staying to fail serves no one.

I left most of my jobs when I wasn't learning anything anymore. I always found the steep ascent of a new job's learning curve exhilarating. I liked it too when it started to flatten out and I started to feel confident. But then I'd get bored. When jobs started to get too easy, I learned to design challenges for myself—some new technology or approach that would keep me engaged. But eventually I'd move on. You only have to see other bored executives to realize you probably don't want to be one. Because although it's hard to change institutions, it seems to be easy for them to change you. They can sap your soul and your spirit—and when they start to, you have to get out to save yourself.

Karen Price

Looking back, I realize that I stuck it out until even the things I liked weren't worth the mental suffering any more. But the change in me, my loss of happiness and loss of self, was SO very gradual, I didn't realize how truly down and unhappy I was becoming. I felt constantly frustrated and was constantly fighting for change. The things I was trying to change WERE changing, but all in the wrong direction it seemed! I can play the games, the politics, that's not the issue. But I wanted us to be more straightforward and realistic. Instead, our company and its direction were becoming more convoluted, the logic of decisions becoming more circular and obtuse. I could have shrugged all this off and said, "They still pay me the same amount to follow stupid directions as smart ones." But I couldn't do this. Something inside of me had gone too far from my own center. Maybe it was too many years playing as one of the boys. I had had enough. The stress of trying to be true to what I believed was literally destroying my health. Everyone could see it on my face.

One day, sitting in my office with one of my close female associates, I sat down and cried. Four or five years prior she too had quit and taken a hiatus from work. She said, "Karen, I think you've hit the point. You're ready to go. It's okay." She was right. I was tired of trying to tell people that the emperor had no clothes, with no one listening. I deserved more and better. I resigned a month later. The day I left my job, I felt that a huge weight had been lifted off my shoulders. I felt I had pushed myself out from under a giant boulder that had been blocking out the sun.

Karen had to get out because staying was destroying her—physically and mentally—and it threatened to destroy her reputation. No matter how big the industry or the company, when you start doing things you feel uncomfortable with, adopting standards that are well below your own, you have to remember that these will attach themselves to you. Your reputation is an asset you must protect. I can remember hearing gossip about a close friend and how vicious she was with vendors. I knew she wasn't—but her boss was and his reputation was rubbing off on hers. I warned her about this and she got out in time.

When it feels like the entire institution stands against you and your values, the question is no longer whether you can win—but whether you can escape succumbing to the madness around you.

Chris Carosella

I left because the environment became toxic to me. I was tired of frequent relocations, constant travel and the only emphasis being on the short-term bottom line. No thought was given to the future beyond annual numbers. Priorities and objectives from the chairman and the president of our division were inconsistent and arbitrary.

The way people (employees and customers) were treated was abysmal. Constant reorganizations just brought chaos. It did feel as if the inmates had taken over the asylum.

Institutions exert a gravitational pull. They are our routine, determining the shapes of our weeks, the pace of our days, sometimes even our home addresses. We become profoundly identified with our work, our teams, our projects—and while those thrive, that identity feels strong and creative. But when those institutions become crazed, corrupt, confused, we start to wither, losing the ferocity we need just at the moment we need it most. At moments like this, it sometimes takes the rough intrusion of the real world to remind us to put ourselves back at the center of the picture. It's time to make a plan, again.

Chris Carosella

There was some talk of sending me to an assignment in corporate but one thing I always heard was "never go to Corporate because it'll suck the life out of you." And then I had a cancer scare. While waiting to hear if it was benign or malignant I knew that, if malignant, I did not want to go out as the queen of the company. There were too many things I hadn't done yet. I made the decision while on sick leave to leave.

The tumor was benign. When I came back to work, I took some time to make sure I wasn't just reacting to the illness and to make my plans. Everything felt much better knowing that I had made the decision to go. I knew it was right.

We stay in jobs for too long because leaving feels like surrender, like a defeat. We would do better to remember that the system we are trying to fix is not of our making—and that to build a better world, the first thing we have to do is stay strong, stay focused on the value we bring. The women I most admire understand this from the outset. They know immediately when it is time to go. They don't linger for quixotic reasons, they don't agonize over loyalties, and they're dispassionate about the company's inability to change. They always have a plan.

Cindy Solomon

The minute they realize that the company is not set up for them to be successful, they move to their next position, usually within a

> different company. It doesn't mean to them that they are not good enough, not smart enough and rarely if ever are they hurt by the companies' inability to recognize their worth. They just move somewhere they can more effectively contribute.

I wish I could emulate women like this. I think I've usually stayed in jobs long after I should have moved on. I was waiting for absolute certainty and confidence and I was probably hoping that someone would just notice that I was bored and come along and save me. Just as, at the start of our career, we hope something will "just happen." Instead, of course, as I waited, I just grew bored, frustrated, and defensive. Once I'd finally found my way out and started a new job, I felt so strong and inspired, I wondered why I'd hesitated.

When a job is destroying your soul, it is tempting to imagine storming off in a thrilling moment of high drama. We fantasize about the devastation we leave behind, delighting in a misguided sense of revenge. We are also impatient—once you've made your mind up to go, nothing can move fast enough. But leaving smart is always preferable to leaving fast.

The biggest roadblock (and, sometimes, mental block) is usually financial. For most of my career, I couldn't leave a job until I had another one to go to. If you don't have severance pay, and haven't saved F.U. money, you have to start looking for another job while remaining in your present one. And then the subterfuge starts: the sick days, the imaginary dentist appointments and funerals. No one likes this; it feels juvenile and I wonder how many people it really fools. But walking away with nothing serves no one. Everyone knows it is easier to find a job when you are in one—and everyone knows you don't really want to end up working in McDonald's.

For many women, trapped in the same predicament, layoffs and redundancies come as blessed relief. Legions of women have been liberated by layoffs and severance packages. Money gives us permission and confidence to go.

> *Donna Collins*
>
> I was laid off shortly after going part time after the birth of my daughter. I knew that my career would be sidelined when I made this decision but those are the sacrifices you make as a mother. It actually happened to be one of the best things that ever happened to me. I got a six month severance package to be home with my

then seven month old daughter and the very same company that laid me off offered me a consulting opportunity. I had never considered being self employed but I parlayed the one contract into four contracts and now I'm working three days a week, making more than I had in my full time job. It is the best of both worlds. I won't be a CEO in a large company but I am the CEO of my own. It is a powerful feeling!

When we stay in jobs for too long, it is often because we focus on the risks of leaving—forgetting the bigger, more knowable risk of staying. Staying in a dead-end job isn't safe—it can be lethal. That consideration has to be part of your risk analysis. The only effective way to make leaving feel less risky is to have a plan and to have some savings. Joan Silver's Ph.D. thesis followed a cohort of women who left their corporations to set up businesses of their own.

Joan Silver

The culture had diminished their confidence and grown their fear, until, when they finally had the courage to leave, they felt things couldn't get any worse. "If all else fails, I can always go and work at McDonald's." They *all* said that!

Almost everyone I knew felt that leaving was risky but they all had some kind of nest egg to reduce the risk. I asked them if they'd ever go back. Every single one of them said, "NEVER AGAIN!" Once you've tasted freedom, you never want to go back.

Having saved the money and marshaled our reasons and plan for leaving, the last roadblock is often loyalty. We can disassociate ourselves from the toxic bosses and alien environments, but if we've enjoyed any success at all it has been because of individual relationships that have enriched our work and our lives. We're loyal to the people who've helped us and even more loyal to the people whom we've helped. We don't want to let them down. Leaving our friends at work is harder by far than leaving the company.

I remember a colleague coming over to me one Friday evening and handing me a glass of white wine. "I don't know how you get out of bed every morning," she said. The paralysis with which our boss had infected the whole company was so painful. Why did I stay? I told myself I had to protect my people, that I was loyal to them. I'd read and admired Shackleton and felt that he represented the pinnacle of responsible leadership, looking after his people against all odds. But he had no choice—he could not quit without dying. But I did have a choice; I was not, after all, in Antarctica! What I didn't realize until later was that my departure would have given everyone else permission to leave. My loyalty trapped all of us in the same abusive situation. It is impossible to take responsibility for others if you don't take responsibility for yourself first.

> *Karen Price*
>
> I think the important thing for women to know—women who want to change things, to do things the way they see is right, that it's okay to give up on a beast that will not change. You are not a failure for your inability to change a 100 year old system. You are not a failure to fit into that system either. You are not a failure for being different.

Exit Smart

"Nothing became his life like the leaving of it" it is said in *Macbeth.* We'd all prefer that our exit not be the best thing about our career—but a stylish exit does everyone good. If you've timed it right, leaving a job can and should be cause for celebration. These rites of passage matter and provide great opportunities for you to articulate how much you value and owe your colleagues. Closure applies to jobs too.

When I left the Boston consulting firm I'd worked for, I was genuinely sorry to be going. The head of the firm had taken a big gamble when he hired me; I appreciated his support. I knew I'd miss him. I also knew he'd be really pissed off that I was leaving. He loved white burgundy, so I bought him a bottle of Batard Montrachet. Presenting it to him, I explained that it was to ensure that my departure didn't leave a bad taste in his mouth. So we stayed pals.

Sometimes, to work up the energy and confidence we need to leave, we demonize our employers; seeing them as totally bad allows us to feel virtuous (or at least innocent) when we leave. This can become a poisonous mind-set. However bad the old job may have been, whatever its faults, you want to preserve your reputation, your network, and your relationships. These are your assets, built with time and effort. Don't throw them away. Crucial to your career, they are also part of what your next company is buying or built upon. More important, leaving in a positive frame of mind is great for your confidence and a stylish way to begin your new life.

Chris Carosella

> I planned a month-long vacation to visit a variety of friends and family around the country before starting my business. I dubbed it the "Carosella '96 Freedom Tour" . . . had t-shirts made with my new company name on the front and the locations I was visiting on the back (kind of like concert tour shirts), sent posters and post-cards announcing the tour and confirming dates/places, gave out the shirts to my hosts and many others along the way. I also had bottles of champagne with engraved glasses made for each person I visited so we could toast my freedom and new business. It was a continuous celebration for me and for them!

If you can see that you will have to leave, don't rush. Take your time. Make sure you leave with everything you are entitled to and everything you need. Many exits are precipitated by negotiations that get out of hand—or that are so painful you just want them to end. This can be a big mistake. I recall one CEO who was threatened with termination and felt so angry and hurt, she quit and went home. She should have stopped the conversation, required that everyone sleep on it, and returned to work with a clear list of what she wanted to get before she left. However senior you are, the waters close over you quickly when you are gone. A dramatic exit is no consolation if you've left money, references, pay on the table.

When I left CMGI, I had enormous difficulty getting anyone to give me a straight answer about my severance package. Nobody wanted to know—and the answers I got were illogical or strangely conflicting. There were unmistakable signs of the buck being passed. Eventually I discovered that I was to be offered something wildly out of keeping with packages offered to my peers. I hired a discrimination lawyer, rallied my network, and fought my way to parity. The process was intimidating and insulting. Nevertheless, I made a point of leaving on good personal terms with my chairman. Why? Because for all the aggravation, I knew I'd learned a lot from working for him. I'd made a lot of money, which gave me freedom I valued. And face-to-face, we had always been straight with one another. His company had fought hard to underpay me—that was their game. I'd fought hard for fairness—that was mine. It wasn't personal.

When I talk to ex-employees of CMGI, I am struck by how bitter many of them are—some with good reason. But they are still angry about events that took place years ago. Stuck in the past, they continue to fight the institutional battles that bedeviled their time there. I've never met an institution that didn't do this to people—but I've met lots of individuals who've resisted it successfully. They do so because ultimately they want to determine their future for themselves—not let it be determined for them by ancient grudges. Instead of staying stuck inside some old corporate game, they refine their own game to win. Their resilience in recovering fast from an abusive workplace leaves them in good mental condition for their next assignment.

You may be asked before you go to do an exit interview. In theory, these are opportunities for you to deliver honest feedback to your employer. In theory, you should be able to tell the truth because, in theory, there shouldn't be any repercussions. In practice, exit interviews usually stay in *your* file—just in case you want to come back. The whole ritual is a staggering waste—not just of time but of information. The one opportunity companies have for hearing the truth is quite often just thrown away.

Joan Silver

When I left, I assumed I'd do an exit interview—I was the one who'd designed the form! They just weren't expecting it. After I'd done it, the head of HR said, "I can't really do anything with this," so I told her I'd taken the liberty of sending it to the CEO. "I care about this organization," I said, "and I want you to know how I feel." No one expected me to do this and HR just felt emasculated.

The organization didn't want to know; they only wanted to hear the good stuff. They didn't want to know if something was broken. In male organizations, the idea of truth telling without punishment doesn't exist; if you tell the blunt truth, you get shot. I don't expect to hear back from the CEO.

Most highly successful women get fired at some point in their careers. It's always a shock, it always feels humiliating, and it is always enormously emotional. It can be tempting to make a grand gesture on leaving, trying to make others feel as devastated as we feel ourselves. This is always a mistake. If ever there is a moment to seize the moral high ground and stay there, this is it. Once someone has decided to fire you, acts of revenge merely confirm their opinion. Acts of grace leave them puzzled, even respectful. It's a far better way to go.

Starting Here, Starting Now

The Belgians used to issue a retirement guide that began, "In the morning, get out of bed and put on your socks." It was typically pedestrian advice that disguised an important idea: you have to keep moving. Whether you are taking a break, going to a new job, or starting a new business, change is disruptive and can be a shock.

Linda Alepin

When I took a year off, it was like looking into an abyss. I had no idea what to do with the time. I realized I was married to titles! In retrospect, I can truly see how I swallowed the male paradigms of money, power and title hook line and sinker. I strove for many years in corporate America on behalf of obtaining these. I succeeded. I was an officer for a F300 company and then the founder and CEO of an Internet startup. It was only as I came to possess these much sought-after parts of an identify that I experienced the hollowness of them. This was not indeed immeasurable personal satisfaction.

Stripped of corporate paraphernalia and excuses, you learn a lot about yourself—some expected, some not.

Liz Dolan

I used to blame Nike. It was always Nike's excuse that I never had any dates—I was working too hard for Nike. Then when I left, I realized: it wasn't Nike, it was me! I love working![1]

Many women feel intensely lonely without the automatic camaraderie of an office. So much of their identity has been tied up in work that they may lose confidence just when they need it most. When you leave to have children, the disturbance to your sense of identity can be even more severe. Janet Hanson started her network for Goldman Sachs women after she'd experienced the loneliness and loss of identity that hit her on maternity leave. Bereft of the identify bestowed by work, she found it impossible to shift smoothly from an intense, high-powered job to small talk in the playground about lunch boxes.

With or without children, at this point, networks can be lifesavers. If you're starting a new business, you know that—but if you are taking a break or just starting a new job, networks remind you who you are and that your value is intrinsic—not a function of title or office size. When you're bereft of the trappings of business success—office, title, staff—your networks remind you of your accomplishments, know-how, and value. Your professional networks are just as important when you're not working as when you are—and may contain riches in areas you never expected. And if you are starting a new job, your networks help you do that new job better.

Career breaks (with or without children) are increasingly common and many women find them essential. Especially if we've been in abusive workplaces, we need time to put our lives and values back together again. Time to recharge and reorient our thinking—and to make solid plans for reaching our new goals. Watching many of my friends recover from abuse, discrimination, discouragement, and burnout, I see how important it is to take time to recover. It may take a long time—often longer than you think. Your girlfriends will tell you not to date when on the rebound and the same can apply to jobs too.

Karen Price

> Several months later, when I thought I was ready to go back to work, I interviewed for a management position and received positive feedback from the company. But when I didn't get the job, I was so relieved!! You see, when I had walked into that office building, with its casual dress code that made them think they had a modern management style, I felt that weight returning to my chest. I felt tightness in my breathing. I saw myself going back in time. New company but same corporate business approach underneath the casual dress code. Back to the boys club, the playing along with the guys, the corporate politics, the sucking up to the boss. Back to seeing the truth and not being able to follow it. It became apparent to me that going back to the corporate world was not for me, at least not as I currently was.

You can leave for a new title, you can leave for a bigger salary. But leaving can be a big wrench—so make sure you're doing it for substantial improvements in the things you care about. Moving from one toxic environment to another isn't progress. Time away from work may help you to identify and plan how radical a change you want to make. Eventually, Karen decided to set up her own company; at the heart of it are the values of fairness and honesty that she is determined to nurture and protect. The women that Joan Silver studied found that, having made what felt like a very risky decision, they'd finally found a safe place to work.

> *Joan Silver*
>
> The women I studied were all more successful in their first year than they had been in past jobs—they got more esteem, they made more money. Most of them could not tell their clients they were leaving—but their clients found them anyway. "We worked with you in the company because we liked working with *you,*" they said. "We knew you would tell us when something was a bad choice. We didn't want the party line and we knew you would give us a good solution." Financially, these women were more successful than they had ever been and no one said they were working more hours.

As I watch women leave traditional business structures and as I watch them flourish, I see the beginnings of our parallel business universe arising. It's one in which companies work differently and in which lives are lived honestly—a world of work in which lives are integrated, not delegated. As I talk to women, I hear hope and energy and enthusiasm, unconstrained by convention, time-serving, and face-saving. They know as well as I do that success is not inevitable and that there is no reward without risk. They know that there are no such things as safety and guarantees, and they are strikingly free of inflated promises. Their quiet confidence is in themselves and in the way they do business. They're discovering the source of power, and it is themselves.

Travel Thoughts

- Are you still learning? Are you proud of your organization? Are you still excited by your job? For you to succeed, how much must the organization change?
- If it's time to go, what's your plan?
- What is the risk of staying? Are you getting mad? Stale? Losing your confidence?
- Who are you loyal to?
- How can you celebrate your departure?

Adrian became an entrepreneuse. In many ways, her story is a paradigm for all women who start their own companies. She's resourceful, determined, and focused—but what sets her apart most from her male counterparts is her passion. Passion is what initiated her company and passion is what saw her through its dark days. With your own business, passion is an asset, not a disadvantage; the emotion that traditional corporations view with disapproval suddenly becomes the essential life force of a start-up. This doesn't mean, however, that the life of the entrepreneuse is for everyone. Many women change jobs—but remain employees—and that decision is right for them unless they feel that having their own business is something they just can't forgo.

Amy Millman

> In the ranks of the 300 women I've got to know well, I have about 100—it is the passion of their lives. I think that is what separates the women from the girls. At the Springboard boot camp that we run, I often say "you can see which ones can't NOT do this and which aren't so sure." They've left something safer. And I say if you don't have the passion and take this all the way (even if it doesn't get all the way) if you won't drive it to the end—leave this room right now! Because it's not worth it any other way.

Women are starting businesses at nearly twice the rate of men. In the United States, women-owned businesses represent 48 percent of all privately held firms, employing 52 percent of the private sector workforce and generating $2.46 trillion in sales. Our businesses are not just growing in number but in size. Between 1997 and 2004, estimated employment in these firms grew at twice the rate of all privately held firms. And we're making more money: revenues in women-owned businesses increased more than in other businesses in the same period.[1] In the United Kingdom, a smaller, slower, but nevertheless similar trend is taking place: women run about a quarter of U.K. business and are starting new companies at twice the rate of men. And although we attract less investment, our businesses are just as likely as men's to succeed. As entrepreneuses we aren't gatecrashers; we are leaders.

We start our own companies for many reasons: because we're sick of playing corporate games and want to work our own way, because we're tired of making money for other people and want to make more for ourselves, because we want to achieve something meaningful to us that springs from our values. Contrary to male myth, women are not leaving traditional corporations because they want to spend more time with their families. Instead, according to a 2001 Korn/Ferry study, they leave because they want to "take risks with new ideas and test their personal limits" by joining or starting new businesses.[2] Our "new ideas" hope to create the flexibility and integration that more traditional structures have denied us. We want to find ways to live and work that will draw our passions together—not polarize them. We are passionate because we identify with our businesses and because we want them to embody the things we believe in. So we want them to be fair, flexible, honest—and successful.

Statistically, you are a lot more likely to run your own business if one of your parents did. Entrepreneurialism, it appears, is almost genetic: it's in the blood of many an entrepreneuse. Adrian's father started with nothing, working as a door-to-door salesman, and he ended up with a chain of stores. Her mother opened and ran a successful lingerie store in Long Island.

Adrian Guglielmo

> I worked there when I was a kid. Then one of our friends got breast cancer and my mother looked inside herself and she just said, "I am not going to be happy—my best friend has breast cancer!" She decided she wouldn't be happy selling lingerie unless she could sell products for women who'd had mastectomies. So she got Christian Dior and other designers to design products for them. She was before Breast Cancer Awareness and all that—this was in the 70s. I find that more amazing than my dad going door to door.

Growing up among business owners, being deeply engaged with their companies, is a seminal memory for many entrepreneuses: their earliest training and inspiration.

Risa Edelstein

> Growing up in an entrepreneurial family had everything to do with my desire to have my own business. My family owns a 26-year-old tape business and the entire family is in the business (except for me;->) and they still talk excitedly about it (it bores me to death—but they

still LOVE it!) Business was what we heard and talked most about at dinners which we ate together every night. Early on when my mom and dad started their business, I used to work on weekends stapling price lists together and earning $.01 apiece. I eventually graduated into the accounting department and got an hourly wage. I was always a self starter and realized that my own company would be one of the few places that I could call the shots.

My own mother was like a lot of women: she discovered her talents by doing volunteer work, fundraising for our school. That success gave her confidence in her own ability—and a taste for accumulating money. My father was shocked to discover that, in good years, her small property business made more money for the family than his soul-destroying job with a giant multinational. More money *and* she was having more fun. It was a powerful childhood lesson.

Women who did not come from an entrepreneurial background often point to their mothers as inspiration: it was seeing their mothers solve problems every day that made them understand how much women can do. And perhaps it helped them to understand that starting a new business does not require genius. It just requires passion for a good idea. Good ideas address an opportunity or solve a problem—something we do well every day of our lives. Good ideas are ageless, so there's no moment too soon or too late to be an entrepreneuse; my mother started her last company when she was in her sixties and Doris Drucker started her first one when she was in her eighties.[3]

To build a business, you do not need a revolutionary idea—you just need a good idea. Although Big Ideas That Change the World are regularly hyperbolized in the press, most new businesses are more evolutionary than revolutionary. Doris Drucker's business solved a need—it made a device to alert speakers when they couldn't be heard. Kimberly Bunting became an entrepreneuse when she worked for the government.

Kimberly Bunting

I saw that businesses needed well trained people to hire and the government was spending plenty (more than $10 billion per year) to train people. Yet, companies rarely used the government systems to find potential employees. The programs were designed to meet the needs of the people participating (which is good) but not to meet the needs of the businesses (which is bad—especially if the main goal is to get people employed). I knew there was a way to create a program that met both needs, without sacrificing one for the other. After fifteen years of trying to persuade government programs to redesign themselves, I determined it would be easier to build it myself and sell it to them.

Risa Edelstein combined her entrepreneurialism with a friend's expertise to develop a market that was staring her in the face.

Risa Edelstein

I remember sitting on the floor in my den with my best friend from high school. I was selling computers at Computerland and she was doing her master's at Boston University and was working at Lotus—a great star company at that time. She was planning on returning to Montreal that summer when she graduated and we were trying to think of a business to start. We brainstormed and thought of computer training—with all this new technology—people will surely need to be trained. During her final semester, we found a company that made training videos, went to NYC to meet them and the rest was history. . . . We got more products to sell, landed a very large account in year 2 and the business grew. Why wouldn't it—the demand was massive (in hindsight I see that).

The top growth industries for women-owned businesses between 1987 and 1999 were construction, wholesale trade, transportation, communications, agribusiness, and manufacturing.[4] Contrary to popular folklore, we are not just running bed-and-breakfasts and hair salons; we are expanding into all industries to launch the businesses that drive economies. We are inspired by seeing opportunities waiting to be developed that will also develop us.

A half-hearted entrepreneuse is an oxymoron: you owe it to the business, to the idea, to give it all the courage and commitment you have. That means that, if you have a family, they must enlist too. They don't have to work for the company—but they have to want it to succeed. Before I started my first high-tech company, I discussed with my husband the time, passion, focus it would require. I knew I couldn't undertake the challenge without his explicit support. As my children grew older, they absorbed that commitment—and I think they absorbed the desire to see the business succeed. (Some women, of course, go much further and start their businesses jointly with their spouses. Such copreneurs understand from the outset how invasive and all-consuming a new business can be and they feel that their marriages are strengthened by a shared passion and commitment.)

Becoming an entrepreneuse is not an easy option. I'm always amused when people assume that women start their own businesses to find some easier work-life blend lifestyle than the traditional corporation offered. Nothing about being an entrepreneuse is easy, and you're likely to find yourself working harder than you ever worked for big companies. What makes the difference is that you are working the way you choose to work: the hours may be immense, but the pace, the pressure, the values, the rhythm are all your own. Jekka McVicar started her herb farm to have a business she could run while her children were still at home. She farmed organically to ensure the children didn't encounter poisonous chemicals while crawling and playing as she worked. Jekka's business has never been part-time or less than serious—and her products now dominate a burgeoning market. She has built a profitable market from scratch and found original and creative ways to develop it. But she hasn't had a week off.

How do you get started? Not by incorporating, hiring lawyers and accountants. You start just like Adrian did; you start by talking. It's how you do your research and it's the only real way to test your idea. Great companies aren't incubated in isolation but through constant iteration as every conversation tells you more. Talking to potential suppliers, customers, and employees, seeing the look in their eyes as they understand your idea (or don't get it at all), can be chastening—but every response gives you more data. Will they work with you? How much do they charge? Can they do everything you need or just part of it? Do they know competitors? Do they think you're crazy? Getting immediate, informed responses to your business idea is more relevant, more efficient, and more empowering than any degree. Business, after all, is not an abstract science but a practical mission.

Risa Edelstein

Creating business plans in theory ad nauseam will get you nowhere. You need to go out and do it, make your mistakes, correct them and keep moving forward. Action is what is most important in a small business, especially in the beginning. Don't be afraid to screw up.

I've made tons of mistakes and I often call these mistakes my "Masters degree"—the cost of which is probably a lot cheaper. Mistakes are part of the growing process and you need to account for them—both time wise, money wise and mental wise. You just have to hope that they are not big enough to completely put you out of business!

I'm always struck that, once they start setting up their own companies, women's reluctance to ask vanishes. Perhaps it is because we are not asking for ourselves, but for our business, our company, our idea, our passion. Asking no longer feels selfish, because we are enabling something bigger than ourselves. We don't stand on ceremony but take help wherever we find it.

Adrian Guglielmo

In 1996, I got a meeting with American Express—and I knew nothing about walking into corporate America. And I went into my closet—nothing but rags. No business clothes. And I had a babysitter coming and you know what that's like—of course, the babysitter never showed up. So I got myself together in a mismatching outfit with a two-year-old in tow. It was the most embarrassing moment of my life. Ten men with a 2 year old, wearing not exactly a New York City business outfit.

The 2 year old is going in and out of the table and this one man (if I met him today, I'd buy him a steak dinner) he put the 2 year old in his lap, gave him a yellow pad and the kid scribbled through the rest of my presentation. And I was able to get the first big sale of my company. It was for twenty thousand dollars. Now we get sales of two million dollars—but that one was so important. For my self esteem. This man helped me and Amex helped me.

Improvise, listen, learn. In every meeting and every conversation, you refine and test your verbal business plan. You hear how it sounds in the marketplace. And nine times out of ten you get the help you seek because people want to be part of something new that could be successful. Every new business needs a thousand midwives—and mothers smart enough to understand their value.

Kimberly Bunting

I like to say, "I am the luckiest girl in the world, I had high level executives helping prepare a business plan that they handed over to me with no strings attached." I spent a year working with mentors to

> lay out the groundwork for an "In-Home Learning System" that put computers and Internet access in people's homes, had them log into an online community that was designed around overcoming the obstacles they faced (disability issues, poverty issues, welfare issues) and provided customized online training oriented to their career goals. After a year of planning, we determined the technology involved required that it be run as a for-profit business. I then set about finding a contract to launch the business with. After a formal RFP and six to seven months of negotiations, the Workforce Board in Dallas agreed to contract with my company to design and build the program for 1,000 people.
>
> I had to pledge our pending patent (which one of my mentors helped me file) in the event we did not complete the contract as specified, since we were a start-up company with no references to speak of. I also had to get the mayor of Dallas, the president of the largest employer in Dallas and the county judge to write letters of recommendations for me attesting to my integrity. That contract bought us revenues to last for one year. I immediately hired an operations manager that I knew well and trusted. He helped me identify and interview a leader for our technology area. From there we very carefully added staff as needed.

What I love about Kimberly's story is it is *saturated* with help: mentors, referees, experts. It's her company and her passion—delivered by an army of supporters, well-wishers, allies, and friends. She doesn't feel threatened by their contributions—she knows the life of her idea depends on it. Her passion keeps her focused on what is right for the business.

Women are more likely than men to ask for help with their business—but we often don't have the best networks from which to find the advice we need.[5] Although most of us believe we have better relationship-building skills than men, we don't focus these specifically on business—we have lots of friends but not necessarily lots of experts who can help us. We have to get better at this—but we also have to think more carefully about the networks we do have. When I started an organization to bring live music to the elderly in nursing homes and hospices, it was my husband who pointed out to me that our family doctor would know this market well; I hadn't even seen him as part of my network. And it was the doctor who kick-started the whole thing.

Even when we think we understand our businesses profoundly, when we have a comprehensive business plan and trusted associates, we will make mistakes. As the business grows, each new phase holds new challenges, issues, conflicts. We will never know all the answers.

Kimberly Bunting

I keep an ongoing list called "all the things I have done wrong." Here it is:

- I hired people I liked instead of people with proven skills to do the job
- I didn't watch our revenue/expenses ratio carefully enough
- I didn't end things as soon as I knew they weren't right
- I didn't document processes and establish progress measurements
- I didn't insist on consistent progress reports
- I didn't project our needs far enough into the future and start the process of solving the problems early enough
- I didn't establish checks and balances that created warnings
- I overestimated people's abilities
- I didn't follow up to make sure things got done
- When entering a new market (or playing field) I entered into partnerships too early to know what my best options would be
- I didn't keep good records to help manage our networking connections
- I didn't get enough balls in the air from a variety of different angles
- I didn't establish guidelines for working with vendors and stick to them
- I wasn't able to utilize people for their best strength (only)
- It took me too long to realize that people were stealing from me

Kimberly's business is currently a multimillion-dollar company and has doubled in size each year since the second year. It has a specific business plan to build to $100 million in revenue per year and a more loosely defined business plan to move up to $1 billion. Mistakes, and the learning she derived from them, are inseparable from that growth. Far from curbing her ambition, her learning spurs it on. Since we are all destined to make mistakes, what matters is how much and how fast we learn from them. It's not the mistake, it's the recovery that counts.

We are not afraid to fail. In fact, "taking on challenges in order to learn" is cited by women as the number-one motivating factor in starting a new business.[6] Most successful entrepreneuses have failed at something and many of their best ideas emerge from the ashes of failed ones. Perfection is not the goal—progress is.

> *Adrian Guglielmo*
>
> I would call my autobiography "What Not to Do in My Business." I got a homeowners loan. I signed for personal things. My credit went down the tube in two years. I signed my husband's name to things. I borrowed from everyone. I didn't pay taxes one month and paid them later. I held off on important bills. I learned very slowly. I was tortured. I *learned* from my mistakes. I learned that you should never put your name on ANYTHING. If you have to have it, think about it for twenty-four hours. Now I have a revolving line of credit of half a million dollars from Chase Bank—but when they said they wanted a personal guarantee, I said no way! I learned from my mistakes.
>
> The best bet is to find an angel which I eventually did. He gave me a million dollars and he believed in me. It's so important not to be afraid of asking for help. I talked to everyone. You don't have to walk in like a big shot. I could be honest with a group of people and eventually I found this man. I did the best I could with that money. You see, there is always someone who will believe in you.

We have high hopes for our companies—but that doesn't always translate to high aspirations. Adrian was smart and found the funding she needed for growth. In doing so, she was highly unusual. Women's businesses are routinely underfunded (by friends and credit cards) and often fail to achieve their potential because they are starved for cash. Women receive only 4.4 percent of venture capital—a pathetic percentage that didn't budge in the boom years of the Internet. In some cases, the absence of venture funding is deliberate; women want to retain ownership and believe there's a genuine benefit to bootstrapping the business.

Kimberly Bunting

Business Access has bootstrapped its way from day one to now and I am eternally grateful that we have. I spent about a year looking for capital in our second/third year. What I saw was a bunch of old school idiots who totally missed the fact that they were looking at a project that is obviously the way things will be going in the future. Maybe they overlooked it because I was a woman. More probably, they overlooked it because my plan didn't fit into their unbending formulas.

The advantages of bootstrapping have been important to Business Access. Our prices are based on our real expenses at the predicted volumes of business. When our revenues are affected, our expenses have to follow (and vice versa). There is a clarity of cause and effect that permeates our company. Quality assurance isn't a buzz word, it's a financial reality.

Bootstrapping has given us time to grow into higher levels of functioning. By virtue of the fact that we cannot do "everything we ever dreamed of right when we want to do it" we analyze things more closely. We look for the most inexpensive way to do things. We prioritize. We compromise. We have real pain when we make the wrong decisions. These are skills that will be valuable to our company for all of our years to come.

The disadvantages are that it's hard to see employees be overworked and underequipped. A certain amount of working for Business Access is being committed to the cause. If you have to have everything guaranteed, it's not the best place for you. There are many times that I wish I could do more for the people that have really dug in to get things done.

Historically, some of the strongest, most enduring businesses have been founded during recessions when money is tight. Not having money emphasizes self-sufficiency, ingenuity, responsibility. How much capital a company has becomes an ineradicable part of a company's DNA and it makes a huge difference if you can get it right from the start. Too much cash and the company becomes spoiled, political, and wasteful—we all saw this happen at the height of the Internet bubble. But undercapitalized businesses can just die, starved of money. My first software company attempted to build with six engineers a piece of software that I subsequently understood really required dozens; I wasn't thrifty, I was wrong.

Those Internet ventures that survived were not necessarily the ones that spent the least—but the ones that spent most appropriately to their market at the right time. Intrinsic to every product or business is a fundamental capital need; consumer products need more money than service businesses. What matters is to get the *right* capitalization for your business.

Amy Millman

There is a great company in Boston, perhaps it's going to be our first IPO. They came in and said, "We want to raise $3 million to launch a consumer product." And I say, "You need $3m? That won't even buy you an ad!" She was insistent. Up to this point, they'd done everything with grants and government funding and strategic funding. But for the consumer market, you need significant money. Finally they agreed to this and decided that they couldn't do what they wanted with less than $15m. That was bottom—and that's what they got.

With that, they became first in the market and it is a success. With $15 million (the bare bones of what they really need) they can get traction. But it was like pulling teeth to get her to realize! And it may be a one-shot deal.

Women are reluctant to seek investment because they've heard that venture capitalists operate an old boy network and it is only the guys who get the cash. They are right—VCs are mostly male and they can be pretty macho at that. Although women start more businesses than men, the venture capital world is, in the words of the Kauffman Foundation, "overwhelmingly male. . . . Few female venture capitalists gain sufficient experience to become partners and to achieve high visibility within the industry." Not only are there very few women in the VC world—but those that enter it are more likely to leave.[7]

But the VCs will tell you that the reason the guys get the cash is because the guys ask for cash; twice as many men as women say they expect to seek venture capital.[8] Women don't ask because they don't want to be rejected—but being rejected is learning, too.

Amy Millman

Men are used to asking women for dates and being rejected so they get used to rejections. Women aren't used to it and don't like it—

but they learn. We tell women to pick ten investors and hit every one of them. If you are rejected, then pick ten more. Don't get upset about it. Pick yourself up. Keep your eye on the prize.

I've known VCs who have said they would never invest in a company run by a woman and I've known female CEOs who were told that they could get funding if they would agree to step aside for a man. (Of course they refused.) But occasionally, being a woman can be an advantage. Carol Vallone could not have built her technology company, WebCT, without venture capital and she found that being a woman had one huge advantage: all the VCs remembered her. They saw so few women that she stood out in their minds. And she knew how to turn rejection into an asset.

Carol Vallone

I always say to people: raising money is no magic, it is like selling anything. It is understanding what values does your investor have, what metrics are they setting around success? That probably is the most important thing: what does success mean to *them* at what point in time? And clearly articulating and identifying that. You have to have an alignment of interests, alignment on vision, and alignment on returns—otherwise, it is not going to happen. And I also find, through my whole funding cycle, people really want to help you. If someone said to me "no, we aren't interested" I would say "what kind of people do you think would be?" And that is how I built my venture network, by people saying "not our stage, our type, our investment level—but so and so does it."

Incorrectly gauging how much capital your business needs is perhaps one of the few fatal mistakes an entrepreneuse can make: too much and you start with a rotten culture; too little and you never gain the momentum you need to assert a presence in the market. But everyone makes these mistakes, men and women. What the numbers show is that we are more likely to undercapitalize our businesses. This may mean that our business will not grow as fast, or as big, as it could. In fearing and resisting growth, we do ourselves—and others—a disservice.

Risa Edelstein

I wish I had known to sell my company earlier at the peak. I was very young when I started the company—23. Most small tech companies need to be sold at the right time to survive. Had I been more business savvy, I would have tried to do that two years earlier.

Most entrepreneuses I've known want to stay with their business. Few want to sell them—and even those who do hope to go with the sale. Such women make a striking contrast to the guys who want to cash out and retire.

Adrian Guglielmo

If we got bought, I'd want to stay with the business for at least two or three years, long enough to know it was safe and sound. I think my business probably will eventually be acquired by a large marketing company when it reaches $100m. Either that or we will be first women-owned disabled company to go public.

When we start businesses, we want them to succeed, of course. But we want more than that. We want their *values* to succeed. We want to build businesses that last, that treat customers and employers with respect, that are sustainable and make the world a better place. As a consequence, our businesses are more likely to offer flex time, tuition reimbursement, and profit sharing; we are more likely, too, to participate, and encourage employees to participate, in volunteering. We don't do this because we're selfless—of the entrepreneuses studied by Korn/Ferry, more than half earned over $100,000, one-fifth earned more than $300,000, and one-tenth topped $500,000. But we encourage volunteering because we know that giving people a life, giving them time to pursue values and meaning, is a smart way to manage our businesses. As entrepreneuses, we are both realistic *and* idealistic, because setting up our own companies allows us the opportunity to create business afresh—free from toxic bosses, stereotypes, anachronistic career paths, hierarchies, and power struggles. We want to build businesses in which values are central to each person's work, not slapped on top of poisonous cultures, the sugary icing on a rotten cake. We are nothing if not ambitious, in the deepest sense of the word.

Kimberly Bunting

The best part of running Business Access is seeing how much it helps people. Watching our employees realize the difference they are making in someone's life. Seeing employees grow into more mature managers and workers. Hearing other people say how great BA and our product are. Seeing spouses and kids of employees and knowing that BA is supporting the foundation of those families. Knowing that we're doing something really important.

The toughest part is not being able to give our employees everything they ever wanted and not being able to do this for every single person on welfare in the US right now.

Paige Arnof-Fenn

For me, it is being able to see how you have made a difference and the impact with the people you touch every day, knowing you have helped them get to a place they wouldn't have been able to get to on their own. Seeing that their business or situation is better now than when you met them—you moved the needle forward. We put our blood, sweat and tears into helping them build their business so it has to be something we believe in. It's about quality and relationships. I think Mavens & Moguls can be as big as I want it to be. I only want it to be as big as it can be where I am still having fun and enjoying the journey—otherwise, what's the point?

Glenda Stone

I'm a business owner and not an employee because my strength is innovation, impatience and competitiveness. I was always the class leader at school—I adore power, challenge, new ideas, and pushing yourself. I have always wanted to run a business to use power wisely, to make money, and get to do something you truly feel strongly about. For me it's all about making money from doing what you love and believe in (i.e., I couldn't sell toilet seats no matter how much the profit margin.)

There have always been three goals for my business: (1) make money; (2) improve the world of business for women, (3) love what I do. Success = 3 × P: Profit + Passion + Power. And thankfully, I can tick each one.

This focus on values and relationships makes our businesses profoundly relevant to the modern marketplace, otherwise characterized by "a chasm of rage and despair between customer and supplier."[9] It is entirely sympathetic and meaningful to those consumers—85 percent of them women—who care about sustainability, ethics, and the environment. Our businesses aren't just relevant; they are also a vital economic engine. Because despite receiving less funding than other businesses, despite exclusion from old boys' networks for finance and procurement, despite resorting to credit cards and families, revenues from our businesses have increased 32 percent over the last five years—compared to 24 percent for other private businesses. Our companies are *staying* in business at twice the rate of men's and are creating more and more jobs.[10] The 18 million businesses we own employ more people than the Fortune 1000, and in times of economic downturn it is our companies that fuel job creation. Our business strengths represent a gigantic natural resource; just imagine what we could do with real funding, real support.

When we run our own businesses, we find ourselves in a domain in which we excel *because* of who we are—not despite it. We don't have to fight, assimilate, equivocate to fit it. As entrepreneuses, our natural strengths—passion, intuition, alignment with the customer—are essential assets. Research studies show that we outshine men in almost every measure of management: motivating others, fostering communication, and producing high-quality work. There is nothing at all soft about these talents. The same studies gave women high marks for being more concerned with overall success than with personal achievement.[11] What better qualities could a new business want in its leader?

We are profoundly in tune with our market and perfectly placed to address it successfully. So let's not play small. Let's not see growth and size as some macho obsession. Let us instead see that as our businesses grow we become more able to change the world.

Adrian Guglielmo

I measure my success on the change that I make in corporate environments on behalf of those with disabilities. If they walk out and say, "I get it, they are just like us," then I feel I am successful.

If everyone ran business the way I do, nobody would be lacking in anything. Everyone that needed help would get it. Corporations would be taking care of everyone, not just one segment. People would be taken care of with new products and new services. The

> disabled can now all get rental cars. What about getting on a plane? How easy is it to get through an airport? If everyone got hold of our ideas as Avis did, we would have a better world. I am going to try to make that difference. Very slowly. I am forty-three years old, I have another thirty years.
>
> I make money. I call it capitalism with a cause. I also am changing a little corner of the world because I'm changing the mind of corporate America and I give jobs to people with disability. It teaches my kids by example and not by mouth. It teaches us a way to be living and be comfortable with what we do and our precious time.

Tom Peters insists, "There is a set of attributes, more commonly found in women than in men, that match the requirements of the new world. Women practice *improvisation skills* with much greater ease than men. Women are more *self-determined* and more *trust-sensitive* than men. Women appreciate and depend upon their *intuition* more than men do. Women, unlike men, focus naturally on *empowerment* (rather than on "power"). Women understand and develop *relationships* with greater facility than men" (Peters's emphasis).[12] In other words, we have what it takes. We are smart, determined, pragmatic, and disciplined. We have high standards, for ourselves and everyone we work with. We refuse to accept that business must be dishonest and dehumanizing. So let's not sell ourselves short. Stand tall. Think big. We don't have to be gatecrashers. We can throw our own party.

Travel Thoughts

- What's your idea? How would you feel if you never pursued it?
- Who do you know—among everyone you've ever met—that can help?
- What mistakes have you made—and what have you learned from them? What about your employees—can they make mistakes too?
- Where can you go for funding? Do you know what they need? What did you learn from meeting with them?
- How much investment do you need? What difference would it make if you could raise twice as much?
- How big can your business get? What problems does it solve? For whom? Do they have money?
- How do you measure success?

Chapter Eleven

The Parallel Universe

They said don't try to change the world
You're just a girl
So it's me against the world today
I'm gonna do it my own way
And though nobody understands
I'm gonna make a one girl stand
It's not Independence Day
I can't waste time on what they say
If we believe when we have faith
We're gonna change the world someday
—SUPERCHICK, "ME AGAINST THE WORLD"

"Our way of doing business is broken." So said a senior vice president of one of the largest media companies in the world. Not a radical young woman but a middle-aged white American man. And he said it a year before the Enron, WorldCom, Tyco, Arthur Andersen, Credit Suisse First Boston, AOL, RiteAid, ImClone, Adelphia, Citigroup, Global Crossing, Merrill Lynch, Qwest, and mutual-fund scandals broke.

Our way of doing business *is* broken. Companies know this but don't know what to do about it. Despite a 50 to 80 percent failure rate, they persist with mergers and acquisitions. Despite public outcry and shareholder fury, they continue to pay CEOs vast amounts for both success and failure—while laying off and reducing benefits for swaths of employees. In a 2003 Korn/Ferry poll, over 80 percent of executives said they were "unimpressed" by the way their management handled the recent economic downturn.[1]

And despite a whole raft of new legislation, in a 2002 Gallup poll, CEOs were regarded with contempt and distrust—only just above car dealers and HMOs—and the selfishness and venality of business executives were deemed to be widespread and a threat to our future.[2] Despite legislation, women continue to be underpaid and underpromoted by large corporations, and they continue to leave.

Business schools find themselves questioning the value of their MBA. Is it relevant, useful, worth its cost in time and money? Why are schools just beginning to think ethics is an important subject to teach? Why has it proved impossible for them to get female enrollment above 35 percent—at a time when other professional schools experience no difficulty achieving parity? Why do teenagers—especially girls—reject business as a career on the grounds that it doesn't help others, doesn't make the world a better place, and isn't exciting?[3]

Individuals wrestle with the existential questions of who they are and how to live their lives, unconvinced that their companies will help them. In the Korn/Ferry poll just cited, over 70 percent of respondents said that they would look for a new job when the economy recovered. Ask a thousand women, as Cindy Solomon did, and nine hundred of them say they want a change.

The old bifurcations—wife at home, husband at work—don't work because they're not economically viable and because they are unfair. No woman can feel comfortable with having to choose between poverty and stress. How to balance personal commitments with work commitments remains the primary chronic problem that employed people struggle with. They're rarely satisfied with the solutions offered up by corporations. Flex time, part time, and paternity leave, where available, are ignored by employees fearful of being branded losers by their bosses. Slapped on top of unchanging cultures, these policies convince no one—and that skepticism is borne out when hard economic times lead to cancellation of the policies. As individuals, we feel no sense of intrinsic alignment between our personal lives and our corporate lives; instead, we find ourselves in a time warp: modern, sophisticated adults who want control of our destinies, confronting Henry Ford's assembly line. And when our friends die young—whether in major terrorist attacks like those of September 11 or through breast cancer—we feel the immense urgency of confronting this central anachronism in our working lives.

Which is when being a gatecrasher reveals its advantages. Women don't carry the accretion of ugly traditions and managerial narcissism, the freemasonry of collusion, deception, and self-perpetuation that male management has evolved. Because we didn't build the system and aren't so invested in it, it's easier for us to see how antihuman—and antiwoman—the contemporary workplace is. We watch from a distance as more regulation piles on top of more rules to reinforce a command-and-control mentality that simply can't cope with the realities of modern-day life. And we know that it doesn't work.

We aren't superior—we just got left out and now find ourselves relatively untainted by a system that feels like it's on its last legs. Left to our own devices, we have had to evolve different ways of working, identify different kinds of power, and build underground railroads and overground networks that get things done in different ways. "I watch my wife in wonder," George Gendron, the editor of *Inc.* magazine once said to me. "It's like she, and the rest of the women she works with, inhabit some parallel universe, where everything gets done but in ways and languages that are so different, I can't see what's happening."

So what is happening?

Changing the Company's Game

If George is looking for the female Neutron Jacks and Chainsaw Al Dunlops, he won't find them. Because that isn't the way we do things. We don't especially value ego—not because we are shrinking violets, but because we think there's a more powerful way to work. Many women remain within large organizations, changing them from within. Their tempered radicalism aims not at wholesale revolution but at a myriad of infinitesimal changes that gradually erode the old toxic way of doing things and replace it with a different set of values and habits. Women like Gail Rebuck, who changed the culture at Random House, or Betsy Bernard at AT&T, who insists that her senior managers sit on boards of non-profits. Such women slug it out on a daily basis, changing how people think and transforming how they work.

I'm in awe of such women because I can't do what they've done. Perhaps I'm too impatient—a bad-tempered radical instead. I don't like cleaning up other people's messes and I'm horrified by the humiliation and pain that I see corporations inflict on women on a daily, systemic basis. I applaud the women who can last long enough to do good; we need them, badly. But I sometimes feel that, as the saying goes, we can't get there from here. Starting with the status quo requires too much destruction before the creation can begin.

So I'm inspired by the women of the parallel universe who are, in their millions, building businesses their own way, according to the values they hold passionately. Many of them are in their twenties and really don't care how things were done in the past. They're proud to be women, proud to be smart, and determined to succeed on their own terms. The *Legally Blonde* generation is not interested in compromise or assimilation. It wears its femininity with pride and seeks success on its own terms. Rather than fight the system, these women seek places to work that value individuals and individual lives. They don't simply pay lip service to work-family balance; they start from a different place altogether. They start from the premise of a life, not an office, and—more important—from the idea of service rather than success.

The economist Shoshana Zuboff, in her analysis of twentieth-century managerial capitalism, makes the argument that the old way of doing business was built by men, for men who did not want to appear to serve in public the women that they dominated in private. In other words, they took a male concept of power (domination) and built corporate structures that served it (the pyramidal hierarchy). But because most customers were women, anything that reeked of service had to be outsourced; dominant men did not want to be seen to be in a role subservient to women. It just didn't suit their concept of power. Service, for them, was a dirty word.

But we don't do that. As gatecrashers, we never were at the center of the picture, so we had to look at the periphery. And what we saw there was very, very powerful. As gatecrashers, we embrace the idea of service and put it at the heart of the female model of leadership. Anyone who thinks that is weak or mealy-mouthed is in for a surprise. "Our true power," said Brenda Rivers, CEO of Andavo Travel, "lies not in the need or ability to control but rather to release control and allow the group to help you. The most compelling lesson for me about power is the power of leading from behind."

When we put service at the heart of leadership, we change the game. Instead of obedience, we seek participation. The women I talk to—in architecture, software, consulting, engineering, construction, pharmaceuticals, marketing, and sales—don't describe their work as killing competitors or trashing the opposition. They talk in detail about reaching deep down inside organizations to understand real needs. They value not how high up in the organization they get, but how deep down they touch people. Their whole way of looking at things is different: valuing values, excellence, and long-term sustainability. All the women I've talked to describe with enthusiasm a way of work that is about exchanges between equals—not about dominating minions. They don't have a mental model of being ordered around and they don't think that power means handing out orders. And they aren't thinking this way because some recent guru has decreed it the latest fashion. They do so because they just can't *not* do so.

As CEOs, we serve our companies, we serve our employees. We don't ask "what do I want?" but "what is best for the business?" It is not that men don't ask themselves these questions. They do; I've watched several of them up close as they struggled with these issues, trying to define their companies, trying to identify priorities. These men were by no means stupid or vicious or mean, but they could not, finally, put the business ahead of their ego—not least because of the contempt they feared from their male colleagues.

Far from being humiliating, service is ennobling—and highly profitable. Because service lies not at the periphery but at the heart of business. Far from demeaning us, serving customers gives us everything we need for success.

The turnaround of Continental Airlines provided a stunning example of how profoundly leading from behind can transform a company. The year 1994 saw Continental as the worst airline in America, en route to bankruptcy court; by the first half of 2001, it was one of only two major U.S. airlines to turn a profit. It has now won five consecutive J. D. Power Awards and is the only Fortune 500 company to make the *Fortune* magazine "100 Best Places to Work" list for five years running. Bonnie Reitz, who pioneered what she calls "Inside/Out" leadership in the company turnaround, believes that putting others first was the lynchpin of the company's turnaround—and of its resilience after September 11.

Bonnie Reitz

What used to drive businesses, what drove the U.S., was products and services and mass production. But that meant that everyone got treated the same way. And people don't want to be treated the same. Now really what you have is the marketplace turned upside down—where customer has the power, driving what companies have to do.

Today I believe that new wealth creation is not product innovation but relationship innovation. If you can take your core trust factor principles and get that same relationship with customers and you have that ongoing relationship, customers train you into what they want from you. It is not necessarily a lot—but it starts to grow itself. A continuous cycle of elevation of engagement of employee and customers. It is the most phenomenal thing to be watching happen. You get a much more profitable company because of relationships and so much more pleasant experience. It is human nature not rocket science. If you listen, you will be heard.

Listening to customers instead of blaming them, hearing employees rather than silencing them, surfacing emotions rather than suppressing them: these represent truly powerful aspects of leadership. The old command-and-control approaches, inherited from the military, not only don't suit us; they don't work any more. Customers feel insulted, employees feel infantilized—and emotions don't just go away. The leaders of the parallel universe change the game by embracing reality, not by trying to order it into submission.

Cindy Solomon

My experience is that women leaders tend to have more of their people stay with them longer (loyalty) or they tend to get more people promoted as they spend significantly more time developing them and touting them to their managers. As women continue to rise to higher levels of authority, they are starting to lose their fear and lead the way they have always wanted to lead.

Once you abandon the illusion of control, all kinds of things become possible. Networks replace pyramids; fairness and respect become requirements, not optional extras. Virtual companies, of the kind that Nancy Frank and Paige Arnof-Fenn run, become perfectly feasible, serving projects run by world class executives of a caliber and variety that no office building or corporate 401(k) could ever attract. I'm interested in the ever-increasing number of companies that have abandoned the traditional work week, demanding instead only that the work is completed to the satisfaction of client and colleagues. I talk to women who work almost everywhere *except* the corporate headquarters—at home, in cars, on planes, in hotels—workblending thousands of miles away from overseers. I'm intrigued by the rise in direct selling, the freedom and autonomy it offers to millions of self-employed women whose joy and expertise is relationship building. What I see all around me are millions of women inventing and discovering ways of working that are direct, fair, honest, and that earn them respect for who they are.

We are not afraid. More than any other characteristic, what excites and inspires me is that the women who are changing the game are so fearless. They aren't afraid of emotion. They know it's inevitable where people are contributing time. They aren't afraid of conflict. They aren't afraid of employees. They aren't afraid of customers. They know that leading from behind banishes fear. So we aren't afraid to be honest.

A guy once described my penchant for honesty to me as "Margaret's little habit." Well, it's a habit we just can't kick—and won't kick. I'm always struck, when I talk to women individually or in large groups, by their honesty, their directness, their lack of conceit. Honesty is a way of releasing energy, the kind of energy that business badly needs to embrace. The kind of honesty without which business turns into posturing and paralysis. If there is one experience that unites all business women, it's that moment when we realize that, underneath all the meetings and titles and oak doors, the mystique and gravitas that men seem to adore, business is just common sense, and we can do it too. That, in fact, it's *easier* to do it without all that baggage—and that if those guys would get out of the way, we could even show them how to enjoy it.

Service instead of success, freedom instead of control, honesty instead of secrecy. These are the hallmarks of the parallel universe. A universe designed to create the structures and cultures in which people can thrive, places in which men and women can stop faking it and instead unleash their hearts and minds on businesses that respect their capabilities, their commonalities, and their differences. While pessimism and cynicism remain persistently fashionable, I persist in obstinate optimism. The scandals and losses of recent years have made many people open to, even hungry for, change, more aware than ever that business is broken for all of us. And we do not fight for change alone; everyone is changing.

Mary Giery Smith

Changing the game has ALWAYS been women's mission, even if it was unconscious. Throughout history, when men were off fighting wars, women kept civilization alive. Now we are changing the business world and we will continue to do so with an increasing rate of return in the coming years. I think the biggest reason that we will continue to change the workplace is that more and more men in recent generations have been raised by working mothers.

Natural Allies

Nowhere is change more important than in men. Many men dislike the anachronistic stereotypes as much as we do—and they feel just as trapped, belittled, and alienated by them. Men don't suffer the same financial and political penalties that women do—but, increasingly, they feel as insulted and frustrated by the remnants of the old-boy culture. In August 2002, I received this email from an executive at a Fortune 100 company:

Jason Miles

My career is moving quickly and I feel fortunate for the recognition and pay that I receive. That does not, however, mean that I am happy about the environment in which I work. In fact, if I would agree to play more golf (which brings me no joy), would agree to let my suppliers take me out to $75 dinners (I'd rather spend the time with my wife) and would stop pointing out the fact that my senior management team routinely over-states my company's competitive advantages, I'd probably be much higher up the chain of command right now.

I agree with you (and the statistics) that there are far too few women in top positions in corporate America, and that many women are under-paid. I am happy that you point out that there are plenty of men (myself included) who detest the old-boy networks that have such a strangle-hold on our companies. What I never pieced together before was that the barriers that professional women face are, in fact, the same barriers that I face. I have had allies around me all of this time and just never realized it.

About a year after this email, Jason decided to make some changes in his life. He changed jobs and he changed departments. He decided that he'd spent too much of his career battling toxic bosses and that it wasn't worth the battle any more.

Jason Miles

The battle only serves to feed their egos. Having sought and found a place in my company that is not ruled by toxic bosses, I have finally won something—and that something is the right to control my own career. I look around me now and I see a group of individuals who have all sought out that same right, and we make a great team. It may only be a pocket within my company, but it is a good place to work and grow just the same. I used to feel like I was always struggling alone against the things that I saw as wrong in my work environment. Now I feel like I have joined a quiet, but growing movement to make that environment better.

Jason now works for a woman in a department run by a woman. And he's right: it is a growing movement. The search for self-determination, the right to live a life according to values, is driving more and more men to question the old paradigms—and to find them old, stale, and unproductive.

John McGarr

In male-dominated companies earlier in my career, the responsibility to solve the problem falls to the manager responsible for the business unit encountering the problem. This poor chap is expected to go into his office, lock the door, sift through all available information until he emerges like a battle-weary gladiator with the Holy Grail solution to the problem. It is then offered for Royal Assent—any hesitation or inability to go through this corporate hazing is viewed as a sign of weakness under pressure, prompting the vultures to begin circling for the kill.

At our place now, there is a value that you will never succeed without the collaboration of your peers. Instead of being isolated with the weight of the world upon one's shoulders, you are expected to bring forth the problem, and toss it into a group discussion for all

> to problem-solve. The process forces all to release the pursuit of individual glory for the betterment of the group.
>
> As I ponder the dynamic it occurs to me that the traditional culture of organizations, modeled after the military, is a "survival of the fittest" one, where the dominant lion gets the most respect. Whereas this culture seems to focus much less on individual success and just focuses on "winning" as an organization, where the most supportive and forthcoming get the most respect. And apart from delivering incredible business results as an organization, it is a whole lot more fun working day to day in this environment than worrying about getting my "game face on" as I enter the coliseum. And if the company is focused on winning as a unified team, how do you think the market would view the (female) CEO as they turn in remarkable business results year in and year out?

That John's company is so successful challenges the old excuse that macho management styles and structures are commercial imperatives. And now those companies that cling to these old extremes aren't just losing their women; they're losing the men too. I hear regularly from men in investment banks who walk away from huge salaries because they want to prioritize personal values over corporate rewards. Like women, these men want to make their own choices, not choose from a severely limited corporate menu. They seek to reclaim their humanity—which, more often than not, takes the shape of providing for their wives some of the backup and support that they themselves received earlier in their career. The fairness they struggle with at home has a profound impact on how they think about work. It changes everything.

Jason Miles

> It used to be normal for me, two to three days a week, to arrive home from work in a bad mood and spend an hour or two by myself, just mulling over the things about my job that upset me. For the most part I haven't experienced that feeling or need in the past few months. Also, by opening up to the realities that I face at work, I've learned a lot about myself. I've reached a comfort level with my own career, in which I am no longer terrified of the prospect of someday being fired, or quitting my job without a new position lined up. That comfort level has spilled over into my personal life, and the results have been great.

I find now that I'm more aware of the feelings that my wife and friends are experiencing from their own careers, and that I can support them not just by listening, but also by coaching. Take my wife, for example. I've always done my best to support her in her career decisions. Recently, I've been more active in helping her to think about alternative solutions to her concerns and issues. One concern has been around the impact of gender in her office. Many of her male colleagues in similar roles have been promoted ahead of her. A few months ago, I encouraged her to attend a negotiations course to help address this concern. She ended up attending a seminar designed for women, on how to better negotiate salaries and promotions. Just last week she went to her annual review and made it clear to her management that she felt she deserved a promotion, and wanted to know what it was going to take to get it. She walked out of that meeting with a commitment from her management to file the paperwork the next day, and her promotion will be official shortly. We were both thrilled, obviously.

Men supporting women takes many forms. When Alan Milburn left the British government, in which he served at cabinet level for many years, he did so because he could no longer stand the toxic lifestyle that government required. He wanted time with his family, he wanted more time for himself—and he wanted to be fair to his wife.

Alan Milburn

Women have been on the front line traditionally of juggling responsibilities and managing the work/life balance. But that's changing and changing fast. And I think more and more men nowadays want to be more involved in the upbringing of their children, and I think that's a good thing.

Ruth had already given up a huge amount. She'd been training to be a consultant for a lot of years and had had to make a lot of sacrifices. Partially because we'd had kids but also to make space for me and my career. She trained part time rather than full time which meant that the people that she was at university with as medical students were already qualified, and getting on with their careers as consultants, while she was still a Junior Doctor. She had supported me throughout all of this and I felt I owed a responsibility back. Relationships can only work if there's give and take.[4]

Making choices consistent with values feels hard—but its effects are liberating and profound. Alan Milburn found that he not only gained time with his children, but the quality of his conversations with people changed. Many men describe how spending time with their children changes how they think, what kinds of stories they're proud to bring home. John McGarr found that escaping a toxic work environment changed every one of his relationships.

John McGarr

> The change that has resulted from the new culture was brought to life for me just this past weekend as I was enjoying a sunny fall Friday afternoon (after working at home for the day) teaching my daughter to ride her two-wheeler, while her younger sister squealed with delight and my son did consecutive cartwheels across the lawn. I paused for a moment and said to my wife "Ya know, this would never happen if we had not moved. I wouldn't be here right now and I would miss all this." Not only would I not have been there physically, I also would not have been there mentally or emotionally. To me that is the greatest cost of the military-model culture. Now that my mental and emotional energy is less overtaxed, I can more equally contribute at home. My relationship with my wife is at its zenith—we both feel it getting stronger, not weaker over time.
>
> The other interesting "side effect" is that both my wife and I are much more comfortable making tough choices in our day to day life—in regard to the friends we keep, the things we buy (or choose not to buy), the activities we choose to participate in. We tend not to pursue relationships with old friends who have bought into the traditional work culture—we find ourselves out of sync with them, and have been opened to a new group of friends who share our values. We focus our discretionary income on inexpensive activities all can enjoy together, rather than toys or events that keeps us apart from one another.

Some commentators describe this change as the *feminization* of work; women often avoid the term because they feel it invites attack. I tend to see the trend as the *humanization* of work, a movement in which women undoubtedly are the leaders. The ideal we all increasingly move toward is not one of military-style command and control but something far more feminine. Asked who they most admire in the world, five hundred business men and women did not cite military or political leaders, they did not even cite a man. They cited their mothers.

Men like Jason Miles, Alan Milburn, and John McGarr make me optimistic because they are not alone. I've spoken to hundreds of men who feel as they do. Men who described every day at work as a battle—and hated it. Men who are teased by their peers with Mother's Day cards and demeaning nicknames. Men who struggle to achieve fairness at home, with their wives and children—and then find they can't abandon that struggle at work. As men spend more time with their children, this changes who the men are, what they want, and what they teach. This represents profound, systemic change. Work starts to assume a different location in the topography of all of our lives, presenting a fundamental challenge to managements that still use the old maps.

In my own career, I've watched myself undergo tremendous change, from working like a man to, finally, working like myself. From a punitive management style to an empowering one (which was both more effective and a lot easier). From ideas of control to concepts of service. Certainly the emotional dynamic of my life is a lot richer and feels a great deal more sustainable. I know that I am truer to myself than I used to be—and a lot less interested in fitting into men's ideas of what I should be. This also means that my relationships with women have improved and I am more curious about what they've discovered in their quest for better ways of work. I'm immensely concerned that the old ways I've left behind are so tenacious, and I've spent enough time battling big institutions to know that they don't surrender or admit defeat. They will change when they have to and then call themselves innovators.

I am confident that, one day, our parallel universe will become the status quo. That we will look back on these years of transition and wonder why everyone couldn't see that. But I'm not complacent. I watch as the number of female directors drops and I know that progress is contingent, not inevitable. The enemies of change are always busy; we have been through dark days and will go through more. As long as we have high schools with the ethos of beauty pageants, proms that teach girls to compete for male attention, a business culture that wants to emulate *Survivor,* and greedy business leaders promoting cynicism, the parallel universe will have to defend itself. We will watch the macho triumphalism that celebrates every time a woman appears to give up and go home—and we will know that the real story is elsewhere. We will continue to be trivialized, marginalized, and discouraged—but we will break through our isolation and find from each other the tactics we need not just to endure but to prevail.

When I started thinking about the lives of women in business, I used to think in terms of catching up with men. But now I see that that is irrelevant, because it is women who are the trailblazers. Our career patterns, which companies see as so eccentric and challenging, are the shape of things to come. It isn't just women who reject submission to the corporate will; men too are leaving for the same excellent reasons that women first voiced: we want a life, we want to know our children while they are children, we seek engagement in our communities, we want to serve seriously the values that companies should learn to cherish. When we try to harmonize work values and life values, we seek to avoid the conflicts that men have endured, and suffered from, for centuries. We don't believe in making bad choices. We believe in redefining them.

The phenomenal growth of women-owned businesses gives me tremendous hope: despite paltry support, they continue to build real jobs with real products with cultures that remain defiantly human. But of all the many brilliant things that I have seen women do, nothing gives me greater confidence in my optimism than watching how women use power. The disenfranchised are always kinder and more generous than the empowered—they have nothing to lose. The acid test comes when they gain power. And the truly fantastic thing about women is that when we gain power, few of us are perpetuating the sins of the past. We work hard not to repeat the sins of our bosses. We reject exclusive cultures. We may have been humiliated, stereotyped, trivialized, and marginalized—but when we build our own businesses, this is not how we treat others. We are not building companies that favor women over men, that humiliate, diminish, or otherwise exclude men. Unlike men, we hire both men and women at equal rates, forging a future that looks very different from the past we've known too well.[5] We employ men, empower men, promote men, support men. We are inclusive. There are no gatecrashers at our parties; the gates are wide open.

Notes

Introduction

1. In D. Marlino and F. Wilson, *Teen Girls on Business: Are They Being Empowered?* (Boston: Simmons College School of Management, 2002).
2. Catalyst Census of Women Corporate Officers and Top Earners in the Fortune 500, 2002.

Chapter One

1. See S. Wellington, *Be Your Own Mentor* (New York: Random House, 2001).
2. Catalyst Census, 2002.
3. Aurora Gender Capital recently introduced a great online tool, Where Women Want to Work, that collects data from both companies and employees [http://www.www2wk.com].

Chapter Two

1. "Women in Leadership: A European Business Imperative," Catalyst and the Conference Board Europe, cited in "Women in Corporate Leadership: Progress and Prospects," published by Catalyst, 1996. Similar figures for Europe can be found in "Study Finds Stereotypes Are Top Barrier for Women Business Leaders" in *Europe Across Regions and Countries* (Scottsdale, Ariz.: National Gender Institute, 2002).
2. U.S. figures are from Families and Work Institute, 2002; U.K. figures, from Office for National Statistics, 2003.
3. "Out of the Doll's House: Just a Girl." Unedited rushes, BBC TV, 1987.

4. See F. D. Blau and L. Kahn, "Gender Differences in Pay," National Bureau of Economic Research Working Paper #7732, June 2000 (U.K. Office for National Statistics, 2003). The closest pay parity—90 percent—is achieved in Belgium.
5. See L. Babcock and S. Laschever, *Women Don't Ask* (Princeton, N.J.: Princeton University Press, 2003).
6. Babcock and Laschever, 2003.
7. *BBC News,* June 13, 2002.
8. S. E. Barnes, "The White Knight Methode," *Executive Female* (Jan./Feb. 1991), 40–42.
9. D. Tannen, *Talking from 9 to 5: Women and Men at Work* (New York: HarperCollins, 1995).
10. S. Wellington, *Be Your Own Mentor* (New York: Random House, 2001).
11. C. K. Goman, Ph.D., "If Women Only Knew What They Know," in *Link & Learn,* Linkage, Inc., Dec. 1, 2002.
12. D. E. Summerville, "Dress Code . . . Appearance Does Matter" [http://www.dcwebwomen.org/resources/wib/981130.html], Nov. 30, 1998.
13. S. Whitely, CEO of Whitely and Co., Women in Business Conference, 2001.
14. "Powerfully Nice: Can Women Get Ahead By Being Nice?" *Good Morning America,* July 16, 2001.
15. R. Gerber, "Bully Broads," James MacGregor Burns Academy of Leadership, University of Maryland, 2001.

Chapter Three

1. J. Coburn, "Sexual Harassment: Why Is Society So Shocked?" [http://www.now.org/nnt/01-97/shocked.html], *National NOW Times,* 1997. A National Organization for Women study came up with the figure of 80 percent. Other studies reckon that "more than one half of women who work outside the home report that they have been sexually harassed" (Equal Employment Opportunity Commission, 2001).
2. *BBC News* reporting on the EOC Review [http://news.bbc.co.uk/1/hi/business/1746689.stm], Jan. 7, 2002.
3. C. Dyer, "£180,000 for Sexual Bullying," *Guardian,* June 28, 2003.
4. Equal Employment Opportunity Commission, 2001.
5. *Sunday Times,* Nov. 24, 2002.
6. Coburn, 1997.
7. BMJ.com editorial, April 2003.
8. *Sunday Times,* Nov. 24, 2002.

9. Women in Corporate Leadership, Catalyst, 2003.
10. Fast Company conference, San Francisco, June 2003.
11. *Guardian,* May 26, 2003.

Chapter Five

1. *Wall Street Journal,* April 21, 1999, page B1. See also Kelly Barron, "Limited Expectations," *Forbes* magazine [http://www.forbes.com/forbes/2001/0305/145.html], March 5, 2001.
2. P. Senge et al., "Looking Ahead: Implications of the Present," *Harvard Business Review,* Sept. 1997.
3. A. H. Eagly and L. L. Carli, "Women and Men as Leaders," in *The Nature of Leadership,* edited by J. Antonakis, R. J. Sternberg, and A. T. Cianciolo (Thousand Oaks, Calif.: Sage, 2004).
4. In addition to defining her skills in interviews, Jane reported saying "things like 'I want this job so bad I can taste it' and 'This is my dream job' (even though I've always heard you should never sound desperate or too enthusiastic). I also asked this question, 'If I were selected for this position, what would you want me to accomplish in the first three months, the first year, and the first two years?' thinking of it as a way to encourage them to view me in that position."
5. "As Leaders, Women Rule," *Business Week,* Nov. 22, 2000.
6. *International Herald Tribune,* June 29, 2001. Also stated by D. Asher in his tips on the hidden job market, cited in "Networking: What It Is and Why You Should Do It" [http://cdc.richmond.edu/studentsalumni/networkingalumni/definition.html].
7. "Executive Sweet," Asian American Wonder Women [http://goldsea.com/WW/jungandrea/jungandrea.html].
8. Babcock and Laschever, 2003. See also data from Hagberg Consulting Group.
9. Data from Hagberg Consulting Group and others, 2000.

Chapter Six

1. In J. Lever, "Office Sex and Romance Survey," *Elle,* 2002, and in "Workplace Dating," a study by the American Management Association, February 2003. See also S. Shellenbarger, "A Nation Failing to Get a Life," *Wall Street Journal,* Oct. 24, 2003.
2. E. Smith, J. D., "The Love Contract Debate" [http://www.srcpro.com/Articles-HumanCapital/The_Love_Contract_Debate.htm].
3. *Wall Street Journal* Women in Business Conference, London, 2003.

4. Other companies, like Shell, have learned how to do this. They used to appoint company chairs from corporate headquarters; now all company chairs are local employees, thus reducing the company's need to relocate so many people.
5. There were about 3.6 million copreneurs in the United States in 2001—and more than two hundred thousand in the United Kingdom. Both numbers are on the rise. Center for Media Research, Apr. 16, 2001, and "Taxman Accused of Killing Family Firms," *Guardian,* Sept. 11, 2003.

Chapter Seven

1. A. Crittenden, *The Price of Motherhood: Why the Most Important Job in the World Is Still the Least Valued* (New York: Henry Holt, 2001).
2. BT, for example, has a return and stay rate of 96 percent, according to Patricia Vaz, managing director of BT's Retail Customer Service.
3. In the 1870s, Edward C. Clark warned women that a college education would make brains get heavier and cause wombs to shrink.
4. L. Belkin, "The Opt Out Revolution," *New York Times,* Oct. 26, 2003, and M. Driscolle, "Selling Out," *Sunday Times,* Sept. 14, 2003, are just two in a very long line of similar pieces.
5. Some of the most alarming assertions that working mothers are shortchanging their kids are based on "evidence" that upon close inspection melts away. One allegation—that U.S. parents spend 40 percent less time with their kids than in 1965—is simply false. This number originally came from a report produced by John Robinson, a preeminent authority on how Americans use their time. Robinson later claimed that he had made a mistake and that his 1985 numbers were in error. In 1996, he was still furious over what he characterized as "the misuse of social science data by the family values groups. They take data out of context and use it to promote their narrow point of view." He believes that exaggerated reports of a parental time famine are based on a willful misinterpretation of data by ideologies whose agenda is to get women back into the home.
6. Data from *Women: The New Providers* (New York: Families and Work Institute, 1995).
7. U.S. Census Bureau, cited in *Business Week,* Oct. 20, 2003.
8. Women's Life Insurance Society (USA), 2000.
9. U.S. Department of Labor. Also *Guardian,* Sept. 13, 2003.
10. Working mothers in Britain say they have less than 10 percent of their salaries left when they have paid for child care and domestic help. *Guardian,* Aug. 28, 2003.

11. Crittenden, 2001.
12. P. M. Senge, *The Fifth Discipline* (New York: Currency, 1994).
13. "Why Women Executives Leave Corporate America for Entrepreneurial Ventures," a study by Korn/Ferry International, Columbia Business School, and the Duran Group, October 2001.

Chapter Eight

1. G. Epstein, "Breaking the Glass: More Women Reach Top Spots But Sexism Persists," *Barrons,* May 26, 2003.
2. Women in U.S. Corporate Leadership, Catalyst, 2003.
3. A. Eagly, "More Women at the Top: The Impact of Gender Roles and Leadership Style." Paper presented at Gender: From Costs to Benefits, the sixth symposium on gender research at Christian-Albrechts University of Kiel, Germany, Nov. 15–17, 2002.
4. S. Appold et al., "The Employment of Women Managers and Professionals in an Emerging Economy: Gender Inequality as an Organizational Practice," *Administrative Science Quarterly,* 43 (1998), 538–565. The authors persuasively argue the relevance of their findings to both developed and developing economies. In S. Zuboff and J. Maxmin, *The Support Economy: Why Corporations Are Failing Individuals and the Next Episode of Capitalism* (London: Allen Lane, 2003), pp. 127–130.
5. Women in U.S. Corporate Leadership, Catalyst, 2003.
6. "Empowering Women in Business," Feminist Majority Foundation [http://www.feminist.org/research/ewb_myths.html].
7. I am indebted to Joan Bakewell for this insight. She worked on the program.
8. Zuboff and Maxmin, 2003.
9. "Changing Places," BBC Radio 4, Sept. 5, 2003.
10. M.E.P. Seligman, Ph.D., *Authentic Happiness* (London: Nicholas Brealey Publishing, 2003).

Chapter Nine

1. Fast Company conference, San Francisco, June 2003.

Chapter Ten

1. *Women-Owned Businesses in 2004: Trends in the U.S. and 50 States* (Washington, D.C.: Center for Women's Business Research, April 2004).

2. Korn/Ferry, 2001. Of the 425 women executives studied, 272 left to start businesses and 153 left to join them.
3. Doris Drucker's management guru husband, Peter Drucker, helped by doing the taxes—but otherwise, she was on her own. She tells the great story of her business, RSQ, in *Inc.* (October 1997).
4. According to the U.S. Small Business Administration, cited in *WOW! Facts 2002,* Business Women's Network [http://www.ewowfacts.com/index.html]. Perhaps even more interesting is the growth rate of these women-owned businesses over the last ten years: 171 percent in construction, 157 percent in wholesale trade, 140 percent in transportation and communication, 130 percent in agribusiness, and 112 percent in manufacturing.
5. Women Entrepreneurs Study: A Joint Research Project by Cheskin Research, Santa Clara University Center for Innovation and Entrepreneurship, and The Center for New Futures, Jan. 2000.
6. Ibid.
7. C. Brush, N. Carter, E. Gatewood, P. Greene, and M. Hart, *Gatekeepers of Venture Growth* (Kansas City, Mo.: Kauffman Foundation, 2004).
8. Cheskin Research, 2000.
9. Zuboff and Maxmin, 2003.
10. Women-owned businesses over the last five years have increased employment by 18 percent, compared to 8 percent in other businesses, according to research presented in 2004 by Project Tsunami, a trilateral organization aimed at increasing rates of female entrepreneurialism around the world.
11. Hagberg Consulting Group and others, 2000. See also "As Leaders, Women Rule" in *Business Week,* Nov. 20, 2000.
12. T. Peters, *Re-Imagine* (New York: Dorling Kindersley, 2002).

Chapter Eleven

1. Korn/Ferry poll, 2003.
2. Gallup poll, cited in *Penn State Smeal College of Business News,* July 2002.
3. D. Marlino and F. Wilson, *Teen Girls on Business: Are They Being Empowered?* (Boston: Simmons College School of Management, 2002).
4. "The Choice," BBC Radio 4, Nov. 11, 2003.
5. Center for Women's Business Research. Women-owned businesses have workforces that comprise 52 percent women and 48 percent men, whereas men-owned businesses employ, on average, 38 percent women and 62 percent men.

Web Resources

Advancing Women
http://www.advancingwomen.com
AllBusiness.com
http://www.allbusiness.com
American Business Women's Association
www.abwa.org
American Woman's Economic Development Corp.
http://www.awed.org/
Aurora Women's Network
http://www.busygirl.com/
BlueSuitMom.com
http://www.bluesuitmom.com
British Chambers of Commerce
http://www.chamberonline.co.uk/
British Federation of Women Graduates
http://www.bfwg.org.uk/
Business and Professional Women UK
http://www.bpwuk.org.uk/
Business and Professional Women/USA & BPW Foundation
http://www.BPWUSA.org
Business Bureau UK
http://www.businessbureau-uk.co.uk/
Business Link
http://www.businesslink.gov.uk/bdotg/action/home
Business Women's Network
http://www.bwni.com
Career Women.com
http://www.careerwomen.com/
Career.com
http://www.career.com
Catalyst
http://www.catalystwomen.org

Center for Women, Leadership, and Management, Simmons School of Management
http://www.simmons.edu/gsm
Center for Women's Business Research
http://www.nfwbo.org
Diversity.com
http://www.diversity.com
Engender
http://www.engender.org.uk
Entrepreneur.com
http://www.entrepreneur.com
Entreworld.org
http://www.entreworld.org
Equal Employment Opportunity Commission
http://www.eeoc.gov
Equal Opportunities Commission
http://www.eoc.org.uk
European Women's Lobby
http://www.womenlobby.org
EveryWoman
http://www.everywoman.co.uk/
Executive Woman
http://www.execwoman.com/
Families and Work Institute
http://www.familiesandwork.org
Fawcett Society
http://www.fawcettsociety.org.uk
Federal Trade Commission
http://www.ftc.gov/
Feminist.com
http://www.feminist.com
Financial Mail Women's Forum
http://www.fmwf.com/
Forum for Women Entrepreneurs
http://www.fwe.org
Girls Inc.
http://www.girlsinc.org
Home Based Working Mums
http://www.HBWM.com
HomeWorkingMom.com
http://www.homeworkingmom.com/
Leadership America, Inc.
http://www.leadershipamerica.com

Mother at Work
http://www.motheratwork.co.uk/
National Association for Female Executives
http://www.nafe.com
National Association of Women Business Owners
http://www.nawbo.org/
National Business Association
http://www.nationalbusiness.org/
National Organization for Women
http://www.now.org
National Women Business Owners Corporation
http://www.nwboc.org/
National Women's Business Council
http://www.nwbc.gov/
Network for Successful UK Women
http://www.topwomenuk.com/
Office of Women's Business Ownership
http://www.sba.gov/financing/special/women.html
Small Business Service
http://www.sbs.gov.uk/
SmallBusinessAdvice.org.uk, National Federation of Enterprise Agencies
http://www.smallbusinessadvice.org.uk/sbas.asp
StartUpBiz.com
http://www.startupbiz.com/
SwiftWork.com
http://www.swiftwork.com/
The Bag Lady Global Directory of Women in Business
http://www.the-bag-lady.co.uk
The Real Deal, Channel 4
http://www.channel4.com/life/microsites/R/realdeal/
Where Women Want to Work
http://www.www2wk.com
The Women's Company
http://www.thewomenscompany.com/
The Work Foundation
http://www.theworkfoundation.com
U.S. Department of Labor, Women's Bureau
http://www.dol.gov/wb
United Nations WomenWatch, Division for the Advancement of Women
http://www.un.org/womenwatch/daw/
Women and Equality Unit, Department of Trade and Industry
http://www.womenandequalityunit.gov.uk

Women at Work
http://www.womenatwork.co.uk/
Women Entrepreneurs, IBM
http://www.ibm/businesscenter/us/womens
Women for Hire
http://www.womenforhire.com
Women in Leadership Summit, Linkage Inc.
http://www.linkage.com/conferences/leadership/wil/
Women Unlimited
http://www.women-unlimited.com/
Women Working 2000 and Beyond
http://www.womenworking2000.com/
Women's Business Center
http://www.womensbusinesscenter.org/
Women's National Commission
http://www.thewnc.org.uk
Women's Work
http://www.wwork.com/
Work & Family Connection
http://www.workfamily.com

Bibliography

American Management Association. "Workplace Dating: 44 Percent of Office Romances Led to Marriage, AMA Survey Shows." [http://www.amanet.org/press/amanews/workplace_dating.htm] Feb. 10, 2003.

Appold, S., Siengthai, S., and Kasarda, J. D. "The Employment of Women Managers and Professionals in an Emerging Economy: Gender Inequality as an Organizational Practice." *Administrative Science Quarterly,* 1998, *43,* 538–565.

Asher, D. "Networking: What It Is and Why You Should Do It." University of Richmond Career Development Center [http://cdc.richmond.edu/studentsalumni/networkingalumni/definition.html].

Babcock, L., and Laschever, S. *Women Don't Ask: Negotiation and the Gender Divide.* Princeton, N.J.: Princeton University Press, 2003.

Barnes, S. E. "The White Knight Method." *Executive Female,* 1991, 40–42.

Barron, K. "Limited Expectations." [http://www.forbes.com/forbes/2001/0305/145.html] 2001.

Belkin, L. "The Opt Out Revolution." *The New York Times,* Oct. 26, 2003, p. 42.

Blau, F. D., and Kahn, L. M. *Gender Differences in Pay.* NBER Working paper no. w7332, (published as "Black-White Earnings Over the 1970s and 1980s: Gender Differences in Trends," *Review of Economics and Statistics,* 1992, *74*(2), 276–286), National Bureau of Economic Research, June 2000.

Bowman, D. "The Problem of Sexual Harassment." TTG Consultants [http://ttgconsultants.com/articles/sexHarass.html], July 31, 2003.

Carter, H. "Study Finds 90 Percent of Mothers' Wages Spent on Home Help and Childcare." *Guardian* [http://money.guardian.co.uk/womenandmoney/story/0,11505,1030699,00.html], Aug. 28, 2003.

"Census of Women Corporate Officers and Earners in the Fortune 500." Catalyst [http://www.catalystwomen.org/press_room/factsheets/COTE%20Factsheet%202002.pdf], July 22, 2003.

Chang, H. K. "Businesswomen Discuss Career Changes, Global Management, Skills to Reach Top." Stanford Business School [http://www.gsb.stanford.edu/news/2001womensconf.html], Feb. 3, 2001.

Coburn, J. "Viewpoint: Sexual Harassment: Why Is Society So Shocked?" *National NOW Times* [http://www.now.org/nnt/01-97/shocked.html], Jan. 1997.

Conlin, M. "Unmarried America." *Business Week* [http://aol.businessweek.com/magazine/content/03_42/b3854001_mz001.htm], Oct. 20, 2003.

Coward, R. *Sacred Cows.* London: HarperCollins, 1999.

Crittenden, A. *The Price of Motherhood: Why the Most Important Job in the World Is Still the Least Valued.* New York: Henry Holt, 2001.

"Discrimination Payouts Rise 38 Percent." *BBC News* [http://news.bbc.co.uk/1/hi/business/1746689.stm], Aug. 1, 2003.

Driscolle, M. "Selling Out." *Sunday Times,* Sept. 14, 2003.

Drogin, R. "Wal-Mart's Income Gap?" *BusinessWeek.com* [http://www.businessweek.com/magazine/content/03_09/b3822068_mz021.htm], Dec. 8, 2003.

Drucker, D. "Mrs. Drucker Starts a Business." *Inc.* [http://www.inc.com/magazine/1997/1001/1337.html], 1997.

Drucker, P. *Management Challenges for the 21st Century.* Oxford: Butterworth, 1999.

Dworkin, A. *Heartbreak: The Political Memoir of a Feminist Militant.* New York: Basic Books, 2002.

Dyer, C. "£180,000 for Sexual Bullying." *Guardian* [http://www.guardian.co.uk/uk_news/story/0,3604,986718,00.html], June 28, 2003.

Eagly, A. H. "More Women at the Top: The Impact of Gender Roles and Leadership Style." Paper presented at Gender—From Costs to Benefits: Sixth Symposium on Gender Research, Kiel University, Germany, Nov. 15–17, 2002.

Eagly, A. H., and Carli, L. L. "Women and Men as Leaders." In J. Antonakis, R. J. Sternberg, and A. T. Cianciolo (eds.), *The Nature of Leadership.* Thousand Oaks, Calif.: Sage, 2004.

"Empowering Women in Business: Myths about Women in Business." Feminist Majority Foundation [http://www.feminist.org/research/ewb_myths.html], Nov. 24, 2003.

Epstein, G. "Breaking the Glass: More Women Reach Top Spots But Sexism Persists." *Barrons* [http://online.wsj.com/barrons/article/0,,SB1053729317616867OO,00.html?mod=b_this_weeks_magazine_main], Dec. 8, 2003.

"Executive Sweet." Goldsea [http://goldsea.com/WW/jungandrea/jungandrea.html], Sept. 15, 2003.

Faludi, S. *Backlash: The Undeclared War Against American Women.* London: Vintage, 1993.

Families and Work Institute. *Women: The New Providers.* New York: Whirlpool Foundation Study, 1995.

Fisher, H. *The First Sex: The Natural Talents of Women and How They Are Changing the World.* New York: Ballantine, 2000.

Fletcher, J. *Disappearing Acts: Gender, Power and Relational Practice at Work.* Boston: MIT Press, 2001.

"Gender Pay Gap: April 2003 Difference Smallest on Record." Office for National Statistics [http://www.statistics.gov.uk/CCI/nugget.asp?ID=167&Pos=4&ColRank=1&Rank=144], Oct. 16, 2003.

Gerard, J. "And It's a Big Kiss-Off from Her." Interview with Kate Bleasdale. *Sunday Times,* Nov. 24, 2002.

Gerber, R. "Bully Broads." [http://www.academy.umd.edu/AboutUs/news/articles/09-12-01.htm], Sept. 12, 2001.

Goman, C. K. "If Women Only Knew What They Know." Link&Learn newsletter [http://www.linkageinc.com/newsletter/archives/knowledgemanagement/if_women_knew_goman.shtml], Dec. 1, 2002.

Hanauer, C. *The Bitch in the House: Twenty-Six Women Tell the Truth About Sex, Solitude, Work, Motherhood, and Marriage.* New York: Morrow, 2002.

"Highlights of the National Study of the Changing Workforce: Executive Summary." Families and Work Institute [http://www.familiesandwork.org/summary/nscw2002.pdf], 2002.

Hochschild, A. R. *The Time Bind: When Work Becomes Home and Home Becomes Work.* New York: Henry Holt, 1997.

Hughes, M. "Single, Female and Worst Off in Retirement." *Guardian* [http://money.guardian.co.uk/pensions/story/0,6453,1040769,00.html], Sept. 13, 2003.

Inman, P. "Taxman Accused of Killing Family Firms." *Guardian* [http://www.guardian.co.uk/business/story/0,3604,1039615,00.html], Sept. 11, 2003.

Jampol, J. "Looking for a Job? Networking Is Best Bet." *International Herald Tribune* [http://www.iht.com/articles/24746.html], June 29, 2001.

Kanter, R. M. *Men and Women of the Corporation.* New York: Basic Books, 1993.

"Key Facts." Center for Women's Business Research [http://www.womensbusinessresearch.org/key.html], July 11, 2003.

Lever, J. Office Sex and Romance Survey database. Findings posted on http://www.ELLE.com and http://www.MSNBC.com.

"Like War, Retail Is Hell, According to the Limited." *Wall Street Journal,* Apr. 21, 1999.

LoVerde, M. *I Used to Have a Handle on Life But It Broke: Six Power Solutions for Women with Too Much to Do.* New York: Fireside Books, 2002.

MacLeod, C. "Dinosaurs in the Gallery." *Guardian,* May 26, 2003.

Marlino, D., and Wilson, F. *Teen Girls on Business: Are They Being Empowered?* Boston: Committee of 200 and Simmons College of Management, 2002.

Micklethwait, J., and Wooldridge, A. *The Company: A Short History of a Revolutionary Idea.* London: Modern Library, 2003.

Minton, T. "Caught in the Pact: Couples Involved in Office Dalliances Required to Sign Love Contract" [http://www.businessweek.com/2000/00_47/b3708146.htm], 2001.

"One in Four Women Has Office Sex." *BBC News* [http://news.bbc.co.uk/1/hi/business/2042540.stm], Oct. 20, 2003.

O'Reilly, C. A., and Pfeffer, J. *Hidden Value: How Great Companies Achieve Extraordinary Results with Ordinary People.* Cambridge, Mass.: Harvard Business School Press, 2000.

Orenstein, P. *Schoolgirls: Young Women, Self-Esteem, and the Confidence Gap.* New York: Anchor Books, 1995.

Orenstein, P. *Flux: Women on Sex, Work, Love, Kids, and Life in a Half-Changed World.* New York: Anchor Books, 2001.

Pearson, A. *I Don't Know How She Does It.* London: Random House, 2002.

Perlow, L. A. *Finding Time: How Corporations, Individuals, and Families Can Benefit From New Work Practices.* Ithaca, N.Y.: Cornell University, 1997.

Perlow, L. A. *When You Say Yes But Mean No: How Silencing Conflict Wrecks Relationships and Companies—and What You Can Do About It.* New York: Crown Business, 2003.

Peters, T. *Re-Imagine!* New York: Dorling Kindersley, 2003.

Pfeffer, J. *Managing with Power: Politics and Influence in Organizations.* Cambridge, Mass.: Harvard Business School Press, 1994.

"Powerfully Nice: Can Women Get Ahead by Being Nice?" On *Good Morning America,* ABCNews.com [http://abcnews.go.com/sections/GMA/GoodMorningAmerica/GMA010716Bully_Broads.html], July 16, 2001.

Quinlan, M. L. *Just Ask A Woman: Cracking the Code of What Women Want and How They Buy.* New York: Wiley, 2003.

Rapoport, R., Bailyn, L., Fletcher, J. K., and Pruitt, B. H. *Beyond Work-Family Balance: Advancing Gender Equity and Workplace Performance.* San Francisco: Jossey-Bass, 2002.

"Results on Office Sex and Romance Survey by Cal State L.A. Professor Released." California State University [http://www.calstate.edu/newsline/Archive/01-02/020514-LA.shtml], May 14, 2002.

Rubin, Ht. *The Princessa: Machiavelli for Women.* New York: Doubleday, 1997.

Ruderman, M. N., and Ohlott, P. J. *Standing at the Crossroads: Next Steps for High-Achieving Women.* San Francisco: Jossey-Bass, 2002.

Ruhe, J. A., and Davis, J. H. *Gender Differences in Ethical Orientation in Different Educational Settings.* Unpublished research paper, 2003.

Ruhe, J., and McElroy, J. "Spirituality and Ethics for Women in the Workplace." Paper presented at the eighth annual conference of the International Association for Business and Society, 1997.

Seligman, M.E.P. *Authentic Happiness.* London: Nicholas Brealey, 2003.

Senge, P. M. *The Fifth Discipline.* New York: Currency, 1994.

Senge, P. M., Drucker, P. F., Dyson, E., Handy, C., and Saffo, P. "Looking Ahead: Implications of the Present," *Harvard Business Review,* Sept. 1997.

"Sexual Harassment Is No Joke, Says EOC." Equal Opportunity Commission [http://www.eoc.org.uk/EOCeng/EOCcs/News/press_releases_2001_35.asp], Aug. 29, 2001.

Sharpe, R. "As Leaders, Women Rule." *Business Week,* Nov. 20, 2000.

Shellenbarger, S. "A Nation Failing to Get a Life: Unromantic Side of Office Romance." *Wall Street Journal* online [http://online.wsj.com/article/0,,SB1063841919558902OO,00.html], Oct. 24, 2003.

Smith, E. "The Love Contract Debate." [http://www.srcpro.com/Articles-HumanCapital/The_Love_Contract_Debate.htm] 2001.

Spence, B., and Wellington, S. *Be Your Own Mentor.* New York: Random House, 2001.

Summerville, D. E. "Dress Code . . . Appearance Does Matter." [http://www.dcwebwomen.org/resources/wib/981130.html] Dec. 14, 1998.

Tannen, D. *Talking from 9 to 5: Women and Men at Work.* London: Virago, 1994.

"Trusting Big Business." Penn State Smeal College of Business, 2002.

"Where Female Execs Do Better: A Scorecard." *Business Week* online [http://www.businessweek.com/2000/00_47/b3708146.htm], Nov. 20, 2000.

"Where the Women Are." Center for Media Research [http://www.mediapost.com/research/cfmr_briefArchive.cfm?s=80293], 2001.

"Why Women Executives Leave Corporate America for Entrepreneurial Ventures." Korn/Ferry International [http://www.kornferry.com/Library/Process.asp?P=PR_Detail&CID=217&LID=1], 2001.

Williams, J. *Unbending Gender: Why Family and Work Conflict and What to Do About It.* Oxford: Oxford University Press, 2000.

Women and Diversity: WOW! Facts 2003. (4th ed.) Washington, D.C.: Business Women's Network and Diversity Best Practices, 2003.

"Women Entrepreneurs Study." Cheskin Research, with Santa Clara University Center for Innovation and Entrepreneurship and The Center for New Futures [http://www.debmcdonald.com/womenentrepreneurs.pdf], 2000.

"Women in Leadership: A European Business Imperative." In *Study Finds Stereotypes Are Top Barrier for Women Business Leaders in Europe Across Regions and Countries.* Scottsdale National Gender Institute [http://www.gendertraining.com/sngi_press_study_finds_stereotypes.html], July 18, 2003.

"Women in U.S. Corporate Leadership." Catalyst [http://www.catalystwomen.org/press_room/factsheets/WomenInUSCorporateLeadership.pdf], 2003.

Women's Institute for a Secure Retirement. "WISER Special Report: and . . . the Pay Gap's Connected to the Retirement Gap!" [http://www.wiser.heinz.org/special_report_pay_equity.html] 2003.

Women's Life Insurance Society. "Distressing Facts." [http://www.womanslifeins.com/html/navbar/commitframe.html] 2003.

"Workplace Bullying." BMJ.com [http://bmj.bmjjournals.com/cgi/content/full/326/7393/776], July 25, 2003.

Wurtzel, E. *Bitch: In Praise of Difficult Women.* New York: Anchor Books, 1999.

Zeldin, T. *An Intimate History of Humanity.* New York: HarperCollins, 1996.

Zuboff, S., and Maxmin, J. *The Support Economy: Why Corporations Are Failing Individuals and the Next Episode of Capitalism.* London: Allen Lane, 2003.

Acknowledgments

This book would not have come about without the support of Alan Webber. Because he challenged me to produce something "worth publishing," I wrote a cover story, "The Female CEO, c. 2002" for his *Fast Company* magazine. I knew he wouldn't publish it unless he thought it was worthwhile, and when he did, he was rewarded for his risk. The magazine and I received thousands of replies to the piece and that tidal wave generated this book. I am deeply indebted to Alan for supporting my desire to tell the truth as I saw it.

Clare Alexander first suggested that I might write a book about something—and has been enormously patient and selfless as I tried to figure out what it was. Talking about our children, and their expectations of what the work world held for them, was the initial inspiration for this book and I'm indebted to Clare for her confidence that I could write it.

Likewise, Fiona Wilson's first response to the earliest draft of this project persuaded me that I was not wasting my time. She and Rob Wilson, along with Jan and John Troha, sustained me though many interview trips. I would like to thank Joyce Fletcher, Deborah Merrill-Sands, and Deborah Kolb of the Simmons College School of Management, who, as academics, were generous enough to endorse and encourage a practitioner. Anne Pace kept me focused on the positive, reminding me of my optimism and persuading me it wasn't foolish.

Fast Company magazine has been like a surrogate family to me. Their tremendous editorial, event, and research team—Linda Tischler, Gina Imperato, Elizabeth Busch, Polly LaBarre, and John Byrne—provided insight, feedback, and market intelligence that have always proved sound. Simmons College also provided feedback and resources that have been greatly appreciated.

Every interviewee in this book has contributed far, far more than is apparent. In particular, Chris Carosella, Cindy Solomon, Jill Silverstein, and Glenda Stone have been enormously helpful in deepening my thinking, broadening my research, and challenging my assumptions. Alice Eagly at Northwestern University and Jack Ruhe at St. Mary's College were extremely generous in sharing their research with a nonacademic.

Jennifer Mack is a promising businesswoman in her own right. Her stalwart research, together with her attention to detail, have informed a great deal of this book and we have both learned a lot working on it together. I am immensely grateful to her for her patience, perseverance, and good humor, and I hope the experience has helped to lay the foundations of a flourishing career. It goes without saying that any mistakes are mine—but there would be far more without the experience and insight of so many supporters.

Many people have helped me though the career that informs this book: Anne Barton, the late Gordon Clough, Piers Plowright, Trudy McGuinness, Roy Foster, Roy Davies, Deborah Perkin, Pippa Holloway, George Faber, Nick Bicat, Kate Leys, Peter Armstrong, Alan Yentob, Rob Goffee, Jan Schubert, Heather Mansfield, Jane Lighting, Nancy Braid, Vanessa Levy, Jane Balfour, Mario Cavalli, Paul Duggan, Steven Magruder, Francis X. Meaney, Guy Bradley, Harry Forsdick, David Wetherell, John Evans, Avram Miller, Felice Kincannon, Bob Crestani, Pamela Esty, Kate Bernhardt, Daphne Kuo, Roger Graef, Mollie Petrie, Guy Edwards, and Alan Rickman. I feel immensely privileged to have worked with such a rich array of artists, historians, lawyers, accountants, thinkers, leaders, and visionaries.

No parent can write a book without a lot of help. Denise Lynn and David Nicholson, Thoro Samuel, Rebecca Nicholson, Lisa Stokes, Jean Ivory, and Liz Edwards have all made it possible for me to concentrate without guilt. Their generosity sets a high standard.

I owe my biggest debt, of course, to my family. To my sister, Pamela Stewart, who has been generous with her insight and wisdom. To my late father, whose love of business turned out to be, after all, contagious and whose resilience in overcoming obstacles remains an inspiration. To the late Michael Heffernan, who taught me courage. To my children, Felix and Leonora, who teach me about patience and flexibility every day. To my husband, Lindsay, whose quiet style is the tip of a very deep iceberg. Thank you for believing in me.

M.A.W.H.N.

The Author

MARGARET WINDHAM HEFFERNAN was born in Texas, grew up in Holland, and completed her education at Cambridge University. Working in BBC radio and television, she produced prize-winning films, documentaries, and comedies. She was managing director of IPPA, a trade and lobbying association for the film and television industries. She worked with film and TV production companies to make them more competitive and also founded a small independent gas-trading company.

Moving to the United States, she developed software products with Tom Peters, Peter Lynch, Intuit, The Learning Company, and Standard & Poor's. She was CEO of ZineZone Corporation and iCAST Corporation and sits on the boards of several companies and institutions in the United States and the United Kingdom. She is married and has two children. Heffernan can be contacted at Margaret@mheffernan.com.

Index

This page constitutes a continuation of the copyright page.